THE SCIENTIFIC
REVOLUTION
IN GLOBAL
PERSPECTIVE

THE SCIENTIFIC REVOLUTION IN GLOBAL PERSPECTIVE

by

WILLIAM E. BURNS

New York   Oxford

OXFORD UNIVERSITY PRESS

Oxford University Press is a department of the University of Oxford.
It furthers the University's objective of excellence in research,
scholarship, and education by publishing worldwide.

Oxford   New York
Auckland   Cape Town   Dar es Salaam   Hong Kong   Karachi
Kuala Lumpur   Madrid   Melbourne   Mexico City   Nairobi
New Delhi   Shanghai   Taipei   Toronto

With offices in
Argentina   Austria   Brazil   Chile   Czech Republic   France   Greece
Guatemala   Hungary   Italy   Japan Poland   Portugal   Singapore
South Korea   Switzerland   Thailand   Turkey   Ukraine   Vietnam

For titles covered by Section 112 of the US Higher Education
Opportunity Act, please visit www.oup.com/us/he for the
latest information about pricing and alternate formats.

Published by Oxford University Press
198 Madison Avenue, New York, New York 10016
http://www.oup.com

Oxford is a registered trademark of Oxford University Press

Library of Congress Cataloging-in-Publication Data
Burns, William E., 1959-
    The scientific revolution in global perspective / by William E. Burns.
       pages cm
    Includes bibliographical references.
    ISBN 978-0-19-998933-1
  1. Science--History. 2. World history. 3. Social change--History. I. Title.
    Q125.B9497 2016
    509--dc23
                                                           2014033999

Printing number: 9 8 7 6 5 4 3 2 1

Printed in the United States of America
on acid-free paper

To Evelyn McCleary

CONTENTS

LIST OF FIGURES

LIST OF MAPS

ACKNOWLEDGMENTS

I thank the Folger Library, the Gelman Library of the George Washington University, and the Washington Regional Library Consortium for access to their resources. JSTOR and academia.edu were invaluable. This book has benefited from conversations with Paula Findlen, Margaret Jacob, and Dane Kennedy. Much of the material was presented to my classes in the Scientific Revolution at the University of Mary Washington, who gave valuable feedback. Chapter Two was read to a discussion group of the History Department at George Washington University, where I received several helpful suggestions. In preparation for the publication of this book, I benefited from the invaluable feedback of several readers: Andrew Keitt, University of Alabama at Birmingham; William Kimler, North Carolina State University; Brian Jeffrey Maxson, East Tennessee State University; Julia Hudson-Richards, Penn State Altoona; Devin Pendas, Boston College; Anthony N. Stranges, Texas A&M University; Erik L. Peterson, University of Wisconsin–Madison; Amy E. Foster, University of Central Florida; and Bruce J. Hunt, University of Texas. My editor at Oxford University Press, Charles Cavaliere, was a believer in this book from the beginning. Greatest thanks, as always, go to Evelyn.

ABOUT THE AUTHOR

William Burns is a historian who lives in the Washington, DC metro area with interests in the early modern world and the history of science. His previous works include *The Scientific Revolution: An Encyclopedia* (2001), *Science in the Enlightenment: An Encyclopedia* (2003), *Science and Technology in Colonial America* (2005), *and Science in World History* (2011).

MAPPING THE SCIENTIFIC REVOLUTION

The Scientific Revolution was an event not just in time, but also in space. Cartography helps us understand the spread and globalization of science in the early modern period, a phenomenon inextricable from the other changes in science that make up the Scientific Revolution. Scientific societies spread north from their origin in Italy. Isaac Newton's *Mathematical Principles of Natural Philosophy* (1687) drew not just from English and European observations, but from the Americas, Africa, and Asia as well (Map 1).

There were several centers of the global circulation of science. Rome was the headquarters of the Jesuit order, a scientific leader in both the Spanish colonies in America and the Philippines and represented throughout much of Asia as well (Map 2). Paris in the late seventeenth century was the headquarters of numerous institutions, including the Royal Academy of Sciences, the Paris Observatory, and the Royal Botanical Garden, as well as the French government, which had scientific interests of its own. Together they generated a stream of expeditions in the Atlantic, to China, and in Europe, the Middle East, and Africa embracing a range of sciences from astronomy to botany. London's Royal Society, not nearly as well funded as its Parisian rival, did not yet have the same global reach; however, it had a dense network of contacts with Britain's American colonies. Less dominated by scientific organizations, Dutch science expanded with the reach of Dutch trade and the development of the Amsterdam market (Maps 3–5).

As part of this expansion, the individual scientist was also growing more mobile (Map 6). Few were as well traveled as Edmond Halley, who traveled throughout the Atlantic basin and Europe (Map 7). Halley's travels were often in the role of a civil servant—a presage of the development of scientific professionalism in the service of the state in the centuries to come.

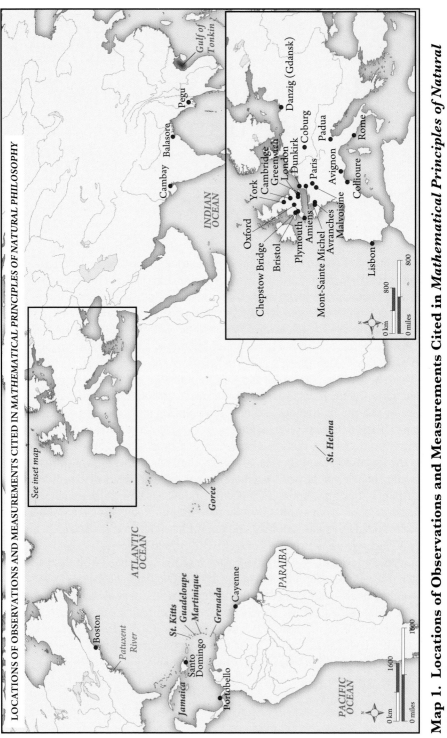

LOCATIONS OF OBSERVATIONS AND MEASUREMENTS CITED IN *MATHEMATICAL PRINCIPLES OF NATURAL PHILOSOPHY*

Map 1. Locations of Observations and Measurements Cited in *Mathematical Principles of Natural Philosophy*

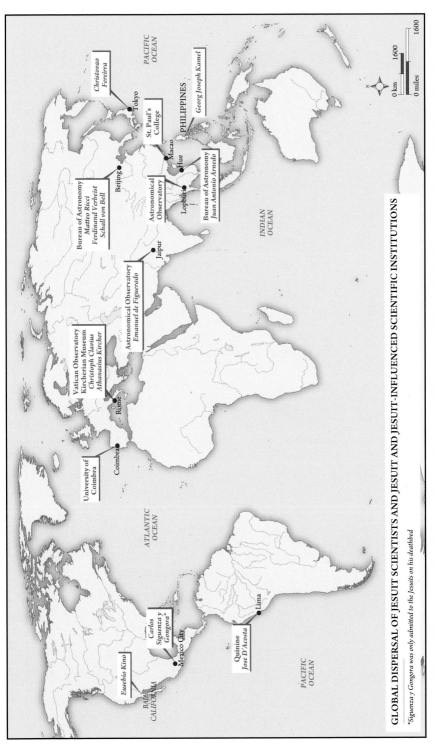

GLOBAL DISPERSAL OF JESUIT SCIENTISTS AND JESUIT AND JESUIT-INFLUENCED SCIENTIFIC INSTITUTIONS

*Siguenza y Gongora was only admitted to the Jesuits on his deathbed

Map 2. Global Dispersal of Jesuit Scientists, and Jesuit and Jesuit-Influenced Scientific Institutions

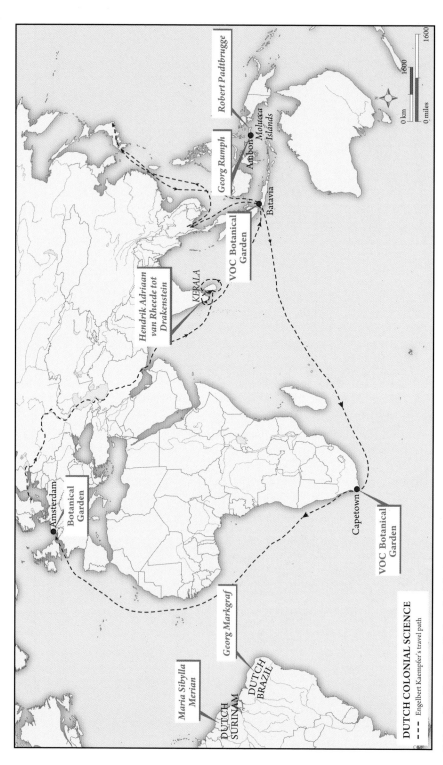

Map 3. Dutch Colonial Science

Robert Padtbrugge

Georg Rumph

Molucca Islands

Ambon

Hendrik Adriaan van Rheede tot Drakenstein

KERALA

VOC Botanical Garden

Batavia

Amsterdam Botanical Garden

Georg Markgraf

DUTCH SURINAM

DUTCH BRAZIL

Maria Sibylla Merian

Capetown

VOC Botanical Garden

DUTCH COLONIAL SCIENCE
- - - Engelbert Kaempfer's travel path

0 km   1600
0 miles   1600

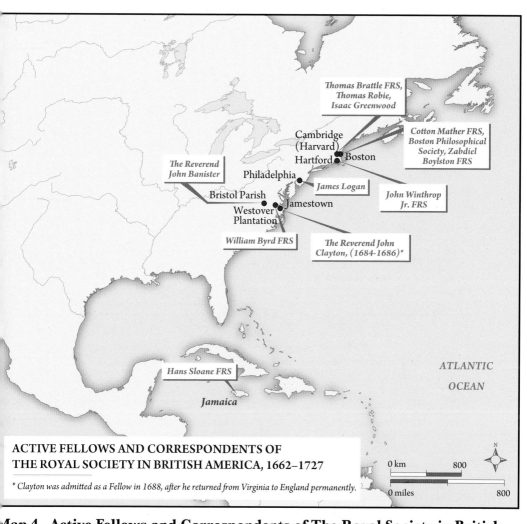

Thomas Brattle FRS, Thomas Robie, Isaac Greenwood

Cotton Mather FRS, Boston Philosophical Society, Zabdiel Boylston FRS

Cambridge (Harvard)

Hartford • Boston

The Reverend John Banister

Philadelphia

James Logan

John Winthrop Jr. FRS

Bristol Parish

Westover Plantation • Jamestown

William Byrd FRS

The Reverend John Clayton, (1684-1686)*

Hans Sloane FRS

Jamaica

ATLANTIC

OCEAN

ACTIVE FELLOWS AND CORRESPONDENTS OF THE ROYAL SOCIETY IN BRITISH AMERICA, 1662–1727

* *Clayton was admitted as a Fellow in 1688, after he returned from Virginia to England permanently.*

0 km   800

0 miles   800

N

Map 4. Active Fellows and Correspondents of The Royal Society in British America, 1662–1727

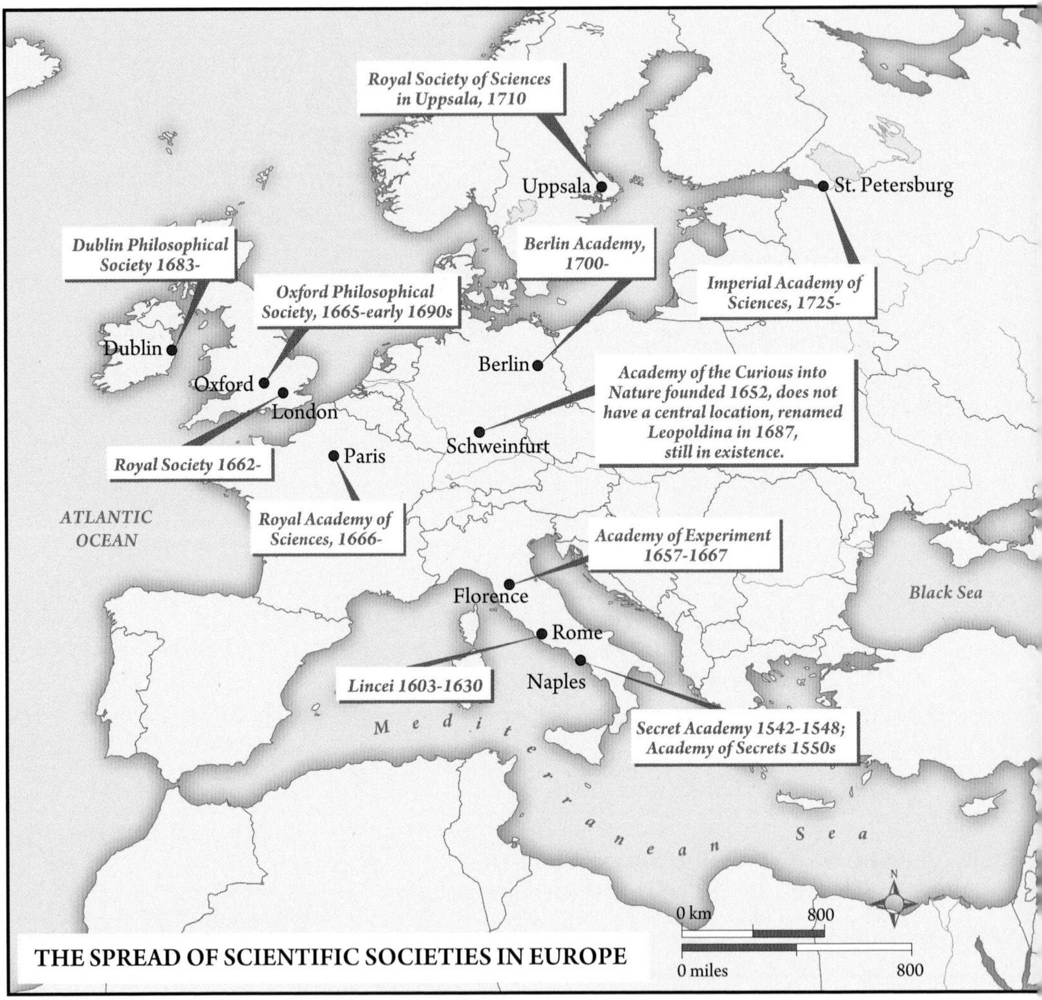
Royal Society of Sciences in Uppsala, 1710
Uppsala
St. Petersburg
Dublin Philosophical Society 1683-
Berlin Academy, 1700-
Imperial Academy of Sciences, 1725-
Oxford Philosophical Society, 1665-early 1690s
Dublin
Berlin
Oxford
London
Academy of the Curious into Nature founded 1652, does not have a central location, renamed Leopoldina in 1687, still in existence.
Schweinfurt
Royal Society 1662-
Paris
ATLANTIC OCEAN
Royal Academy of Sciences, 1666-
Academy of Experiment 1657-1667
Florence
Black Sea
Rome
Lincei 1603-1630
Naples
Mediterranean Sea
Secret Academy 1542-1548; Academy of Secrets 1550s
0 km
800
0 miles
800
N
THE SPREAD OF SCIENTIFIC SOCIETIES IN EUROPE

Map 5. The Spread of Scientific Societies in Europe

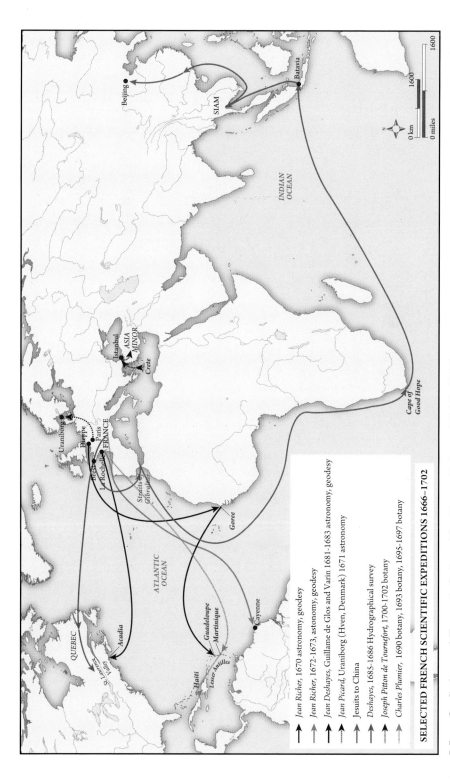

Map 6. Selected French Scientific Expeditions 1666–1702

SELECTED FRENCH SCIENTIFIC EXPEDITIONS 1666–1702

Jean Richer, 1670 astronomy, geodesy

Jean Richer, 1672-1673, astronomy, geodesy

Jean Deshayes, Guillame de Glos and Varin 1681-1683 astronomy, geodesy

Jean Picard, Uraniborg (Hven, Denmark) 1671 astronomy

Jesuits to China

Deshayes, 1685-1686 Hydrographical survey

Joseph Pitton de Tournefort, 1700-1702 botany

Charles Plumier, 1690 botany, 1693 botany, 1695-1697 botany

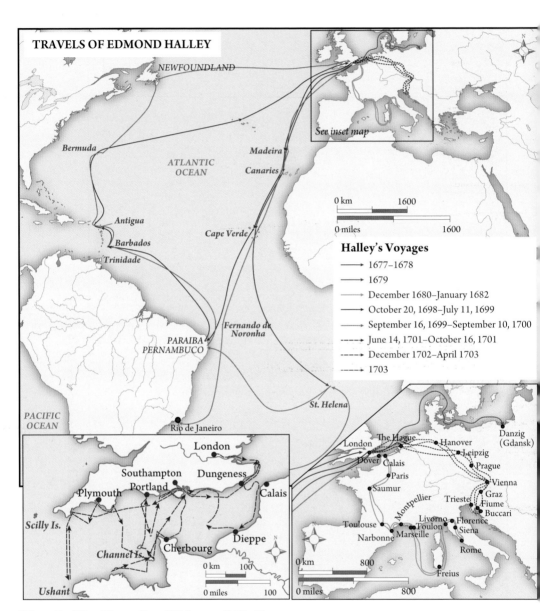

TRAVELS OF EDMOND HALLEY

NEWFOUNDLAND

Bermuda

ATLANTIC
OCEAN

Madeira

Canaries

See inset map

0 km   1600

0 miles   1600

Halley's Voyages

→ 1677–1678
→ 1679
→ December 1680–January 1682
→ October 20, 1698–July 11, 1699
→ September 16, 1699–September 10, 1700
⇢ June 14, 1701–October 16, 1701
⇢ December 1702–April 1703
⇢ 1703

Antigua

Barbados

Trinidade

Cape Verde

Fernando de
Noronha

PARAIBA
PERNAMBUCO

St. Helena

PACIFIC
OCEAN

Rio de Janeiro

London

Southampton   Dungeness

Plymouth   Portland

Calais

Scilly Is.

Dieppe

Channel Is.   Cherbourg

0 km   100

Ushant

0 miles   100

London   The Hague   Hanover   Danzig
(Gdansk)

Dover   Calais   Leipzig

Paris   Prague

Saumur   Vienna

Montpellier   Trieste   Graz
Fiume

Toulouse   Livorno   Buccari

Narbonne   Toulon   Florence

Marseille   Siena

Rome

0 km   800

Freius

0 miles   800

Map 7. The Travels of Edmond Halley

Introduction

We live in a world of science. Science possesses intellectual authority and provides wonder in the vistas of the universe. It employs millions of people and lies at the core of education throughout much of the world. Science provides a universal language enabling people to communicate across cultures, religions, and political systems.

Yet science has not always played this central cultural role. As late as the European Renaissance, science, or "natural philosophy," was a marginal activity. The change that led to our modern scientific culture is called the "Scientific Revolution." The term refers to changes in Western science—the science of Christian Europe and its colonial offshoots in America and elsewhere—in the sixteenth and seventeenth centuries. Both the content of science and in its institutional and cultural roles were transformed. The term "Scientific Revolution" was not used by people in the sixteenth and seventeenth century themselves to describe these changes, as the words "scientific" and "revolution" did not have the meanings they have today. However, the perception that the knowledge of nature was changing radically in the period from the early sixteenth to the early eighteenth century was widespread, with the use of terms such as "New Philosophy." The term "Scientific Revolution" itself was invented in the twentieth century, and one of the greatest debates in the history of science addresses whether or not it is an accurate description of what happened centuries earlier. (The idea of a Scientific Revolution has also been generalized, so that some historians speak of "scientific revolutions" plural, describing the introduction of evolution by natural selection in the nineteenth century as a "scientific revolution" in biology.)

One aspect of revolutions is that they are relatively sudden. However, while political revolutions often transpire over a few years or even days, intellectual revolutions can take longer to unfold. While the millennia since the ancient Greeks had seen slow, incremental developments in science, with periods of stagnation that sometimes lasted for centuries, the sixteenth and seventeenth centuries saw unprecedentedly rapid change in a variety of scientific disciplines, and

1

since then science has never returned to long-term stagnation and many disciplines have continued to develop at a rapid pace. The acceleration of scientific knowledge in the three centuries since the Revolution far surpasses the relatively slow development of science before it. Changes in scientific knowledge in the early modern period could also be called revolutionary in that they completely overthrew old ways of looking at things and introduced ideas and practices that, if not always completely new, were new to many participants. The best known of these are the linked changes from Ptolemaic, Earth-centered astronomy and qualitative Aristotelian physics to Copernican sun-centered astronomy and mathematical Newtonian physics. However, there were many other "revolutionary" innovations in science at the time, from the discovery of the circulation of the blood in medicine to the establishment of new kinds of institutions, such as the scientific society and the journal of science. A plethora of new instruments, such as the telescope, microscope, and air pump, changed the practice of science. The Revolution took science from a marginal cultural position, practiced by a few specialists with little impact on other areas of human thought, to a position well on the way to its current role as the ultimate arbiter of truth.

The Scientific Revolution is most analogous to a political revolution in its overthrow of long-established authorities. These authorities dated back to the time of the ancient Greeks, in some cases as long as two thousand years before the Scientific Revolution itself. During the Scientific Revolution science went from an activity largely built on ancient texts to one built on empirical and mathematical methods as well as the instruments that extended the reach of human senses. As in other revolutions, the overthrowers of ancient authority often differed among themselves (although violent conflict was at least kept to a minimum) but agreed that the old order had become intolerable.

WAS THE SCIENTIFIC REVOLUTION
A WORLD REVOLUTION?

The story of the Scientific Revolution has been told and retold by historians and scientists in many ways, but always as a European story. This "Europe" was not the entire continent, but the Europe that was religiously Catholic and Protestant, with Latin as its language of learning. The great names of the Scientific Revolution are all European—Nicolaus Copernicus the Pole, Galileo Galilei the Italian, France's René Descartes, Isaac Newton the Englishman, as well as many others in different European countries and cultures. Not only the heroes but also the villains, like the conservative Aristotelian professors or the Roman Inquisition that tried Galileo, have been Europeans. Although Arab scientists have sometimes been given credit for their important scientific role in the Middle Ages, the Scientific Revolution itself has always been framed in European terms.

But the age of the Scientific Revolution was also the age of the expansion of European interests and knowledge over much of the world, with an unprecedented level of physical and cultural contact with different environments, peoples, and states. This expanding contact embraced both areas previously known to Europeans, such as India and China, and those previously unknown, most importantly the Americas. The age of Copernicus was also that of the explorers and conquerors Cristopher Columbus, Vasco da Gama, and Hernán Cortés; the age of Newton was also that of the establishment of the English colonies in North America, the Atlantic slave trade, and the worldwide missionary effort of the Catholic Church. Many European phenomena, such as the rise of capitalism and democracy, have been reevaluated in global terms. Is the Scientific Revolution an exception?

The European culture from which the Scientific Revolution emerged was also the product of millennia of interactions between civilizations. The formation of European culture from the ancient Mediterranean, its long-term contacts with the Islamic world, and its more intermittent contacts with India, China, and other areas of Asia as well as Africa shaped its science along with the rest of its culture. The "contributions" of these areas are generally acknowledged for the medieval science that the Scientific Revolution overthrew, but can they also have influenced the Revolution itself?

The immediate impact of the Scientific Revolution as well as its origin has usually been limited to Europe, and within Europe, the focus has usually been on the northwest, England, France, the Netherlands, and Germany. But even as early as the seventeenth century a variety of cultures outside Europe, both European colonies and non-European societies, were interested in some of the new scientific ideas. These ideas were made available beyond the lands of their origin by missionaries, traders, and scientists. Rulers, physicians, and numerous other individuals and classes outside Europe adopted or promoted these ideas for their own purposes. Europeans could not, as they could in later centuries, "force" the adoption of Western scientific principles on the states and peoples of Asia, but some of their ideas were attractive enough that Asians adopted them of their own accord. Was the Scientific Revolution a revolution in world as well as European science? Can the later domination of the world by Western science, to the point where in most places it has become synonymous with "science," be traced to the Scientific Revolution?

The centuries following the Scientific Revolution would also see the growth and development of the European domination of the rest of the world that reached its height in the early twentieth century. What role did the Scientific Revolution play in transforming Europe from one among several regions of Eurasia to a temporary hegemon of the world? How was the Scientific Revolution related to the powerful belief of European and European-descended people in their own superiority over the other peoples of the world, whether cultural or "racial"? Both inside and outside Europe, did science betray the liberating principles of the first challenges to the ancients to lay the foundations of new despotisms?

THE WORLD AS A NEW SUBJECT
AND PLATFORM FOR SCIENCE

Before the early modern period, the collection of knowledge about nature was usually restricted to the area occupied by one civilization and its immediate neighbors. Word from distant regions about their flora, fauna, people, and geography was intermittent and often encrusted with myth, such as the dog-headed men that both Western and Chinese ethnographers identified as living in Central Asia. More direct evidence about far-distant places was rare. The Romans brought a hippopotamus to Rome from Africa, but it was the last hippopotamus in Europe until the nineteenth century. On rare occasions, Chinese people could look at giraffes from Africa, but they could not examine them in their native habitat. A whole world of plants, animals, and peoples flourished in the Americas with no impact on how Afro-Eurasians thought about the world, and vice versa.

European expansion in the early modern world made Europe the most global of civilizations, the first to bring together the Americas and Afro-Eurasia. European ships called in ports from western Africa to China to Peru, and Europeans ruled territories as distant from Europe and each other as Goa in India and Brazil. No other civilization—including the previous contender as the most geographically dispersed and transculturally connected civilization, Islam—could rival this global reach. Although even by the end of the Scientific Revolution some lands— particularly those of the far south, such as Polynesia, Australia, and Antarctica— remained out of the grasp of European power and knowledge, the reach of European empire and commerce enabled Europeans to build the first global science across a variety of disciplines, a truly revolutionary transformation. For the first time, scientists could consider data from this vast area of the world spanning hemispheres, oceans, and continents with which Europeans were in contact, rather than being restricted to a smaller portion in their own immediate neighborhood. This not only affected the obvious case of those sciences based on the diversity of living things—botany and zoology—but also those where a global variety of points of view are desirable, such as astronomy. Since the major textual scientific civilizations were in the Northern Hemisphere, the stars of the southern sky had remained largely unknown to their astronomy until the Scientific Revolution. Europeans were the first people with the ability to compile a truly complete map of the skies of Earth. Furthermore, the mere fact that celestial phenomena could be observed from points distant on the Earth's surface revolutionized the way they were understood.

ONE

THE OLD REGIME IN SCIENCE

Like all revolutions, the Scientific Revolution cannot be understood without understanding first the Old Regime it overthrew.

SCIENTIFIC ISSUES IN PREMODERN CULTURES

For as long as human beings have existed, they have thought about the natural world, including their own bodies. The roots of science extend as far back as the first human being to investigate nature, whose name has long been forgotten. Premodern agricultural societies faced a broad range of issues to which the knowledge of nature was relevant. Maintaining the health of the human body and curing disease led not only to the development of specific cures but also to theoretical systems of medicine. Many, such as the Western theory of the four humors or the Chinese yin-yang approach, treated health as preserved by maintaining a balance. These systems of medicine were embodied in ancient texts such as China's Yellow Emperor's Medical Classic or the writings of Hippocrates and Galen in the Greco-Roman, Christian, and Islamic worlds. The exploitation of plants for medical uses also meant that the study of non-crop plants emerged as a branch of medicine across cultures.

Agriculture made several intellectual demands. Getting water to where it was needed led to the development of basic hydraulics. The need for an accurate calendar to regulate planting and harvesting led to the development of astronomy. Basic botany and the awareness of the nutritional and other needs of plants can be traced to early agriculturalists. The domestication of animals also led to an increase of natural knowledge, although across most premodern cultures interest in plants, which furnished a vastly greater amount of the human diet and lent themselves to medicinal uses, was much more central than interest in animals outside a narrow range of domesticated species.

The needs of navigators to know their position and direction over the open sea also contributed to astronomy. Since the belief that the movements of the stars and planets had meaning for people on Earth can be traced to the earliest civilizations, astrological interpretation also led observers to study the skies.

Examination of the natural environment led to speculation about how it all worked. Particularly in early Greece and China, various schools of interpretation of the natural world flourished. In time, one major school became dominant in most societies after an initial more pluralistic phase, what the Chinese called the age of the "Hundred Schools." In the West, both Christian and Islamic, the Aristotelian school came to be dominant during the Middle Ages. In China, the yin-yang school attracted the majority of inquirers into nature's secrets.

In many cases, religion contributed to the growth of premodern science, both by making questions of cosmology important and by posing specific problems. Religion made bold, sweeping assertions about the nature of the universe, the world, and humanity with scientific implications, such as the theory of divine creation of the entire universe held by believers in the Abrahamic religions— Judaism, Christianity, and Islam—that dominated western and central Afro-Eurasia. Religion also posed technical problems requiring scientific answers. The problem of fixing the date of Easter was a spur to the development of astronomy in the Christian world, while in the Islamic world Muslims developed trigonometry from its Greek and Indian roots in part to be able to ascertain the direction of the holy city of Mecca, the focus of Muslim prayers, from different spots on the globe.

Philosophers, priests, physicians, and technologists across the early modern world pondered the great questions of nature, studied ancient texts and traditions, and came up with a number of answers. Although much of the work was done by individuals in informal settings, a few institutions, such as the universities of Europe or the Chinese bureau of astronomy, also dealt with theoretical as well as practical issues of the natural world. Some traditions, such as the sophisticated Mayan calendar or Aztec medicine, would be destroyed by invaders along with the societies that produced them, a few fragments perhaps surviving to be incorporated into the science of the conquerors. Among the survivors, one, the science of Christian Europe, would acquire a narrow but definite superiority over its rivals in a few crucial areas during the Scientific Revolution, and eventually become the basis of world science.

THE ORIGINS OF WESTERN SCIENCE

A continuous tradition of science leading to the Scientific Revolution can be traced from the roots of western Afro-Eurasian civilization itself, to the societies of Egypt and Mesopotamia.

Babylonians pioneered astronomy and astrology, making and recording close observations of celestial phenomena and correlating them with earthly events. Other civilizations, such as the early Britons who built Stonehenge, also observed the courses of the stars, but the Babylonians are remembered as the pioneers due to their production of written texts. Egyptians were among the first to practice geometry and to systematize medicine, separating the work of the physician from that of the priest.

The greatest ancient contributors to the tradition of Western science were the Greeks, who drew upon the achievements of previous civilizations but further pioneered nearly every branch. One area of inquiry introduced by the Greeks was "natural philosophy," a discipline that examined the fundamental nature of the "physical" (a Greek word) universe. Greek natural philosophy was integrated into philosophical systems that also covered ethics and metaphysics—questions about the fundamentals of being that went "beyond" physics—along with other subjects. In addition to Aristotelianism, the major systems included Platonism, Stoicism, and Epicureanism. The fifth major school, Skepticism, criticized the truth claims of the others rather than putting forth its own theories.

The most influential of the Greek natural philosophers was Aristotle (384–322 BCE). Aristotle's surviving works cover a wide range of topics, from physics to ethics to biology—a greater range of topics than covered by the surviving works of any other Greek thinker. Aristotle saw the world as made of substances and qualities. Things existing in the natural world were compounds of substance and qualities such as color. The material world itself was divided into four elements, earth, air, fire, and water, in various combinations. The universe, centered on the Earth, was divided between the corruptible "sublunary sphere," containing all beneath the moon, and the perfect and unchanging heavens. (This belief would prove very compatible with the Christian contrast between earthly corruption and God's perfection.)

Aristotelian natural philosophy viewed natural things as endowed with purpose, the so-called Final Cause. Things fell, for example, because the Earth was the proper place for them—they possessed the quality of "gravity." Other things, like the stars, did not fall because the heavens were the proper place for them. Motions were divided into natural motions (expressions of a body's true nature) and violent (those imposed on a body from outside). The hurling of a rock, for example, combined natural motion (the rock's eventual falling to the ground) and violent motion (the rock's going in the direction it was thrown). A body's natural motion included phenomena we would now call change and development as well as motion; Aristotle viewed the growth of a tree as a form of motion. Stars and planets moved naturally in eternal perfect circles, because heavenly things were perfect and Aristotle believed that only circular motion was suitable to perfection.

Greek Mathematical Science

Aristotle made little use of mathematics, but the Greeks also possessed a strong tradition of mathematical science. Greek mathematicians made several advances, mostly working from a geometric base. Perhaps the most influential textbook of all time is the geometer Euclid's *Elements*, written around 300 BCE, a work on planar geometry covering triangles, circles, and parallel lines, among other basic topics. Applying mathematics to natural phenomena was more of a challenge.

The few phenomena that were considered amenable to mathematical analysis included harmonics, simple mechanics, optics, and astronomy. The science of musical intervals, their concordance and discordance, was pioneered by the philosophical school centering on Pythagoras (570–490 BCE), which was oriented to mathematics.

Greek mathematical astronomy began after the Greek leader Alexander the Great (356–323 BCE) conquered the Persian Empire. Greeks assimilated the astronomical data that had been gathered for centuries in Babylon and subjected it to their own powerful mathematics, attempting to come up with formulas to account for the regularities in the movements of the heavenly bodies and to predict their courses. The most influential ancient Greek astronomer, Ptolemy (100–170 CE), came at the end of this tradition, when Greece and most of Greek civilization were ruled by Rome, centuries after Alexander's conquests (Fig. 1-1). Ptolemy's *Almagest* presented a powerful synthesis of Earth-centered, or "geocentric," astronomy. Ptolemy was more concerned with "saving the phenomena," enabling astronomers to make accurate predictions of the positions of the celestial bodies, than with presenting a physically accurate picture of the cosmos. (One Greek astronomer, Aristarchus of Samos [310–230 BCE], had put the sun at the center of his cosmos, but he would have far less influence than Ptolemy.) Subsequent astronomers would mostly follow in Ptolemy's footsteps, leaving the question of the "real" nature of the universe to natural philosophers, who in turn usually had little acquaintance with mathematical astronomy.

The application of mathematics to mechanical problems was pioneered by the Greek scholar Archimedes (287–212 BCE). In addition to inventing several techniques in solid and plane geometry and numerical reckoning, Archimedes established the mathematical principle of the lever and the principle of displacement. He also pioneered applied mechanics, possibly inventing the "screw of Archimedes," a kind of pump, and inventing engines of war for the government of the city of Syracuse. Although Archimedes himself was a Sicilian, Greek mathematics would be further advanced mostly by scholars in the city of Alexandria in Egypt, named after Alexander. However, Greek mathematics proved unable to develop mechanics much further beyond Archimedes.

Medicine and Natural History

For the Greeks, the study of living things mostly took place in the discipline of medicine (a major exception was Aristotle himself, who did several studies of animals that would not be followed up on in a serious way for over a millennium). Even botany was mainly devoted to identifying plants of medical use, as it would remain through the Scientific Revolution. The most important Greek physicians were Hippocrates (460–377 BCE), generally viewed as the "founder of medicine," and Galen (130–200 CE), who systematized Greek medicine in a way that would shape learned medical traditions for centuries. Galen's work, based on extensive experience gathered by physicians through the centuries as well as theoretical

Figure 1-1. Armillary Sphere with Ptolemy. An early printed edition of Ptolemy's *Almagest* shows the Ptolemaic astronomical system in the form of an armillary sphere.

approaches, dominated thought about human anatomy and physiology into the Renaissance, even though he was forbidden, like all physicians at the time, to dissect humans and had to dissect animals instead.

Greek medicine as synthesized by Galen saw the essential problem as maintaining health through a balance of "humors" or bodily fluids. Knowledge of anatomical details was less important than monitoring and if necessary modifying what went into and came out of the body. A common Galenical technique was bloodletting, cutting to remove a quantity of blood from the body, as many diseases were believed caused by an excess of blood.

Botany, often treated as a subdiscipline of medicine, was far more advanced than zoology among the Greeks. Two major botanical writers were Theophrastus (370–286 BCE), a disciple of Aristotle, and the physician Pedanius Dioscorides (40–90 CE). Theophrastus wrote about plants in the way that Aristotle wrote about animals, seeking a philosophical explanation for why they were the way they were. Dioscorides was the major ancient "herbalist" whose writings survived. He was concerned with compiling information about plants and their healing properties for the use of physicians.

Ancient Science in Latin

In the second and first centuries BCE, most of the lands inhabited by or ruled by Greeks were taken over by the Romans, whose language was Latin. The Romans as an ethnic and cultural group were not innovators in science (and it was a Roman soldier who killed Archimedes), although such later Greek scientists as Ptolemy and Galen were Roman citizens and thus "Romans" in the political sense. However, Latin writers were interested in Greek science and produced much derivative science in the form of popularizations, adaptations, and compilations. These writings would become particularly important because Western students would be cut off from direct contact with Greek writings after the fall of the Roman Empire when Greek was forgotten but Latin would become the language of learning. Significant Roman writings in science include Titus Lucretius Carus's epic poem on Epicurean philosophy, *On the Nature of Things*, lost for most of the Middle Ages but rediscovered in the fifteenth century; the *Natural Questions* of the Stoic philosopher Lucius Annaeus Seneca (4 BCE–65 CE); and Pliny the Elder's voluminous if not very critical *Natural History*, a compilation of facts and anecdotes about the natural world drawn mostly from Greek sources (Fig. 1-2).

Christianity and the Decline of Ancient Science

Ancient science declined significantly after the second century BCE and lost most of its intellectual drive after the era of Ptolemy and Galen. One reason for the diminished interest in science in the later Roman Empire was an increased focus on otherworldly concerns. This can be traced across a broad range of religious and philosophical positions, but ultimately its greatest impact was in the

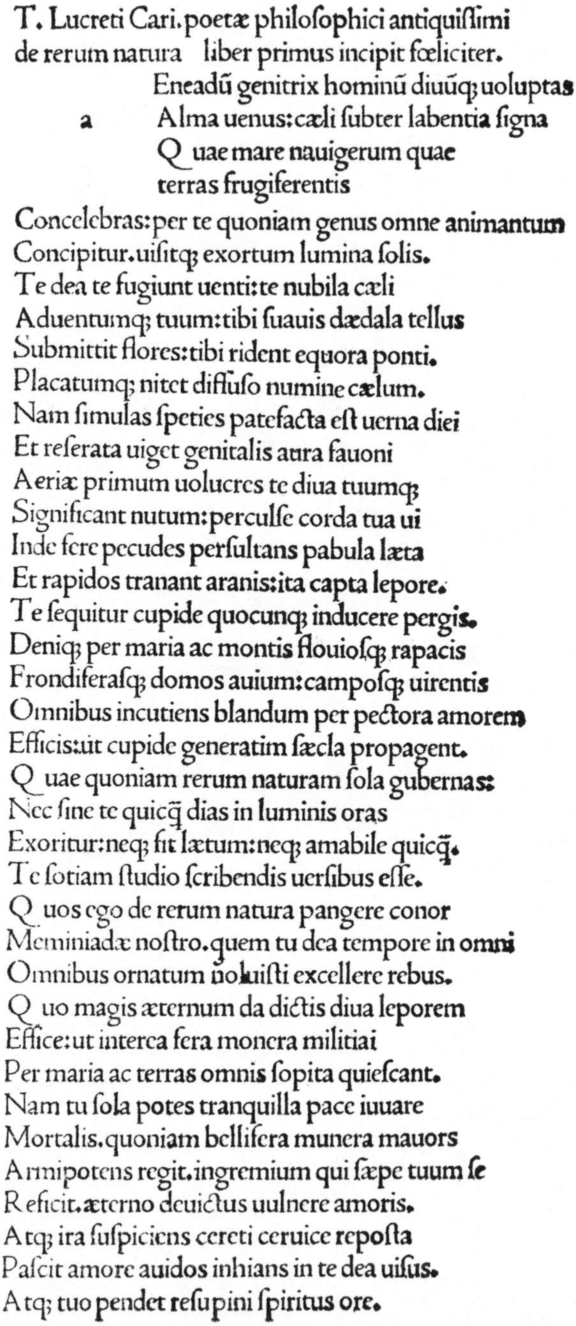

T. Lucreti Cari.poetæ philofophici antiquiſſimi
de rerum natura liber primus incipit fœliciter.

     Eneadũ genitrix hominũ diuũq; uoluptas
a   Alma uenus:cæli ſubter labentia ſigna
     Quae mare nauigerum quae
     terras frugiferentis
Concelebras:per te quoniam genus omne animantum
Concipitur.uiſitq; exortum lumina ſolis.
Te dea te fugiunt uenti:te nubila cæli
Aduentumq; tuum:tibi ſuauis dædala tellus
Submittit flores:tibi rident equora ponti.
Placatumq; nitet diffuſo numine cælum.
Nam ſimulas ſpeties patefacta eſt uerna diei
Et reſerata uiget genitalis aura fauoni
Aeriæ primum uolucres te diua tuumq;
Significant nutum:perculſe corda tua ui
Inde fere pecudes perſultans pabula læta
Et rapidos tranant aranis:ita capta lepore.
Te ſequitur cupide quocunq; inducere pergis.
Deniq; per maria ac montis flouioſq; rapacis
Frondiferaſq; domos auium:campoſq; uirentis
Omnibus incutiens blandum per pectora amorem
Efficis:ut cupide generatim ſæcla propagent.
Quae quoniam rerum naturam ſola gubernas:
Nec ſine te quicq̃ dias in luminis oras
Exoritur:neq; fit lætum:neq; amabile quicq̃.
Te ſotiam ſtudio ſcribendis uerſibus eſſe.
Quos ego de rerum natura pangere conor
Meminiadæ noſtro.quem tu dea tempore in omni
Omnibus ornatum noluiſti excellere rebus.
Quo magis æternum da dictis diua leporem
Effice:ut interea fera monera militiai
Per maria ac terras omnis ſopita quieſcant.
Nam tu ſola potes tranquilla pace iuuare
Mortalis.quoniam bellifera munera mauors
Armipotens regit.ingremium qui ſæpe tuum ſe
Reficit.æterno deuictus uulnere amoris.
Atq; ira ſuſpiciens cereti ceruice repoſta
Paſcit amore auidos inhians in te dea uiſus.
Atq; tuo pendet reſupini ſpiritus ore.

Figure 1-2. Page from an Early Edition of Lucretius. The rediscovery of Lucretius shortly before the introduction of printing enabled Epicurean philosophy to circulate in an unprecedented way.

rise of the new religion of Christianity. Early Christianity cannot be described as either pro- or anti-science, but many Christians did view excessive focus on the things of this world, including nature, as distracting from the far more important world of the spirit. The intellectual dominance of theological issues was reinforced by the adoption of Christianity as the Empire's official religion in the fourth century. Theological issues, not scientific ones, were the ones that divided the Empire and led to voluminous controversies as both sides sought the support of the Imperial government. The fall of the Roman Empire in the west in the fifth century ended written science in the western Mediterranean, except for a few texts saved through the work of monastic copiers.

Although the Empire survived in the east with its new capital at Constantinople, in the Greek world of the time most intellectual energy continued to go into theology. The ancient scientific heritage dwindled in the care of its original possessors. The last major scientific writer in the ancient tradition was the Aristotelian commentator John Philoponus (c. 490–570), who significantly renounced philosophy in the second half of his career to concentrate on theology.

ARABIC SCIENCE

In the early medieval world, the inheritance of Greek science was pursued most vigorously in the Islamic lands. The religion of Islam emerged out of Arabia, an area that had never been ruled by Greeks or Romans, in the early seventh century. The early Muslims established an empire that stretched from Spain in the west to central Asia in the east. Not all of the scientists in this huge region were Muslims or Arabs, but they worked in a society where Islam was the dominant religion and Arabic the language of learning. There was a massive effort, sponsored by the Abbasid caliphs, leaders of the early Islamic Empire, to translate Greek works on philosophy, natural philosophy, and medicine into Arabic. Arabic science was important both for preserving the Greek heritage—some works of Greek science have been lost in their original language, surviving only in Arabic—and for innovating within that tradition.

Arabic science was marked by the integration of elements of Greek, Persian, and Indian science, as well as some influence from China. One of the most significant adoptions was the Indian system of numerals, which later became known in the West as Arabic numerals. This system of notation was far more flexible and efficient than anything previously used in classical or medieval Western civilization, such as Roman numerals or associating letters of the alphabet with numbers. Other aspects of Indian mathematics adopted by Arab mathematicians and later by the West were innovations in trigonometry such as the use of sines rather than chords. The idea of an "elixir of life," which would greatly influence Western alchemy, appears to have first entered the Islamic world from China, eventually passing to the West.

Areas where Arabic scientists further advanced the tradition of Greek science include optics, where Ibn Haytham (965–1040) pioneered the development of experimental science, and astronomy, where Ptolemy's system was refined with new observations and more sophisticated mathematical models. The Islamic world established the astronomical observatory as an institution. Major observatories include the Maragha Observatory founded in 1259, where astronomers developed some of the mathematical techniques that would later be used by Copernicus. The Maragha Observatory is associated with a greater willingness in the Islamic world to criticize the Ptolemaic model and to relate astronomy to an actual physical picture of the cosmos rather than merely "saving the phenomena," the same intellectual project that would lead to the "Copernican Revolution" in Europe.

Arabic medicine built on the Galenic tradition, applying Galenic reasoning to a vast range of physical conditions and adding many more plants to the pharmacopeia. Medicine was particularly important in that many of the leading Arabic-speaking natural philosophers, such as Abu Bakr Muhammad Ibn Zakariyya Al-Razi (d. 925), known in the Latin West as "Rhazes"; Abu Ali Al-Husayn Ibn Sina (980–1037), "Avicenna"; and Abu'l Walid Muhammad Ibn Rushd (1126–1198), "Averroes," were also physicians. Ibn Sina's medical encyclopedia, the *Canon of Medicine*, would be one of the most influential texts, not just in the Islamic world but in the West as well, into the seventeenth century.

SCIENCE RETURNS TO THE WEST

The revival of Western science can be traced to the growing prosperity of the West in the eleventh century. The growing intellectual class, nearly all "clerics" affiliated with the Catholic Church, supported by the slightly more productive economy first became interested in the surviving Latin writings such as Pliny's *Natural History*. However, the Latin writings by themselves were thin gruel, and for a more theoretical approach it was necessary to turn outside the corpus of Latin literature. Beginning late in the eleventh century there was an influx of translations from the Arabic, both of originally Greek texts translated into Arabic and of originally Arabic ones. Islamic Spain was the center of this translation effort, which was supplemented by another effort to translate works directly from Greek based in southern Italy. (The third area where the Latin world came into direct contact with the Islamic, the Crusader states, represented an intellectual backwater and contributed nothing to the translation effort, although physicians in the Islamic tradition did practice at Crusader courts.) In the Middle Ages, the translations from Arabic had more impact than the ones directly from Greek.

The most important translator from the Arabic in the twelfth century was Gerard of Cremona (1114–1187), an Italian who worked in Toledo, Spain. Gerard's translations of Arabic versions of Greek works included Ptolemy's *Almagest*, Euclid's *Elements*, and Archimedes' *Measurement of the Circle*. Gerard was a Christian, but Jewish translators also played an important role as cultural intermediaries. The translation effort continued into the thirteenth century—Ibn Haytham's foundational work on optics was not available in Latin until 1270. The twelfth- and thirteenth-century discovery of these Greek and Arab writers had a radical impact on European culture, making the physical universe an object of intense scholarly interest. Some historians argue that this medieval change is the true "scientific revolution," in that "science" gained an intellectual place and an institutional basis that it was never to relinquish in the West. This base was the university, an institution founded in medieval Europe.

The Medieval Western University and Aristotelian Natural Philosophy

Universities emerged in the twelfth century. They were intimately related to the authority structure of church and state. They were chartered by political and church leaders, run by clerics, and used the language of the church, Latin.

The faculty was divided into an undergraduate college of arts, including natural philosophy and mathematics, and three graduate faculties (theology, law, and medicine, although few universities had all three). The most important for science were the arts and medical faculties, although the theological faculty also played an important role in setting the boundaries of what could be said in natural philosophy. The dominant texts in the medieval natural philosophy and medical classrooms were those of the ancient Greek scientists, physicians, and mathematicians in Latin translation and their commentators.

The dominant school of natural philosophy in European universities between the thirteenth and the late seventeenth centuries was Aristotelianism, although this encompassed a range of philosophical positions and allowed for the incorporation of non-Aristotelian ideas such as a god who actively intervened in the universe. Medieval Aristotelians did not view qualitative science as a discipline divorced from philosophy but as a subdiscipline within philosophy, "natural philosophy." Natural philosophy was taught in university arts faculties principally by commenting on Aristotle's genuine and spurious scientific works along with previous commentaries and other texts. The medieval university played down the empirical side of the Aristotelian heritage in favor of the logical side.

The basic procedure of medieval Aristotelian natural philosophy was taking generalizations about the physical world, originally based on knowledge acquired through the senses, and performing logical operations on them. The basis of the generalizations was not as important to medieval and Renaissance Aristotelians as the logic applied to them. The emphasis on general statements meant that Aristotelians focused on the normal and the typical, and viewed the study of the aberrant as not truly philosophical. Aristotelian philosophers aimed at certain rather than probable knowledge of the world and believed that their procedures offered it.

The greatest challenge faced by medieval natural philosophers was reconciling Aristotle's thought with Christianity, as Muslim and Jewish philosophers had faced similar problems before them. Several Aristotelian doctrines were incompatible with Christianity—notably the eternity of the world, which conflicted with the Christian narrative of Earth's history from creation to apocalypse. The most common approach was to subordinate Aristotle to Christian doctrine, denying the anti-Christian elements of his philosophy while saving as much of the physics as possible. A champion of this approach was the greatest philosopher and theologian of the medieval university, Thomas Aquinas (1225–1274), an Italian who taught at the University of Paris. Thomas's philosophy, known as "Thomism," incorporated Aristotelian logic and natural philosophy along with Platonic elements in a way compatible with Christian dogma.

A very different strategy from Thomas's based itself on the philosophical works of the Spanish Muslim philosopher Ibn Rushd (1126–1198), known in the Latin West as Averroes. Ibn Rushd had asserted a difference between religious and philosophical truth, both of which could be true in different senses despite seemingly contradicting each other. By asserting the autonomy of philosophy, including natural philosophy, from Christian theology, the "Latin Averroists," Christian followers of Ibn Rushd, aroused the suspicion of church authorities, eventually provoking a hostile reaction and a crackdown on independent thinking in the university.

Medieval Mathematics

Mathematics continued to be studied in the Middle Ages, but it did not have the prestige or the institutional presence of natural philosophy, a handicap it would carry into the seventeenth century. It did not play a major role in the university curriculum. Like Greek mathematics, medieval mathematics remained primarily geometric.

The most important development in medieval Western mathematics was not a breakthrough in theory, but the adoption of the Hindu-Arabic system of numerals. This was a slow process, in which the lead was taken not by learned mathematicians but by business people, particularly in Italy, where many cities carried on an active trade with the Islamic world where the numerals were already in use. The one great medieval European mathematician, Leonard Fibonacci (c. 1170–1250), was an Italian from the trading city of Pisa and an "early adopter" of the Hindu-Arabic system, which he learned of while living with his father, a Pisan diplomat in Muslim-ruled Algeria. The numeral system was increasingly popular in the fifteenth century and was the norm for arithmetic and calculation by the early sixteenth century. The increased ease of calculation the new numerals possessed over Roman numerals would immeasurably aid the mathematically based science of the Scientific Revolution.

The "Middle" or "Mixed" Sciences

The boundary between natural philosophy and mathematics was not always clearly drawn. Those sciences that combined aspects of natural philosophy and mathematics were referred to as "middle" or "mixed" sciences. Two of the most prominent were astronomy and optics. Astronomy occupied a marginal position in the Middle Ages. Aristotelian cosmology was about the nature of the universe, not the precise movements of the stars and planets. Astronomy was about predictions of celestial events such as eclipses and tracing the paths of the planets across the heavens. This required mathematics, which was not a major part of Aristotelian natural philosophy. Aristotelian cosmology emphasized the perfect circular movements of the solid spheres that carried the planets around, while Ptolemaic astronomy concerned itself not with the physical nature of the planetary system but rather with the mathematical devices necessary to make accurate predictions. Astronomy was necessary to maintain a calendar and fix the correct date of Easter, both church functions, but it lacked the prestige of natural philosophy.

Optics was another middle science, one that made important advances in both the Islamic and Christian worlds during the Middle Ages. All the middle sciences were considered less "noble" than either natural philosophy or pure mathematics, partly due to their practical applications. The university arts curriculum centered on the "liberal" arts, the knowledge of a free man, and practical knowledge was often viewed as particularly characteristic of slaves and peasants. The Greek heritage tended to treat practical knowledge as "base," inferior to contemplation, and medieval Christians associated practical science with the fallen nature of man, which made it necessary to use practical techniques. However, medieval culture was somewhat more technology-friendly than was that of the Greeks and Romans, with the extensive use of mills and developments in the manufacture of clocks that put the Europeans ahead of the Chinese, the previous leaders in clock making.

Nominalism

The late Middle Ages saw changes in scholasticism that affected natural philosophy. The new school of philosophy originating in the early fourteenth century, nominalism, was also known as the *via moderna* or "modern way," in comparison to the *via antiqua* or "ancient way" of scholasticism. *Nomina* is Latin for "names," and nominalism is the belief that labels and categories are essentially arbitrary and do not correspond to anything in the deep structure of the universe. There had always been a nominalist strain in medieval thought, but it grew more prominent with the late-thirteenth-century church reaction against what many considered the scholastic overemphasis on reason and its close connections with pagan and Islamic philosophy.

The most important of the nominalists was the Oxford Franciscan William of Ockham (c. 1287–1347). Ockham completely denied the existence of universals, the belief that classes of things have real existence. He endorsed a principle of thought that later became known as "Ockham's razor": only necessary abstractions should be used and the simplest explanations are the best. The only knowledge is knowledge of individual entities via sense perception, and metaphysics does not exist.

Theologically, Ockham and subsequent nominalists believed in the essential arbitrariness and freedom of God. Nominalists argued that the classical scholasticism of Aquinas limited God's freedom by subordinating him to reason. They abandoned the scholastic hope of rationally understanding the universe through deductions from first principles. Nominalism contributed to a trend to empirical observation of concrete instances as opposed to theorizing on the basis of generalizations. This led to attempts to develop a logic of induction, reasoning from particular cases to universals, as opposed to the deductive logic that had dominated the Western tradition since Aristotle. Clerical concern over the dangers of an excessive reliance on Aristotle encouraged a greater focus on God's omnipotence, with an increased interest in hypothetical non-Aristotelian cosmologies. These discussions were not assertions of physical reality but remained speculative. When the Parisian master Nicolas Oresme (c. 1325–1382), for example, discussed the anti-Aristotelian idea that the Earth rotated, his influential arguments were directed at demonstrating that it was possible, or at least impossible to disprove, not that it was actually happening. He was making a point about the limitations of human knowledge rather than the motion of the Earth.

DISREPUTABLE SCIENCES—MAGIC, ALCHEMY, AND ASTROLOGY

Not all Arab and Greco-Arab science found a place in the university. Some disciplines, notably experimental science, alchemy, and astrology, were held in suspicion for the taint of magic or heresy or association with fraud. However, practitioners of these sciences did not necessarily view them as magical, but as making use of the natural properties of things. Excluded from the university curriculum, these sciences found homes elsewhere, notably the courts of princes.

The medieval university had little interest in experimentation, which had a disreputable association with magic. The experimentalist's "manipulation" of nature was often difficult to distinguish from that performed by magicians with demonic aid. Aristotelian philosophy devoted itself to nature in its ordinary course, and the artificial distortion of nature that experiments involved was seen as not conducive to natural knowledge. Some university masters might have experimented, but experimentation was not part of the curriculum.

One person who was both a university-trained Aristotelian natural philosopher and an experimental scientist was the English Franciscan friar Roger Bacon (ca. 1214–1292). Bacon argued for experimentation as a road to the knowledge of nature, but his efforts to introduce alchemy and other experimental sciences to the university curriculum failed. Ironically, in legend he was remembered mainly as a great magician.

Although Aristotle wrote nothing, or at least nothing that survives, on magic, he was a legendary magician, and magical works, including the very popular *Secret of Secrets*, were ascribed to him. It was very common to view persons who had distinguished themselves in other fields, including classic figures like Aristotle and the Roman poet Virgil, or medieval ones such as the natural philosopher Albertus Magnus (1200–1280), as great magicians. There were several religious problems with magic and quasi-magical sciences. The ascription of "natural" powers to items, such as magnets or jewels, a staple of medieval magicians, was thought to verge on idolatry. These powers were often referred to as "occult," which in the Middle Ages and early modern period referred not to those powers that were magical, but those whose causes were hidden (*occulta*, "secret things" in Latin). The concept of "occult" science also includes the idea that knowledge of these effective sciences should be kept hidden from those who would misuse them. While natural knowledge was openly taught in the university, many works of occult science used false names for the authors, as well as codes and exhortations to the reader not to tell anyone of the secrets contained within. The title "Book of Secrets" was commonly used. Magicians and alchemists claimed that if the common people got hold of their knowledge, vulgar and ignorant practitioners would give it a bad name.

Alchemy

The most important medieval experimental "magical" science was alchemy. Alchemy covered a wide range of endeavors, including the famous "Great Work," the search for the "philosopher's stone" capable of transforming base metals, such as lead, into precious ones, such as gold. However, it also included more practical applications. Alchemists worked with miners and metal manufacturers in smelting and the mixing of alloys. The shortage of gold and silver in late medieval Europe made this a particularly important issue, and alchemists participated in the devaluation of coinage by mixing precious metals with "base" metals. There was also a medical alchemy dedicated to identifying those substances that could cure disease and promote health, such as the "elixir of life." Many alchemists were also physicians. Alchemy was also viewed in a spiritual sense, as a means of purifying the soul by purifying matter, although this view was more common in the Renaissance than in the Middle Ages. An early-fifteenth-century book described the death and resurrection of Jesus Christ as an alchemical process.

Western alchemy had Greek roots but had been developed by Arabic speakers— the word "alchemy" first appears in Arabic, although there are different theories as to whence it came into the language. Improved communications across Eurasia brought about by the spread of Islam also meant that Islamic alchemists were able to draw on Chinese Daoist ideas, such as the elixir of life, which in turn were transmitted to Western alchemists. The idea of the Islamic East as a source of alchemical wisdom would persist into the seventeenth century.

Knowledge of alchemy seems to have been lost in the early medieval West along with the rest of Greek science, and like other sciences it was recovered from the Islamic world. The first Arabic treatise on alchemy was translated into Latin in 1144. Much of the Western chemical vocabulary still bears traces of its Arabic origin—words such as alkali, naptha, alkahest, and alcohol.

A key role in both the creation and transmission of alchemical knowledge was played by Jews. The association between Jews and alchemy went back to its earliest days: The first Western alchemist whose name is recorded is Maria the Jewess, who lived around the second or third centuries CE and was credited with the invention of the *bain-marie*, a hot-water bath enabling slow and even heating and used in the kitchen as well as the chemical laboratory. (The association is probably apocryphal, inasmuch as the term was not used until the Middle Ages, about a thousand years after Maria's career.) The strong continuing associations of Jews and alchemy can be seen not only in the careers of Jewish alchemists but also the use of Hebrew as a language of power in alchemical texts. Both Muslim and Christian masters claimed to have learned alchemy from Jewish teachers.

Learned alchemy as practiced in both Islam and the West demanded a familiarity with philosophy, often including Aristotelian matter theory. Alchemical theory developed in the basically Aristotelian terms of the four qualities—hot/cold and moist/dry. Alchemy was not a theoretical alternative to Aristotelian natural philosophy in the Middle Ages. Alchemists differed from scholastic natural philosophers in their future orientation: While the scholastics usually presented their work in terms of the recovery of ancient wisdom, alchemists sometimes boasted that their science showed how the works of nature would be perfected by human art, another aspect of their science that aroused religious suspicion.

Alchemy was vulnerable to criticism on several fronts. The alchemical project of creating gold was viewed as fraudulent or demonic. Alchemical fraud was indeed common, as numerous charlatans claimed the ability to create gold, harming the reputation of the science. Laws were promulgated against them. "Spiritual" alchemy was denigrated for its association with mystical and heretical religion by both Muslims and Christians.

The court was a natural home for alchemists who claimed the ability to create precious metal. Rulers had both the financial resources to supply alchemists with the materials they needed and a burning desire for wealth. Some alchemical writers warned against associations with princes, who would ceaselessly pressure the alchemist for gold, but a serious alchemical laboratory was expensive, and many had no choice but to seek financial backing. This also involved risk—if a prince decided he had been defrauded by a fraudulent alchemist, there was no limit to the revenge he might take.

Astrology

Another "disreputable" science was astrology. Medieval astrology was based on the idea that the stars and planets exert an influence on the affairs of Earth. This influence was not necessarily "magical"; it was the enemies of astrology who associated it with magic. Many astrologers seem to have viewed the celestial forces as "natural." Astrology had a long history, intertwined with the history of astronomy. The greatest ancient astronomer, Ptolemy, was also the greatest ancient astrologer, and astronomy was often valued for its usefulness for astrological prediction. Unlike alchemy, knowledge of astrology was never entirely lost in the West after the fall of Rome. However, the astrology of the early Middle Ages was crude compared to that of the ancient world. The era of translation greatly changed Western astrology, transforming it into a learned discipline. Arabic works on astrology, which drew from Persian and Mesopotamian traditions as well as Greek, were translated into Latin along with the writings and charts of Greek astrologers.

Astrology was a complex discipline, demanding a great deal of astronomical skill. The taking of horoscopes involved a complete chart of the positions of the sun, moon, and planets at a particular moment in terms of both their positions in the zodiac and relative to the horizon—the "house." The key to astrological prediction was not just the positions of the celestial bodies against the stellar background but also their positions relative to each other—the "aspects," which could be good or bad. Astrological curiosity was one force supporting astronomy, as it would remain through the sixteenth century.

Astrology raised fundamental religious questions. Jewish, Christian, and Islamic religious authorities opposed it because the claim that the influence of the stars determined events on Earth seemed to infringe on the omnipotence of God. Christians further attacked astrology on the grounds that it deprived humans of free will. Some also feared that astrology would lead to the worship of the stars and planets as gods—mythology continued to influence the perception of the sky as the names of the planets and many of the constellations harkened back to paganism. The general idea that the stars influenced events on Earth was accepted— it was undeniable that the sun influenced the weather and the sun and moon the tides—but many wanted to restrict astrology to general questions rather than the destiny of specific individuals and societies. Scholastic philosophers and physicians were willing to admit that the stars influenced the body but were careful to specify that they could not determine a person's actions—the will remained free, even if a person chose to follow the promptings of the stars.

In response to criticism based on religion, many astrologers were careful to emphasize that the stars did not determine but merely influenced terrestrial events and human choices. Some clergymen practiced astrology and others claimed that significant religious events such as the creation or end of the world could be dated astrologically. The three magi who attended the infant Jesus guided by the star of Bethlehem provided an excellent Christian precedent for astrology.

By the late Middle Ages, astrology had begun to be taught in the university setting. However, like the alchemist, the medieval astrologer was more a "court" than a university figure. The principal job of the court astrologer was not to predict the future but to determine the right times for events. The position of the stars in the heavens determined the favorability of the time for royal enterprises, including coronations, military expeditions, medical procedures, weddings, and even the consummation of marriages. Court astrology also posed its dangers: One of the most severe astrological offenses was predicting the day of a king's death, and the failure of a high-profile prediction could discredit an astrologer. Astrological information was much in demand, by rebels and other enemies of the ruler as well as the sovereign.

TWO

THE ANCIENTS
AND THE MODERNS

European science in the fifteenth century, like science in other Afro-Eurasian civilizations, was heavily dependent on texts. Many of these texts were ancient, having originated with the classical Greeks or Romans and in some cases drawing on still earlier cultures. Some were more recent, having been first written in medieval Latin or Arabic. (The Hebrew Bible, usually read in Latin translation, was even older, but had as yet relatively little impact on the content of science, while the Christian New Testament had even less.) Most of the important texts had also acquired a secondary body of interpretations, abridgements, and commentaries.

The world of textual science in the fifteenth and sixteenth centuries was transformed by two revolutions—one the humanist rediscovery of lost ancient literature and particularly Greek literature and the other the introduction of printing with movable type. These developments enabled the dissemination of dozens of ancient and medieval scientific texts, in astronomy, botany, medicine, mathematics, natural philosophy, and many other disciplines. It also enabled the recovery of several schools of natural philosophy in addition to the dominant Aristotelianism of the Middle Ages. The ancients did not speak with one voice but were a glorious cacophony. The revival of ancient voices, by making early modern natural philosophers aware of a broad range of intellectual options, fostered changes from the scholastic Aristotelianism that dominated medieval thought about nature.

HUMANISM AND SCIENCE

The humanist movement, beginning in the fourteenth century, emerged in the city-states of northern Italy, one of the most economically advanced areas of Europe due to its connection with Mediterranean trade. It was dedicated to the recovery, preservation, and reading of ancient texts, both Greek and Latin. Particularly in the early stages of the movement, humanists were driven by a passion to restore the lost world of antiquity, a period many made no bones about preferring to their own. Many found the culture and institutions of the city-states of ancient Greece and Rome relevant to the problems faced by the Italian cities. Humanists scoured monastery libraries in remote parts of Europe in search of copies of ancient Roman texts. They acted outside the university system, although relations were not always hostile, and strove to recover the ancient writers in their original forms, not translated or encrusted with the centuries of commentaries produced by Greeks, Romans, Arabs, and medieval university professors.

Humanism was not a scientific movement, but its achievement was essential for the Scientific Revolution. Natural philosophy was not the main interest for most humanists, but natural philosophical, medical, and other scientific texts were valued along with other ancient writings. Many of the classical scientific writings of the Greeks and their Roman epigones were recovered and circulated in this period.

The Rediscovery of Greek

The rediscovery of Ancient Greek, including Greek science, was a product of both the humanist movement and the larger changes of the Mediterranean world. With the fall of the Roman Empire, the knowledge of Greek had largely died out in the northwestern Mediterranean, as the knowledge of Latin had disappeared among the Greek Christians of the Byzantine Empire. There were some areas where direct Greek-to-Latin translation did take place in the Middle Ages, notably Sicily and southern Italy where the ancient Greek heritage had never entirely disappeared, but access to Greek manuscripts was limited. Much of the Greek corpus known to medieval natural philosophers was the product of Greek-to-Arabic-to-Latin translation, which was very selective—numerous works of Aristotle had been translated but only two thirds of one dialogue of Plato's, the *Timaeus*.

The Byzantine Empire had been hostile to the Westerners since the fall of its capital at Constantinople to the Fourth Crusade in 1204, a hostility that did not end with the restoration of the Empire to Constantinople in 1261. However, by the late fourteenth century, the growing power of the Muslim Ottoman Turks and the wealth of the Italian city-states were bringing Eastern and Western Christians closer together. The threat of the Turks, who had crossed over into Europe and begun to conquer the Christian kingdoms of the Balkans, caused Greek and Latin Christians to explore new alliances. Byzantine royalty intermarried with Italian nobles, Greek scholars represented the Byzantine Church at Western church councils, and ambassadors from the emperor at Constantinople pleaded for help at European courts. In its last centuries the Empire also underwent a cultural revival, with increased interest in the writings of Plato and other ancient philosophers. The various meetings of Eastern and Western dignitaries fostered more contact between intellectuals. The desperate condition of the Eastern Empire, which fell to the Turks in 1453, also encouraged many

Greek-speaking intellectuals to think of a future in the West. One of the earliest and most influential of the Greek teachers, Manuel Chrysoloras (1355–1415), arrived in Italy as a teacher after he had first visited as an ambassador. Humanist scholars from Italy also journeyed to Constantinople to bring back previously unknown manuscripts.

Greek scholars knew that Western humanist intellectuals, librarians, and manuscript collectors hungered for classical Greek writings. By bringing the Greek language with them, the Byzantine immigrants also ensured that the new texts could be read in their original as well as translated forms. Even old Greek texts known for centuries in Latin translation, including the works of Aristotle, could now be read in their original language and translated directly into Latin and European vernaculars without going through an intermediate language like Arabic.

As much as they revered ancient Greek authors, the humanists despised the Arab philosophers, scientists, physicians, and commentators of the Middle Ages. Part of this bias was the belief that the Arabs, like the medieval European Latin commentators, had distorted the true meaning of the ancient texts in the process of transmission. A humanist motto was *"ad fontes"*—to the sources, meaning the original Greek and Latin writers—and humanist science was not an exception to this pattern. The most valuable scientific writers in the eyes of most humanists were those who wrote before the fall of the Roman Empire, and in particular the ancient Greeks like Ptolemy and Galen. Subsequent writers, Latin or Arab, represented a decline.

Many Arab writers, such as Ibn Sina and Ibn Rushd, were also associated with the scholastic university curriculum that many humanists considered outmoded. While the medieval Latin corpus and the university canon included revered and sometimes even canonized Christian thinkers like Thomas Aquinas, whose popularity as a theologian was at its height in the early modern period, the Arabs could be freely rejected and mocked for their Islamic belief as well as their "barbarism." This dislike of Muslims was shared by contemporary Greeks, the last vestiges of whose independence were falling into the power of the Muslim Ottomans. Humanists denied that the Arabs had made any original contribution to knowledge, at best merely passing on the writings of the Greeks. This prejudice would have a long history in Western thought.

THE REVIVAL OF ANCIENT ALTERNATIVES TO ARISTOTELIANISM

An important aspect of the humanist revival of ancient natural philosophy was that readers were presented with a number of alternatives to Aristotelian approaches, some of them radically different. These would be adopted and adapted throughout the Scientific Revolution. The presentation of alternative philosophies fostered the intellectual pluralism of sixteenth- and early-seventeenth-century natural philosophy.

Platonism

Platonism derives from Aristotle's teacher Plato (427–347 BCE), although the Platonic philosophy has taken many forms in the millennia since he taught. Although Platonists have a variety of differences between themselves, their basic approach to the natural world is that it is an inferior imitation of the world of "archetypes"—Plato compared our perception of the universe to people chained in a cave looking at shadows. The realities we perceive through our senses are but the shadows of the true nature of things. Platonism as it was understood in the sixteenth and seventeenth centuries was heavily influenced by the "neo-Platonic" interpretation dating from the late Roman Empire. Neo-Platonists viewed the universe as mathematically structured and number as the secret to the universe. The Platonist emphasis on the unreality of the world of the senses fit in well with mystically oriented Christianity. The Greek Orthodox Church was influenced by neo-Platonism far more than Aristotelianism, and Platonic ideas were advanced by the clerically trained Greeks who came to Italy in the late fourteenth and fifteenth centuries, along with their Italian disciples.

The Platonic view of the actual world as an imperfect embodiment of the "real" world of archetypes or Forms has affinities with the view developed during the Scientific Revolution of the physical world as imperfectly exemplifying real mathematical "laws." The physicist and astronomer Galileo Galilei (1564–1642), for example, sometimes proclaimed himself a Platonist for this reason. The legend was that inscribed above the gate of the original Platonic Academy at Athens were the words "let none enter who are ignorant of geometry," and Platonism awarded mathematics a higher intellectual status than did Aristotelianism. Plato's description of God as a geometer was frequently referred to in the Scientific Revolution.

Neo-Platonic mysticism, with its emphasis on the harmony of number, influenced the astronomy of Copernicus and Kepler. Kepler's *Harmonia Mundi* (1619), a work expounding his new astronomy, had the same title as the Christian neo-Platonic Kabbalist treatise published by the Venetian friar Francesco Giorgi (1466–1540) in 1525. Kepler's scheme for relating the orbital distances of the planets to the regular or "Platonic" solids also drew on neo-Platonism (Fig. 2-1).

However, despite Platonism's growing popularity, Plato's works never seriously rivaled Aristotle's in the university curriculum. Plato's dialogues could not be arranged in a course of study in the fashion of Aristotle's systematic treatises, which covered a far wider range of topics. Despite Plato's long-established reputation as the most Christian of ancient philosophers, anti-Platonists were suspicious of his paganism and his endorsement of love between men. Catholic authorities often looked on Platonism with suspicion as related to magic and heresy, although many Platonists were loyal Catholics. Despite the opposition of conservative churchmen, there were professors of Plato in Italian universities, including Rome's Papal University, La Sapienza, by the 1570s. Although many tried to combine Plato and Aristotle (and both with Christianity), waving the banner of Plato was one way for scientists like Galileo to express their opposition to Aristotle.

Figure 2-1. Frontispiece to Kepler's *Rudolphine Tables*. The elaborate frontispiece to Kepler's *Rudolphine Tables* includes representations of four named astronomers in addition to Kepler himself: the ancient Greeks Hipparchus and Ptolemy and the sixteenth-century astronomers Copernicus and Tycho. This humanist-influenced narrative of progress from the anonymous ancient Babylonian reckoning on his fingers in the back to Copernicus and Tycho omits Arab and medieval Latin astronomers, essentially treating the span of well over a millennium between Ptolemy and Copernicus as an empty space. This approach would greatly influence understandings of the history of science in the West for centuries.

A key individual in the spread of Platonic knowledge in Latin Europe during the fifteenth century was Marsilio Ficino of Florence (1433–1499). Ficino, under the patronage of Cosimo de Medici (1389–1464), banker and political boss of the city-state of Florence, led a group of scholars whose mission was to translate and disseminate Plato's works. This informal group is sometimes referred to as the "Platonic Academy of Florence," although it lacked the formal structure and defined membership of later academies and scientific societies. Ficino, who was fascinated by magic and astrology, interpreted Plato in a "neo-Platonic" way with affinities for magic and mysticism. In addition to Plato's works, the group translated into Latin the *Enneads* of the ancient neo-Platonic philosopher Plotinus (204/5–270 CE).

The *Prisca Sapientia*

Allied to the Platonic revival was the belief in the ancient wisdom, the *prisca sapientia*. The ultimate source of this wisdom was God, who had handed it down to Moses. From Moses the wisdom had been passed down to a variety of legendary and historical figures from various cultures, including Zoroaster the Persian, Pythagoras the Greek, and Plato. (Some viewed Aristotle as one of the inheritors of the ancient wisdom, but Plato was much more strongly identified with it.) One of the most intriguing of these figures was the legendary Egyptian Hermes Trismegistus or Hermes the Thrice-Great, the author of a series of Greek religious and magical treatises known as the Hermetic corpus. In the sixteenth century the Hermetic corpus was thought to be very old, dating to shortly after Moses, although in fact it was written around the second century of the Common Era. (The humanist scholar Isaac Casaubon [1556–1614] revealed the true dating of the Hermetic Corpus in 1614.) The Hermetic writings had been lost to the West in the Middle Ages and rediscovered in the Renaissance. Ficino made them better known with the publication of a Latin translation of thirteen Hermetic tracts in 1471. The Jewish Kabbalah, which had only recently become known to Christians, was also often viewed as part of the ancient wisdom and indeed shared some of the same neo-Platonic roots as the Hermetic corpus.

The content of the *prisca sapientia* could be obscure, but it basically emphasized the connection between God and the cosmos as an emanation or a series of emanations of God. The role of angelic hierarchies as intermediaries between God and man is also frequently invoked. While for astrologers celestial influences could be good or ill depending on which planet was their source, for the *prisca sapientia* all celestial influences tended to the good. The idea of man as a "microcosm" of the universe, the "macrocosm," was also common in the ancient wisdom, as was the idea of a cosmic harmony.

Although many sources of the *prisca sapientia*, including the Hermetic writings and the Kaballah, were not Christian, its supporters viewed it as compatible with Christianity or even, after the Reformation, as offering the possibility of a true reform of Christianity that would heal the division between Catholics and Protestants. The *prisca sapientia* was particularly attractive to believers in magic, particularly since both the Hermetic writings and the Kabbalah were commonly viewed as magical. Ficino was particularly interested, and translated the Hermetic writings into Latin at the behest of Cosimo de Medici. Hermeticism was one source of Copernicus's heliocentrism, and among the believers in the ancient wisdom who saw it as an inspiration for his own work was Isaac Newton. The Hermetic tradition also endorsed the idea of using knowledge for doing things, making it particularly compatible with experimental alchemy.

Epicureanism

The revival of the ancient philosophy of Epicurus was less shaped by the recovery of Greek texts—few original Epicurean works survived—than by the recovery of a Latin epic, the first-century BCE Roman poet Lucretius's *De Rerum Natura, Of the Nature of Things*. Lucretius and Epicureanism generally had been largely forgotten during the Middle Ages and his poem survived in only three copies, one of which was rediscovered and made public by the humanist manuscript hunter Poggio Bracciolini (1380–1459) in the early fifteenth century.

Lucretius set forth in powerful Latin verse the Epicurean theory of a world constructed entirely of tiny, hard, uncuttable bits of matter—atoms—moving in empty space. These "atoms and the void" literally constituted the entire universe. Epicureanism was philosophically materialist, with no room for a spiritual soul, which made it anathema to many Christians. Epicurus was often viewed as particularly repulsive by Christians who respected other ancient philosophers. The medieval Italian poet Dante Alighieri (1265–1321), author of the *Divine Comedy* about his journeys through Hell, Purgatory, and Heaven, put most ancient philosophers, including Aristotle, in the "nice part of Hell," the Limbo of virtuous non-Christians, but Epicurus in Hell proper suffering eternal torment as a denier of the immortality of the soul. The idea, frequently associated with the universe of clashing atoms, that the universe was governed by chance also presented religious problems.

Epicurean physical theory was handicapped in the eyes of Christians by its association with Epicurean ethics, which revolved around pleasure rather than adherence to a moral law, and with Epicurean "atheism"—not the denial of the existence of gods, but the assertion that they were irrelevant for human life. There was no place for divine guidance in the Epicurean universe. Lucretius was hostile to organized religion and would later become a hero of skeptics and atheists. However, since the religion he denounced was classical paganism and not Christianity, this hostility could be explained away.

Even with its numerous thorny religious problems, Epicureanism appealed as a materialist philosophy that did not endow matter with the kinds of sensibilities that Aristotelianism did. Epicurus and Lucretius appealed to those who wished to view the universe in a mechanical way, a position with growing appeal in the seventeenth century. This was not necessarily viewed as anti-Christian—denying that matter was endowed with sensibility could be seen as a way of reserving those qualities to God and the souls he created. The leader of the seventeenth-century revival of Epicurean physics, the French priest Pierre Gassendi (1592–1655), spent much his intellectual labor presenting Epicurus in a way acceptable to Christians—"baptizing Epicurus" as the medieval scholastics had baptized Aristotle. For example, while Epicurus had claimed that the atoms existed without a beginning or end in time, Gassendi claimed that God had created them. Gassendi's project had some success. By the late seventeenth century, even the devoutly Christian if unorthodox Isaac Newton could describe the philosophy of Epicurus and Lucretius as "true and old" although "wrongly interpreted" as "atheism."

Intellectually, the principal problem with Epicureanism was explaining how complex organisms like living things emerged merely from the clashing of atoms in the void. One device was the "clinamen," or "swerve," a mysterious force that drew atoms together. Lucretius had claimed that the clinamen was what kept atoms from simply falling in unconnected paths in the void. However, he provided no explanation for the clinamen, and it remained a problem to vex early modern Epicureans.

Stoicism

Stoicism, the dominant school of Greek and Roman philosophy during the Hellenistic era and the early Roman Empire, had attracted little interest during the Middle Ages but was influential in many areas of early modern life, including law, theology, and politics. The Stoic universe, philosophically monotheistic and dominated by divine providence, was far more compatible with Christianity than that of the Epicureans and arguably than that of Aristotle. (This was logical, as Stoic ideas had influenced the formation of Christianity.) Stoic ethics were also popular among some early modern Christian humanists.

In natural philosophy, Stoicism was particularly influential in cosmology. As in the case of Epicureanism, the principal source of Stoic natural philosophy was not a Greek but a Roman writer. Seneca's *Natural Questions* was by far the most extensive treatment of natural philosophy surviving from an ancient Stoic. The statesman and popularizer Marcus Tullius Cicero (106–43 BCE), whose much-admired works discussed Stoicism alongside other ancient philosophies, including Epicureanism, also helped shape the Stoic legacy to the early modern period. Stoicism had less impact on natural philosophy than Epicureanism, but it did have a unique physical picture that offered an alternative to Aristotelianism without Epicureanism's religious radicalism. While Aristotelianism proclaimed an absolute difference between celestial and terrestrial matter, Stoics viewed the universe as uniform and the same conditions prevailing in the heavens and the Earth. Stars and planets swam through a medium, a form of increasingly rarefied matter called the *pneuma*, or breath, guided by divine intelligences rather than being carried on crystalline spheres as the Aristotelians thought. Early modern cosmologists, including Tycho Brahe and Johannes Kepler, found the Stoic cosmology more suited to their world-pictures than Aristotelianism. The elimination of the crystalline spheres opened the way for intersecting paths, noncircular motion, and other departures from the traditional scheme.

The acceptance of Stoic cosmological models did not necessarily mean support of the revolutionary new astronomy of the Scientific Revolution. Among the supporters of a Stoic approach to cosmology was the Jesuit Cardinal Robert Bellarmine (1542–1621), who strongly opposed sun-centered astronomy and enforced the Catholic Church's strictures against it. Nor did Stoicism raise no religious problems, although its acceptance of a providential universe made it less "blasphemous" than Epicureanism. Stoic natural philosophy, like Epicurean, was materialistic, which contradicted the spiritual universe of the Christians, and like most Greek philosophical systems it was utterly incompatible with the biblical account of creation.

Skepticism

Skepticism was an ancient philosophy that attacked the possibility of certain knowledge. It had been ignored or despised for much of the Middle Ages but underwent a revival in the sixteenth century based primarily on the works of Sextus Empiricus, a second-century CE Greek philosopher. Sextus's works had been virtually unknown in the Latin Middle Ages, but Greek manuscripts were circulating in Western Europe by the late fifteenth century. There were two main schools of early modern skepticism. Moderate or academic skeptics believed that nothing could be known for certain, while the more influential school of radical or Pyrrhonian skeptics like Sextus believed that even the impossibility of certain knowledge could not be known for sure. Skepticism was employed in many arenas during the sixteenth century, including religious dispute. Although ancient skepticism lacked a natural philosophy, its revival had a profound impact on the development of early modern science.

Skepticism was a solvent of the certainties of scholastic Aristotelianism and helped foster interest in new ways of attaining certain or at least reliable knowledge. Although some still hoped that natural knowledge could be founded on a certain basis even after the rejection of scholasticism, the ultimate solution outside mathematics was a mitigated skepticism that assigned to opinions a high degree of probability rather than certainty.

The New Aristotelianism

Aristotelianism retained a massive institutional presence into the early eighteenth century, particularly in the universities of Catholic countries, and many natural philosophers were first educated in it before being exposed to alternatives. Aristotle continued to have his champions among the scientific elite well into the seventeenth century, including William Harvey (1578–1657), the discoverer of the circulation of the blood, who referred to the anti-Aristotelian new philosophers, or "neoteriques," as "shit-breeches."

The revival of ancient learning also changed Aristotelianism. Much of Aristotle's voluminous corpus had been unavailable in the Latin Middle Ages, and what was read was often read under the influence of commentaries like that of Ibn Rushd, the "Commentator," as Aristotle was the "Philosopher." Medieval writers were interested in many of Aristotle's works on subjects like metaphysics but much less interested in his works on biology, some of the most advanced studies of the subject produced before the Scientific Revolution.

The revival of interest in the Greek world led to these hitherto obscure Aristotelian works being examined with new interest. There was also an interest in basing Aristotelianism on Aristotle's original Greek texts, ignoring the Latin translations (many of which had been translations from the Arabic rather than the original Greek) and the commentary tradition—an interest particularly powerful in the Italian universities such as the University of Padua, the most advanced school of medicine and the sciences in the sixteenth century.

By the early sixteenth century, the Italian universities saw a movement toward the study of Aristotelianism in a humanist-influenced, nonscholastic form by men such as Pietro Pomponazzi (1462–1525), a professor successively at the universities of Padua, Ferrara, and Bologna. Pomponazzi claimed to be expounding the original Aristotle cleansed of centuries of Greek, Arab, and Latin commentaries and distortions, although he was not a strict Aristotelian, incorporating Platonic and skeptical elements as well. Pomponazzi's advocacy of the original Aristotle required the removal of the many adjustments that made the Philosopher acceptable to Christians (or, for that matter, Muslims and Jews). Pomponazzi argued that Aristotelianism did not imply the immortality of the soul, and Aristotle himself had denied it. Since there was no example of the soul functioning without the involvement of the body, there was no reason in philosophy to think the soul could subsist without it. He favored natural explanations over supernatural ones in many contexts, arguing that effects that many attributed to angels and devils had natural causes. (Pomponazzi included the influence of the stars as a natural cause.) Despite Pomponazzi's claim that he believed in angels, devils, and the immortality of the soul as a Christian if not a philosopher, these beliefs got him into trouble with the Catholic Church, which remained suspicious of "Averroism," the doctrine ascribed to Ibn Rushd and some of his medieval Christian disciples that a proposition could be both true in philosophy and false in theology.

THE CONTINUATION OF ANCIENT SCIENCE

Numerous scientists, including many of those later identified as "revolutionaries," often viewed themselves as heirs and continuators of ancient scientific traditions rather than their overthrowers. Starting or restarting entire disciplines from scratch had little appeal for most investigators when the ancients and their medieval successors had provided a base to build on.

The creation of new and improved editions of the ancients or commentaries on them was a common vehicle for the presentation of new scientific information. The Siennese physician Pier Andrea Mattioli (1501–1577) dominated mid-sixteenth-century botany by producing a series of expanded editions of his commentary on Dioscorides' work on plants. These editions incorporated new botanical discoveries made in both northern Europe, which Dioscorides did not survey, and in the New World that he had known nothing about. Mattioli became the center of a network of botanical correspondents whose records of plants could be included in the next edition of his commentary. His rival, the Portuguese physician Amatus Lusitanus (1511–1568), also published commentaries on Dioscorides, setting off one of the most vicious scientific controversies of the sixteenth century, in which the combative Mattioli made free use of anti-Semitic attacks on Lusitanus's Jewish ancestry. Other compilations of information on natural history, such as the Swiss polymath Conrad Gesner's *History of Animals*, also combined material taken from the ancients along with the author's own observations, although the ancient writers had devoted relatively little attention to zoology as compared to botany.

Mathematics is a unique case, in that progress in mathematics usually does not involve proving previous mathematicians wrong—Euclid's geometry remains as valid today as the day it was written—but in expanding on their work. The Italian humanist Federigo Commandino (1509–1575) led the revival of ancient mathematics, producing edition after edition of the ancient mathematicians alongside original mathematical work of his own. The logical sequencing of classic mathematic texts such as Euclid's *Elements* led some humanist mathematicians to believe that works surviving only incompletely could be recreated. Pierre de Fermat's discovery of analytic geometry began as an attempt to reconstruct the lost work of the ancient Greek Apollonius of Perga (c. 262–190 BCE).

The two men most frequently identified as scientific revolutionaries in the early sixteenth century, Copernicus and the anatomist Andreas Vesalius, were deeply proficient in the classical authors, Ptolemy the astronomer for Copernicus and Galen the physician for Vesalius. Copernicus presented his new, sun-centered astronomical picture not as a revolutionary break with ancient science but as a return to an ancient Pythagorean and Hermetic tradition. Copernicus was very familiar with the works of Ptolemy, and the structure of argument of his major work, *On the Revolutions of the Celestial Spheres* (1543), was closely modeled on that of the *Almagest*. The basic structure of Copernicus's universe drew on the tradition of Ptolemaic astronomy with its circular orbits and its established devices such as epicycles for making the positions of the planets the theory predicted match the data. Vesalius was deeply learned in Galen, having edited several humanist editions of Galenic texts, and accepted many aspects of the Galenic picture of the body.

The relation of Galileo, frequently identified by historians as a scientific revolutionary in the seventeenth century, to the ancients was more complicated. He vehemently opposed Aristotelian physics (Galileo's adoption of Copernican, sun-centered astronomy was more an anti-Aristotelian move than an anti-Ptolemaic one) but placed himself in the tradition of the ancient mathematician Archimedes as well as invoking Plato, rather than proclaiming a bold break with all of antiquity. Even his rejection of Aristotelianism was not total. Galileo, trained in Aristotelian logic in the Italian university system, used aspects of the Aristotelian method in his investigations and sometimes rhetorically employed Aristotle as an intellectual ally against his dogmatic followers.

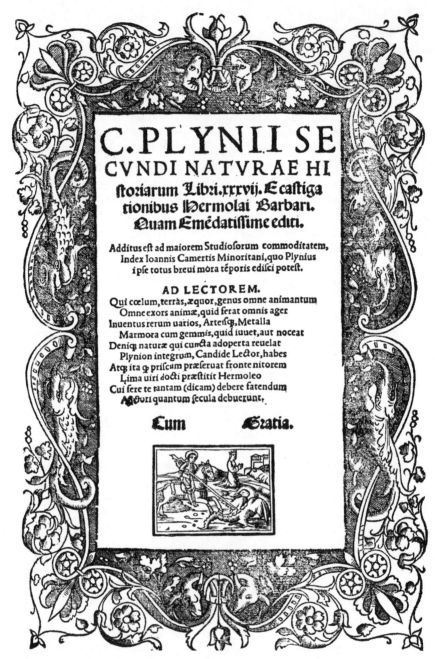

Figure 2-2.   Pliny Title Page. The title page of an early-sixteenth-century edition of Pliny's *Natural History*.

PRINTING AND SCIENCE

Printing was not invented in Europe. By the fifteenth century it had a long history stretching over many centuries in East Asia. Although some historians have claimed that Johannes Gutenberg, the first European printer, was inspired by East Asian precedents, no one has demonstrated how the detailed knowledge of East Asian technologies required to build a printing press on the Chinese model would have reached Gutenberg's home city of Nuremberg. Printing was not itself the cause of the Scientific Revolution. In the centuries that East Asia had enjoyed printing, it had not produced a Scientific Revolution. However, printing unquestionably played a major role in disseminating the new science.

Gutenberg's introduction of printing with movable type in the 1450s enabled for the first time the mass production of hundreds of virtually identical copies of a text. Although some scientists, rejecting textually based scholastic natural philosophy, spoke with scorn of book-learning as compared to the direct study of nature, in practice books remained indispensable for the circulation and preservation of knowledge. Few of the major works of the Scientific Revolution were best-sellers, but the ability of print to circulate and stabilize knowledge enabled science to become fully cumulative for the first time. The great loss of knowledge that had accompanied the decline and fall of the Roman Empire as manuscripts vanished was much less likely in a print culture. Scientists could much more easily obtain and read the works of their predecessors and contemporaries. When combined with the humanist effort to recover ancient texts, print also allowed an unprecedented circulation of ancient Greek and Latin texts, both original and in translation, on natural and mathematical subjects. Not only ancient works such as Pliny's *Natural History*, but major works of medieval Latin natural philosophers were printed, as were Latin translations from Greek and Arabic. Scientific works were also printed in Europe's vernacular languages.

Nor was the circulation of information restricted to classical and medieval Greek and Latin science. New information could also be disseminated on a massive scale, a condition that changed the very nature of scientific investigation. In astronomy, for example, a major problem for astronomers had been simply acquiring the data necessary for elaborating astronomical theories. The printing press made it relatively easy for the aspiring astronomer to acquire the body of available ancient, Arabic, medieval, and contemporary stellar and planetary observations and theory. It also facilitated the dissemination of new calculations and tables based on new astronomical systems, as well as new star catalogues. The wealthy astronomer Tycho Brahe even included a printing press in his observatory complex at Uraniborg, and he owned a paper mill to keep it supplied.

Of course, not all information was freely disseminated. Tycho kept much of his observational data secret, so that his rivals could not preempt him in the development of a new astronomical theory based on his improved data. (Kepler eventually got his hands on Tycho's observations after his death, on which he based his own revolutionary interpretation.) Many governments kept information relating to national interests and resources, such as navigational data, as secret as they could. The Catholic Church and various governments also tried to control the dissemination of printed information via censorship. Although the principal target of most censorship in early modern Europe was religious and political writings rather than scientific ones, censorship could have an impact on science, as when the Catholic Church put Copernican writings on the Index of Forbidden Books. Islamic religious authorities in the Ottoman Empire kept the printing press out of Muslim hands entirely, fearing the dissemination of erroneously printed Qurans. Although Christian minorities in the Empire operated presses, there were no Muslim-operated presses until the eighteenth century, contributing to the isolation of Ottoman Muslims from many of the scientific and intellectual developments of the Christian world.

Learned writings were not the only ones that could be printed and distributed. Basic astronomical and astrological information was widely dispersed through printed almanacs, and "books of secrets" contained basic alchemical and magical procedures. Books of secrets often took a pragmatic view of natural processes, emphasizing the results of procedures rather than theoretical explanations, that influenced the development of the experimental tradition.

Print enabled the reproduction and circulation of images as well as words. Before print, images and maps had been even more vulnerable to corruption at the hands of generations of copyists than had words. Illustrations of plants and animals in natural history books got successively cruder with each generation of copying by hand until different plants were represented by virtually indistinguishable images. Sixteenth-century printed botanical books reversed this process by employing increasingly detailed representations that could be reproduced in hundreds of copies, and the woodcuts or engravings themselves could be preserved so the illustrations could appear unaltered in subsequent editions or even other books.

Printing had a particularly great impact on cartography, which had advanced little since the ancients. The creation of printed maps enabled cartographers to build on others' work to create increasingly accurate representations of the Earth's surface at the same time that Europe was being flooded with descriptions of previously unknown countries and seas.

Anatomy was another area where printing had a powerful impact. The detailed woodcut illustrations of Vesalius's *Of the Fabric of the Human Body* (1543) had an even greater impact on Renaissance anatomy than the text. Amazingly detailed and accurate images could be created by skilled woodblock cutters or engravers and then reproduced over thousands of copies. Anatomical illustrations were often issued separately from the text for the use of students. Printing made possible the distribution of much more precise and standard illustrations of plants, animals, rocks, topographical features, and machines. It also served as an example of how the modern world had surpassed the works of the ancients.

REBELS AGAINST THE ANCIENTS

Not all natural philosophers viewed what they were doing as a continuation of ancient and medieval projects. Some supported a sharp break with both the ancients themselves and the Arab and medieval tradition built on ancient science. By the mid-sixteenth century, the idea of ancient science was coherent enough to provoke intellectual revolt against ancient authority as a whole, rather than simply against Aristotle. (Of course, the revolt against the ancients never implied the rejection of all ancient influence—the ancient scientists and natural philosophers, particularly Aristotle, influenced all early modern natural philosophers in a way that could never be entirely overcome, even if it was desired.) These revolts against the ancients led to the first attempts to formulate a distinctively "modern" scientific program. The revolts were very different from each other, depending on what aspects of ancient science were found objectionable and what program was suggested to replace it.

The Religious and Magical Revolt—Paracelsus

An early champion of the complete rejection of ancient and medieval science and the building of science on a new foundation was the German physician and alchemist Paracelsus (1493–1541). His original name was Theophrastus von Hohenheim. Adopting a Latin name was a common practice among scholars. The name "Paracelsus" meant "equal to Celsus," the Roman medical encyclopedist, and adopting it in itself constituted a challenge to the ancients.

Much of Paracelsus's rebellion against the ancients was driven by what had always been recognized as among the biggest chinks in the armor of ancient philosophy and science—the fact that the vast majority of the ancient authorities were not Christians. This was an effective argument against the Muslim Arab philosophers as well as the ancient Greek and Roman pagans. Even the undoubtedly Christian scholastic philosophers were delegitimized by their dependence on the ancients and the Arabs. There was also an anti-intellectual element to Paracelsus's challenge to antiquity, which went along with an institutional challenge to the university that relied on the ancient and Arab thinkers. His contempt for traditional authority and the Arabs in particular is exemplified by his famous public burning of the *Canon* of Ibn Sina, the basic textbook of medicine. Paracelsus argued that natural philosophers and physicians should, rather than read old books, seek out the wisdom of the common people, including peasants and women. He also believed that knowledge should be circulated as well as gathered from the common people, lecturing in German rather than in the learned language of the university, Latin.

Alchemy, a science without an authoritative body of ancient texts, was particularly attractive for many who wished to denigrate or escape ancient authority. The pragmatic approach of alchemists, who were more concerned with results (whether or not they actually attained those results) than theoretical explanations, was also appealing to those who found the ancients too talkative. Paracelsus was identified with a reform of medicine on alchemical rather than Galenic principles. Paracelsian matter theory, based on three substances he called salt, sulfur, and mercury rather than the Aristotelian earth, air, water, and fire, had alchemical origins but no real roots in antiquity. Like many, but not all, alchemists Paracelsus was identified as a magician. Paracelsus's emphasis on the religious illegitimacy of the ancients and Arabs was followed by other magical writers such as the Italian Dominican and defender of Galileo Tomasso Campanella (1568–1639). His unsystematic medical works were systematized by his disciples, and "Paracelsianism" or "chemical medicine" constituted an alternative to the works of Galen and Ibn Sina into the late seventeenth century. However, his radical challenge was muted by some of his disciples, who sought to blend Paracelsian and Galenic medicine in "eclectic" practice.

The Empirical Revolt—Francis Bacon

Unlike Paracelsus, the English statesman and philosopher Francis Bacon (1561–1626) was deeply learned in ancient culture (although his Latin was considerably stronger than his Greek) and respectful of many aspects of ancient thought. Bacon's revolt also differed from Paracelsus's in having little to do with the religion of the ancient philosophers. It resembled Paracelsus's in being based on what he saw as the practical fruitlessness of ancient natural philosophy. Most ancient philosophers, Bacon claimed, had been more driven by the desire to make money or feed their own egos than by the quest for truth.

Bacon was impressed by the technological advances of his time, particularly gunpowder, the printing press, and the magnetic compass (all Chinese inventions, although Europeans had considerably improved on them, particularly the compass). He saw these innovations, rather than political or religious events, as marking out modern times. None of these inventions had been inspired by the science of the day, which by comparison seemed stagnant. Bacon believed that science had the potential to drive technological change, but for that to happen it had to be fundamentally reformed—and the need for this reform had been created by the weakness of ancient science. "Now the true and lawful goal of the sciences is none other than this: that human life be endowed with new discoveries and powers." Ancient science, he believed, had a rhetorical rather than a practical bent. Bacon's emphasis on the practical applications of theoretical science to increase man's power over nature had no ancient precedent.

The solution to the sterility of ancient science was to reroot science in empirical reality rather than ancient or modern theory, and build new theories on a base created by observation. Bacon envisioned a scientific project devoted to gathering accounts of nature, systematically arranging them, and developing theories based on data rather than ancient or even modern authorities. The knowledge would then be put to use to increase man's power over nature. The projects would require not the work of an individual philosopher in his study but the cooperative effort of many, with different persons assigned different tasks. Bacon did not share Paracelsus's populist interest in the knowledge of the common people but saw natural philosophy as the task of an intellectual and social elite. Unregulated knowledge could itself represent a danger.

Bacon was deeply involved in the politics of England in his time, and this shaped his scientific program. It would require and encourage a far greater involvement by the state in science than had hitherto been the case and certainly more than had been the case in the ancient and medieval worlds, when natural philosophers had worked largely independently of governments. When state-driven scientific societies and academies such as England's Royal Society and France's Royal Academy of Sciences were founded in the second half of the seventeenth century, they would claim inspiration from Bacon. Bacon's orientation to the state also meant that he was much more reluctant than Paracelsus to allow this new knowledge to circulate among ordinary people.

Bacon's philosophy is often described as "experimental." However, Bacon was not usually referring to artificially created experiments, but to close observations of nature. But as "experimental philosophy" and such experimental technology as the prism and the air pump emerged in the mid- to late seventeenth century, the experimentalists, particularly the English experimentalists, placed themselves in a "Baconian" tradition, like Bacon putting experimental "facts" over theory, but unlike Bacon progressing from the experimental data to new natural philosophical ideas.

The Rationalist Revolt—René Descartes

The most thoroughgoing revolt against the ancients was that of the French philosopher and mathematician René Descartes (1596–1650). Descartes, one of the most ambitious minds produced by the Scientific Revolution, wanted to elaborate a complete system of natural philosophy on a new basis to compete with and eventually replace that of Aristotle. Ideally, Descartes' new system would have reorganized the disciplines from astronomy to medicine and served as the basis of a reformed university curriculum.

Descartes was thoroughly educated in ancient thought as a pupil of the Jesuits, whose schools combined humanist and scholastic approaches to philosophy. His attitude to the ancients was less to attack them and deny their authority than to ignore them as much as possible to put forth his own philosophy. The new philosophy would be built on new foundations based on reason. Although Descartes' "corpuscularian" natural philosophy was clearly influenced by ancient Epicureanism and Aristotelianism, he broke with the tradition of proclaiming one's fidelity to one or another school of ancient philosophy to emphasize his own originality. Pierre Gassendi, who proclaimed himself a follower of Epicurus, was one of Descartes' greatest intellectual rivals despite sharing many aspects of Descartes' natural philosophy. Descartes claimed that both metaphysics and natural philosophy could be founded on an introspective basis, by searching one's own soul first and building outward. The physical properties of the universe could be deduced from a set of first principles ascertained through reason and expounded through "clear and distinct" ideas. Cartesianism in the late seventeenth century was openly flaunted as a "modern" philosophy, often written in French rather than Latin, in opposition to the "pedantry" of the university-educated Aristotelian natural philosophers.

The Cartesian program was largely successful as a rival to Aristotelianism and Gassendi's revived Epicureanism in the late seventeenth and early eighteenth centuries. Many universities, particularly in the Protestant world where there was more academic flexibility, adopted Cartesian natural philosophy as part of their curriculum. Many natural philosophers, including some like Newton who later repudiated it, adopted Cartesianism as the most complete system of natural philosophy incorporating modern discoveries like Copernicanism.

THREE

New Worlds of Science

The early modern period saw a tremendous increase in European involvement with and knowledge of the outside world, whether dealing with previously unknown regions like the Americas, or regions previously known only from a distance like India and East Asia. Beginning with the Portuguese African and Atlantic voyages of the early fifteenth century, Europeans encountered, traded with, and invaded much of the Americas, Africa, and Asia. Direct contact with the Americas was initiated by the voyage of Christopher Columbus (1450?–1506), under Spanish patronage, in 1492. Six years later the Portuguese captain Vasco da Gama (c. 1460–1524) circumnavigated Africa, enabling direct contacts between Europe and the Indian Ocean, the center of world commerce. This new knowledge gained from these contacts transformed European science, gradually making it clear that the books of the ancients were not complete repositories of natural knowledge, creating new intellectual problems and making other problems more urgent. European contact with other lands and other cultures shaped the Scientific Revolution by introducing new kinds of information and requiring new ways of thought to deal with it. The new attitudes were less tradition-bound, more practical, and more based on experience (Fig. 3-1).

THE INSUFFICIENCY OF THE ANCIENTS

Exploration revealed the falsity or insufficiency of much traditional European knowledge. Aristotle's belief that the equatorial zone of the Earth's surface was too hot for human beings to inhabit was thoroughly disproved by Iberian sailors and the African and American peoples they encountered. The circumnavigation of Africa demonstrated that the Indian Ocean was not an inland sea, as Ptolemy, who had been the ancient world's authority in geography as well as astronomy, had claimed. Educated belief in the traditional monstrous races such as the people with dog's heads, thought since classical times to be living outside Europe, declined in the early modern period as more was known about the world. (This process

Figure 3-1.   Piri Reis Map. This early surviving map with the American coast marked is not Spanish but Ottoman, a possession of the Ottoman admiral Piri Reis. Its existence testifies to the circulation of geographical information across Mediterranean cultures.

took a long time—as late as the early seventeenth century Sir Walter Raleigh was claiming that Guiana was the home of the traditional "race of people without heads whose faces were in their chests.") Columbus's first letter from the New World specifically mentioned the lack of monstrosities. Astronomers were faced

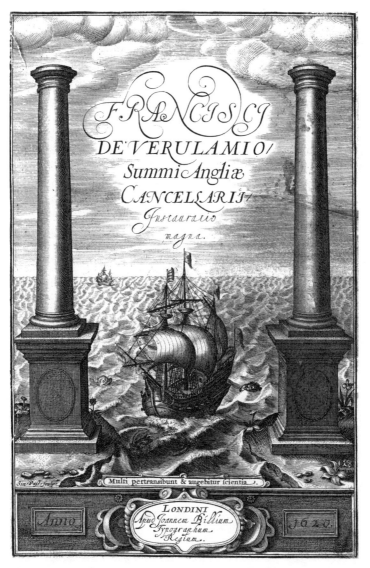

Figure 3-2.   Bacon, *Instauratio Magna* Frontispiece. This frontispiece of Francis Bacon's proposal for the reform of natural knowledge represents a ship sailing beyond the "Pillars of Hercules" that divided the Mediterranean from the Atlantic. It harks back to the great Atlantic voyages of Columbus and his successors as a mark of how the modern world could exceed the ancient.

with the stars of the southern sky, unknown to Ptolemy and the ancient and medieval stargazers (Fig. 3-2).

Parts of Asia and Africa and the Middle East had been known to the ancients and there had been some direct contact with China and Ethiopia during the Middle Ages, but America presented a more fundamental intellectual challenge.

The basic problem, once Europeans abandoned the early idea that the Americas were an extension of Asia, was the lack of awareness of the Americas shown both by the classical Greco-Roman writers and by the Bible, the two main textual sources of European knowledge about the outside world. Not everyone acknowledged this problem. Sometimes Europeans attempted to graft classical and biblical knowledge onto the Americas. The Amazon River was given its name by Spanish explorers who believed it was inhabited by women warriors of the kind that ancient Greek writers had described. Some ethnologists suggested that the Native Americans were the descendants of the ten "lost tribes" of Israel, and even though that was never a majority opinion among European thinkers, nearly all agreed that they could be fit into the biblical framework by tracing their line of descent from one of the sons of Noah. Some argued that America could be found in the Bible, or that various places in the New World were named after biblical figures. Some applied traditional European intellectual categories to the newly found lands and their inhabitants. The debate in Spain over the status of New World peoples and their societies in the mid-sixteenth century was the last major European intellectual debate to be carried out entirely in Aristotelian terms. But Europeans gradually became aware that the Bible and the classics were not very useful in dealing with the specificities of America. Nor was either very useful in understanding the further reaches of Asia. By 1570, Ptolemy's *Geography* was openly referred to as possessing merely historical interest.

European expansion also had a liberating effect on European culture. It became the standard example for those who argued that modern civilization had advanced beyond the classical world, an ideology that would eventually be applied specifically to science, resulting in the idea of "scientific progress." Francis Bacon specifically compared himself to Columbus, and the frontispiece of his influential program for the reform of natural philosophy, *The Great Instauration* (1620), showed a ship sailing past the Pillars of Hercules, the western limit of the Mediterranean and a symbol of the limits of ancient knowledge—an image previously employed by the Spanish royal cosmographer Andres Garcia de Cespedes (1560–1611) in the frontispiece to his *Rules of Navigation* (1606).

NAVIGATION

Exploration, discovery, and conquest also put new problems on the intellectual agenda, perhaps most importantly those of navigation and cartography. Governments offered lavish rewards for new and successful navigational methods, and navigational problems engaged the attention of many of Europe's leading scientists, including Galileo Galilei and Isaac Newton. Instruments and charts became more common and more diverse, and made increasing demands on navigators' technical skills. The earliest European peoples in the Renaissance to face these new and complex navigational problems were the earliest explorers, the Spanish and Portuguese.

Before the fifteenth century most European voyaging was basically coastal, and one of the most useful tools of navigation was the portolan, or coastal outline, a rough map of the closest land mass that gave the navigator a rough idea of where he was and in what direction he was heading. The dominant idea in navigation was to rely on experience, not instruments and maps. The best pilot was the experienced pilot, with his intimate knowledge of land masses, currents, winds, and weather. The experienced pilot was favorably contrasted with the overly theoretical, unpractical "book-pilot" whose knowledge was derived from textual sources rather than practice. Even after 1498, orienting the ship to land masses continued to be a common practice in the island-filled Indian Ocean, where ships spent relatively little time out of sight of land.

The real problem for traditional European navigation was that the Atlantic and Pacific were open oceans where a ship could spend many days or weeks out of sight of land. The lack of land masses to guide by, unfamiliarity with the waters and the southern sky, and the lack of a body of experienced pilots made navigation on these seas an immense challenge, one that was approached through building a technical knowledge through study, rather than relying primarily on experience.

One basic problem was the fixing of the ship's position on both the north–south and east–west axes. This "latitude" problem was relatively simple, based on the elevation of the sun or stars above the horizon. Portuguese sailors were using instruments called quadrants to determine the altitude of the polestar in their West African voyages of the fifteenth century. South of the Equator, where the polestar was no longer visible, it was necessary to use the sun, whose path is more complicated. Printed tables of the variance of the sun's apparent path around the Earth, the ecliptic, from the Equator, assisted in this procedure, but to use them properly required literacy and technical knowledge.

The Longitude Problem

The east–west position, the "longitude," was a far tougher nut to crack and became one of the classic technological problems of the early modern period (Fig. 3-3). As the celestial bodies seemed to rotate around the Earth from east to west (whether the sun orbited the Earth or the Earth orbited the sun made no difference to navigators, whose skills were based on the appearance of the sky, not the underlying reality of the cosmos), they did not offer a way to know one's position on it. Existing methods, based on observation of the moon, or simply estimating the speed one had been traveling for a given time, were maddeningly and even dangerously imprecise. Most approaches to the longitude reduced the problem to that of finding the difference between the time on the ship and the time at a fixed point, usually that of the home port. The difference in time could be translated into spatial terms as the difference in longitude between the two points. There were all sorts of bizarre schemes for this, such as that based on the seventeenth-century English natural philosopher Sir Kenelm Digby's Powder of Sympathy. The powder maintained a connection, or "sympathy," between a wound and the weapon that had inflicted it or other things that had come into contact with it as long as both carried the powder, even over great distances. The author of an anonymous 1687 pamphlet, *Curious Enquiries*,

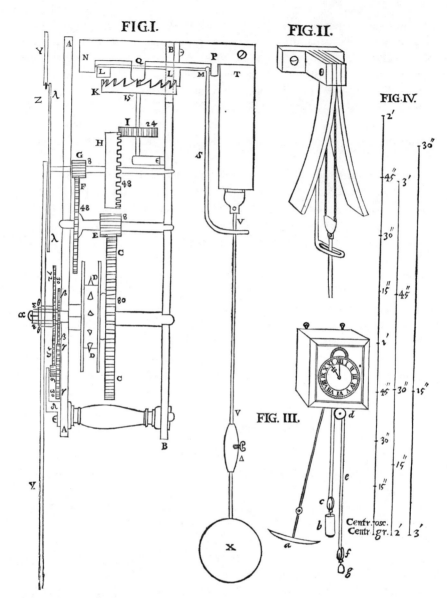

Figure 3-3.   Clock Mechanism Drawings by Huygens. The longitude problem was one factor driving the development of clock technology. This drawing of clock mechanisms was the work of seventeenth-century Dutch scientist Christiaan Huygens, who was keenly interested in the problem.

suggested that ships carry wounded dogs whose wounds would be dusted with the powder. Every hour, bandages from the wound would be dipped in water at the home port, the dogs on the ships would yelp, and the home-port time would be known. It is not known if this was ever tried. Another longitude scheme was to fill the oceans with boats that would fire cannons, thus studding the seas with known points from which sailors could figure their distance.

The two main approaches to finding the time were using astronomical observations to give the correct time and creating a clock able to give accurate time on a moving, rolling ship. If the home-port time of a celestial occurrence was known, all that would be necessary would be to compare the ship's own time on observation of the occurrence. Italian physicist and astronomer Galileo Galilei hoped that the movements of the satellites of Jupiter he had discovered could be the astronomical clock, trying to sell a navigational method based on the moons to both Spain and its mortal enemy the Dutch Republic. But the precise telescopic observations needed could not be taken from the rolling, moving deck of a ship. Making a clock that would function accurately under such conditions also posed challenges insurmountable at the time. The effort to create an accurate marine clock underlay many of the clockmaking innovations of Robert Hooke, Christian Huygens, and other leading scientists of the late seventeenth century, but these efforts were also in vain.

Another approach that attracted some interest was to map the variations in the Earth's magnetic field and then observe the ship's compass to determine its location. This approach was particularly popular in England, and the astronomer and ship's captain Edmond Halley among others worked on it, but to no real avail.

The longitude problem was not merely a matter for sailors and natural philosophers. It was also the concern of governments, particularly those governments who engaged in empire and trade beyond the seas. The governments of Spain, the Dutch Republic, and Great Britain all offered substantial cash prizes for a workable solution. The best known is the British Parliament's offer of twenty thousand pounds in 1714. The problem of the longitude would remain to be solved in the eighteenth century with the invention of accurate shipboard clocks and the near-simultaneous development of the astronomical method of "lunar distances."

The Compass

Nearly as important as position was direction. The magnetic compass, developed in the Middle Ages from Chinese models, became even more important as European mariners sailed across trackless oceans far out of sight of land. That the needle pointed north was known, but why it did remained a mystery. With greater dependence on the compass came a growing interest in how and why the compass worked the way it did, and its improvement helped raise the scientific profile of magnetism, leading to a series of important studies, such as the English physician and natural philosopher William Gilbert's early work of experimental science *De Magnete* (1600), which established that the Earth itself was a giant magnet.

Navigation and Education

The needs of navigation were an important contributor to a revolution in European education. The teaching of mathematics and astronomy in vernacular languages rather than Latin, the language of the university, for men pursuing marine careers was a growth industry in much of early modern Europe and was inextricably linked to the rise of a scientific and mathematical culture. Isaac Newton himself urged the teaching of mathematics to young men being educated for the sea, against conservative sailors who thought it unnecessary because navigational skills could be picked up in practical apprenticeships.

Vernacular mathematics education existed before Columbus's first voyage to the Americas in 1492, principally in Italy, where it was aimed at young business-men. However, navigational education was far more intellectually demanding than teaching accounting or currency conversion. It required knowledge of as-tronomy as well as mathematics. In addition to basic astronomy for the purpose of celestial navigation, young men learned trigonometry to determine the optimal path for a ship on the spherical Earth. Both students and teachers were participat-ing in the creation of a far more numerate and scientifically literate culture.

THE NEW NATURAL HISTORY

Among the disciplines most immediately transformed by the new knowledge coming from the Americas and Asia were natural history, botany, and zoology. Knowledge about previously unknown plants and animals, and sometimes the plants and animals themselves, came to Europe in a flood, particularly from the only recently encountered lands of the West, which had been separated from Afro-Eurasia for millennia and had developed a remarkably different natural world. Asia and Africa too could supply organisms whose alienness would make a particularly dramatic impression, such as the rhinoceros, a gift from the Sultan of Gujarat, which arrived in Lisbon in 1515. The ancients provided little help in working out the nature and properties of these newly known organisms, al-though Europeans gained much knowledge from indigenous informants, rang-ing from the hunter-gatherers of the Amazon jungles to the learned Ayurvedic Brahmin physicians of Portuguese Goa. The importance and the overwhelming quantity of the new knowledge forced Europeans to adopt a more empirical and systematic approach to its collection and organization. It led states, beginning with the Spanish monarchy, to take a more direct role in this process in hopes of finding products that would be economically valuable or otherwise useful.

The myriad of new plant and animal species encountered in the newly known countries eventually made much of classical natural history obsolete. Amerigo Vespucci (1454–1512), the Florentine mariner whose pamphlets on his encoun-ters in the New World were more influential than Columbus's writings in shaping the first European perceptions, specifically pointed out that the abundance of American plants and animals were not to be found in the works of Pliny. These newly encountered species also lacked the traditional cultural and symbolic associations of animals and plants already known to Europeans and could be discussed in a much more empirical way.

Botany was considered a branch of medicine, and Europeans were particularly interested in the medical properties of strange plants. Many of the scientific explorers and knowledge gatherers sent from Europe were eminent physicians, such as the Portuguese Garcia D'Orta in India and the Spaniard Francisco Hernández in Mexico. Europeans were sometimes carried away with enthusiasm over the medical potential of foreign plants. For example, tobacco, a New World plant, was hailed as a wonder drug, capable of curing a wide range of ailments including migraine, kidney pain, hysteria, gout, toothache, worms, scabies, nettles, burns, wounds from poisoned arrows, and gunshots. The French diplomat Jean Nicot (1530–1600), after whom nicotine is named, was a particularly strong booster of tobacco as a medicinal plant and introduced it to the French court, where it became very popular. The belief that cures were to be found in the same places where diseases originated also led to interest in American plants as cures for syphilis, a recently prominent sexually transmitted disease that Europeans believed to have originated in the Americas. The treatment of tobacco as a medicinal plant also helped make it more acceptable for nonmedicinal uses by separating it from its connection with New World peoples and their "idolatrous" religious practices.

The creation of massive natural historical compendia covering an entire region was both a way of taking inventory of a colony's natural resources and staking a textual claim on it. The production of such natural histories, however, required a substantial commitment of resources both to the collection of knowledge and to its publication in book form. The most obvious place to look for these resources was the state, but cash-strapped early modern states were not always willing to provide the necessary funding. Harriot's proposed natural history of Virginia never got past the initial stages due to poor financing and the general shakiness of the English position in Virginia in the late sixteenth century. The German astronomer and schoolmaster Georg Markgraf's *Natural History of Brazil* (1648) was more successful. Ironically, Markgraf, one of the first astronomers to study the stars of the Southern Hemisphere, worked under Dutch sponsorship during their short-lived rule in northern Brazil, and his work appeared after the Dutch had been expelled and Portuguese rule restored.

CARTOGRAPHY

Cartography, the science of mapmaking, also became more important as European power and knowledge extended over the rest of the world. Mapping a territory both made it known to its new "owners" and staked an intellectual claim on it. However, cartography did not only appeal to imperial state authorities: There was a growing interest in having accurate land maps, from traders and scholars as well as landowners and potential landowners.

New knowledge, beginning with the charts of the coast of West Africa and the Atlantic islands produced by Portuguese seafarers in the fifteenth century, stimulated the creation of new maps. The most common form of world map in the Middle Ages showed Asia, Europe, and Africa huddled around Jerusalem at the center of the world. Asia beyond the Middle East, Africa below the Sahara, and the then-unknown Americas did not appear at all. The maps did not purport to give an accurate representation of the world even according to the limited knowledge available at the time, as major features of Europe itself such as the British Isles were not shown.

Growing global awareness led to the creation of maps purporting to give an accurate representation of the world according to current knowledge. Like other visual forms, cartography had been revolutionized in the fifteenth century by printing, which for the first time allowed for the precise reproduction of large numbers of identical maps. The combination of the printing press and the new information flooding into Europe that had to be fixed in maps made cartography a boom industry of the sixteenth century. The two most important cartographers were friends, Gerhardus Mercator (1512–1594) and Abraham Ortelius (1527–1598). Ortelius became official geographer to Philip II, the leader of the Spanish Empire, the world's greatest consumer of cartographic services. Mercator was the first to refer to a collection of maps as an "atlas," but Ortelius's *Theatrum Orbis Terrarum* (1570) is considered the first world atlas.

The necessity of mapping the world led to the creation of a universal system of coordinates by which any spot on the world could be precisely located. Although this idea dated back to ancient Greek geographers, it was systematically applied by Mercator in his world map dated 1569. The "Mercator projection" of the sphere onto the flat map depicted rhumb lines—the circular paths produced by following a constant compass direction—as straight lines, making it useful for navigation, although the distortions as the map approaches the top and bottom mean that it is only useful for the mid-range of the Earth. Even then the distinction between the true north used by Mercator and the magnetic north used by navigators and the inability to reckon the longitude meant that the practical usefulness of the map to navigators was limited. The famous distortion of the Mercator projection, which has led to its abandonment by modern cartographers, is the way that everything gets larger as the map goes north, leading to the notoriously massive Mercator Greenland. (As the map approaches the poles, the space represented approaches infinity, meaning that a Mercator map can never be truly complete.) Mercator did not explain the mathematical principles on which the Mercator projection is based—they were first put forth by the English mathematician Edward Wright (1561–1615) in *Certaine Errors of Navigation* (1599).

Not all maps were made with the geographical knowledge, mathematical precision, and skill of Mercator and Ortelius, nor did they need to be. Maps of the newly acquired and encountered territories in the Americas and elsewhere served many purposes. Some were decorative and some were promotional. The earliest English maps of North America, for example, encouraged investment in prospective voyages and colonizing expeditions by emphasizing easy access to the wealth of Asia through a wide, and, as it turned out, nonexistent, Northwest Passage connecting the Atlantic and Pacific. Such maps were essentially fictional. Even maps with some pretensions to accuracy varied widely. Military maps emphasized fortresses and the connections between them, whereas maps for traders emphasized natural resources and trade routes. Cultural and economic differences influenced mapping styles. Early Dutch maps of upstate New York emphasized waterways and trade routes, reflecting the fact that Dutch settlers in the region were principally interested in buying furs from Native Americans. When the English took over the territory in the late seventeenth century, their maps were organized in terms of delineating the properties suitable for agriculture and the relations of English and French fortresses. Waterways were now shown less as routes for trade than as boundaries.

EUROPEAN SCIENCE AND INDIGENOUS KNOWLEDGE

The peoples Europeans encountered around the globe had their own traditions of knowledge about the natural world, both textual and oral. European attitudes toward indigenous scientific knowledge varied according to the place and the subject. In all places specifically local knowledge of geography, natural history, and local diseases was valued. European visitors to the Islamic Middle East and Iran avidly collected geographic and astronomical manuscripts to "fill in the blank spaces" and improve the accuracy of their own maps. European knowledge of the geography of Africa was greatly advanced by a North African Muslim diplomat, al-Hasan ibn Muhammad ibn Ahmad al-Wazzan, who had been captured by Spanish pirates in 1518 and sent to the Pope as a potential intelligence source. Converting to Christianity (possibly under duress) and baptized as Johannes Leo, he wrote *The Description of Africa,* which was translated into several European languages and remained a major source of European knowledge of North and West Africa.

The importation and cultivation of new crops—tobacco, tomatoes, corn, and potatoes, among many others—required some appropriation of indigenous knowledge of cultivation and preparation, and in some cases, consumption. Europeans received this knowledge mostly orally, as the major civilization of South America, the Inca, had not developed written language, and in Central and North America the Spaniards destroyed nearly all Aztec and Mayan texts on religious grounds, believing that the texts they could not read contained invocations to the "Devils" Native Americans supposedly worshipped. The civilizations of Asia, however, had a long textual tradition. Arabic and Indian texts were treated as valuable sources of knowledge in botany and pharmacology. Arabic medical texts such as Ibn Sina's *Canon of Medicine* had a long history in the medical schools of European universities, but Indian texts were a new discovery. An Italian visitor to Goa, Filippo Sassetti (1540–1588), translated an Ayurvedic compendium, the *Nighantu*, from Sanskrit to Italian.

Accounts of the transmission of Native American knowledge to Europeans vary. Writers like Monardes recounted how Native American healers generously made the medical properties of American plants known to Spaniards. However, one of Monardes's correspondents in the New World, Pedro Osma, complained that Native healers deliberately withheld information from the Spanish, and what little knowledge the Spanish did gain came from Native women involved with Spanish men. The fact that the Spanish were conquerors in America made it difficult for Spanish and Native healers to meet as equals and colleagues, although it could happen in frontier zones. In other areas, such as India, Europeans and the indigenous people were on a footing of greater equality. The Portuguese physician Garcia d'Orta's *Colloquies on the Herbs and Drugs of India* (1563), the first scientific book published in India, rested on a wide range of conversations with Indian Ocean healers, including Persians and Chinese as well as Hindu Ayurvedic practitioners. Garcia d'Orta also drew on his knowledge of Arabic writers, making his work a multicultural synthesis rather than simply an example of "European knowledge."

Botany and pharmacology were areas where Native knowledge was highly prized. But non-European knowledge received much less attention in the more theoretical and abstract areas of natural philosophy. The calendars of the Mayans and Aztecs aroused curiosity and respect from European chronologists, but their techniques were not incorporated into European chronological reckoning. Europeans sometimes examined the natural philosophical theories and observations of "civil" peoples—those who had cities, a written language, and a social hierarchy, such as the Chinese, Japanese, and many Muslims, although all believed European knowledge was superior. The natural philosophy of the East Asian learned tradition, based on a yin-yang dualism and five elements rather than the European four, was discussed by Europeans, but mostly in the context of how to make effective missionary appeals. It was not adopted and did not really influence the development of European natural philosophy. Even the Jesuit missionaries in China who adopted much of Chinese high culture, including the study of the Confucian classics, remained Aristotelian in their natural philosophy.

SPAIN'S EMPIRE OF KNOWLEDGE

The initial impact, intellectual and otherwise, of the New World discoveries was greatest by far in Spain. Spain possessed a monopoly over the New World (with the exception of the Portuguese settlements in Brazil), although one of decreasing effectiveness, and received by far the greatest flow of information thence. Europeans outside Spain curious about the newly discovered lands were often forced to rely on translated Spanish texts. Spanish investigators dominated New World natural history, producing a long series of works, of which the earliest notable example is the Spanish official Gonzalo Fernández de Oviedo's *Natural History of the Indies* (1526).

Knowledge was essential if Spain were to effectively control and exploit the resources of its empire. In addition to the knowledge of American plants and animals, the Spanish were also interested in improving techniques for silver mining and the refining of metallic silver out of ore, an area in which Spanish Americans made several technical innovations. The Spanish government took a lead in gathering and organizing knowledge. The Crown sent detailed questionnaires on the newly discovered lands, the "*relaciones geográficas*," to thousands of local officials and compiled the information received. Royal officials evaluated the efficacy of new technical processes using empirical criteria. The connections of the Spanish monarchy elsewhere in Europe also proved useful—Italian mariners like Columbus and Vespucci; German miners like Juan Tetzel, a founder of the copper mining industry in Cuba; and Flemish cartographers all served the Spanish ruler.

Entrepreneurial Spaniards working outside the government bureaucracy also helped circulate the new natural knowledge. One leader was the Seville physician Nicolas Monardes (1493–1588), who became mid-sixteenth-century Europe's leading expert on American nature without ever, as far as we know, crossing the Atlantic! Seville was the only port in Spain allowed to send and receive ships to and from the New World, and Monardes used his access to New World products to become a rich man. His fortune was originally founded on a purgative called "Michoacan root," which he learned about firsthand from a user. Much of his information he obtained firsthand from people coming to Seville from the Americas or from Spanish American correspondents. Monardes maintained a garden of New World plants, and his *Medical History of things found in our Western Indies* (1565–1574) identified and gave the medical uses of dozens of American plants. (Monardes is particularly remembered for his enthusiasm for tobacco, which he regarded as a cure for many diseases.) Like other Spanish books on the New World, Monardes's work was translated and plagiarized in several languages, often alongside material on Asian remedies.

Spanish manuals of navigation and books on the New World and its nature were widely translated into both Latin and vernacular languages. The impact of the new Spanish knowledge on the rest of Europe was limited, however, by the Spanish penchant for treating it as a Spanish possession that should be kept secret. This was part of the Spanish program for maintaining a monopoly over the New World and its valuable resources.

The First Scientific Institute—Spain's Casa de Contratación

Before Columbus, the major institutions for pursuing science in Europe had been general educational institutions, particularly universities. The Spanish discovery of the Americas was followed in a few years by the founding of Europe's first scientific institute, the Casa de Contratación or House of Trade, founded in 1503. The Casa regulated trade and movement between Spain and its new American possessions, but it was also a place for the gathering, organization, and dissemination of knowledge on Spain's new empire and the routes thither and back.

Much of the Casa's work focused on navigation and the creation of theoretically aware ship's pilots. The Casa trained pilots and captains in the arts of cartography and navigation, making navigation a more textual body of knowledge, as opposed to something passed down orally. The Senior Pilot of the Casa was responsible for both the training and testing of new pilots and for examining and certifying maps and navigator's instruments. The work of the Casa became more specialized and technical with the creation of the post of Senior Cosmographer in 1523 and the establishment of a chair of navigation and cosmography in 1552. Several leading Spanish, Italian, and Portuguese cosmographers held these posts in the sixteenth century, some of whom wrote books on navigational science. However, the Casa was not just a teaching institution devoted to the handing down of old knowledge; it was also a scientific and technical institute, devoted to the creation and dissemination of new knowledge. The "Royal Pattern," a cosmographic pattern continuously updated with new information from Spanish pilots, was kept at the Casa from 1612. Casa cartographers researched the problem of consistently projecting the surface of the spherical world onto a flat map. The culture of the Casa, however, worked against making this research public—its researchers were employees of the Spanish ruler, and the tendency throughout the sixteenth century was to treat the knowledge they created as a state secret. The culture of the Casa extended to the Spanish court with the foundation of the Mathematical Academy of Madrid in 1582, an institution designed to teach navigators and cosmographers which lasted until around 1630.

Although Portugal, the other leader in European expansion, lacked an institution comparable to the Casa, the Portuguese were also making innovations in navigational science. The Portuguese Joao de Castro (1500–1548), a Viceroy of Portuguese India, made the first study of magnetic declination, and another Portuguese, Pedro Nunes (1502–1578), demonstrated that sailing on a great circle on the surface of the spherical Earth was a shorter way of getting to the destination than sailing in a straight line. (Nunes held the chair of mathematics founded in 1537 at the Portuguese University of Coimbra to train navigators. Among his students at Coimbra was the German Christoph Clavius, the last great Ptolemaic astronomer.) Astronomical observatories were founded to provide more accurate astronomical data using the latest technologies to serve navigational needs. The need for more accurate navigational data underlay the founding of France's Paris Observatory in 1667 and England's Greenwich Observatory in 1675, two of the major scientific institutions of the Scientific Revolution.

Francisco Hernández and the Natural History of Mexico

Among the most prominent state-sponsored scientific projects of the sixteenth century was the natural history of Spanish Mexico undertaken by the physician Francisco Hernández (c. 1517–1587). Hernández had already established himself in Spain as a leading medical botanist and physician, as well as a skilled humanist who was working on a Spanish translation of Pliny's *Natural History*. In 1570 King Philip II (r. 1556–1598), an amateur gardener and botanist himself, ordered him to Mexico to study its natural history with a view to medical uses. Hernández arrived in Mexico in 1571, staying until 1577. He traveled extensively throughout the colony, gathering specimens, illustrations, and descriptions of plants. Hernández, like all students of medical botany in European colonies, consulted with indigenous healers. He learned the indigenous Nahuatl language of Mexican scholars and translated some of his materials into it for their use.

Whatever the original plans to make use of Hernández's materials, they were not published on his return to Spain, possibly because he died shortly afterward and possibly because the chronically short-of-cash Philip II was not willing to pay for an elaborate publication of all of Hernández's material with his illustrations. Abridged versions were published in Mexico in 1579 and 1615, marking the early presence of a Mexican audience interested in the natural history of the place where they lived. In Europe, Hernández's work circulated in manuscript copies and was included in other books on New World natural history. The first European publication of Hernández's work was sponsored by the Italian natural philosopher Prince Federico Cesi and his scientific society, the Accademia dei Lincei, in Rome in 1628. (The lynx was believed to have very keen eyesight, hence the name.) The fact that the Lincei was also interested in publishing Hernández's work indicates the broadness of its scientific interests and the important role of "exotic" natural history in forming scientific communities.

Science and "Race" in the Spanish Empire

One of the most fundamental debates provoked by the Spanish conquests in the Americas was the nature of American indigenous people. Some argued that the people of the Americas were not even human—an argument very much to the advantage of Spanish landowners in the newly established colonies, who could exploit their Native servants as brutally as if they were animals. This theory was opposed by the Catholic Church, which held that the Natives, like all humans, had souls that could be saved and therefore fell under the spiritual jurisdiction of the Church. This issue was settled definitively in favor of the Church position by the papal bull *Sublimis Deus* issued by Pope Paul III (r. 1534–1549) in 1537. The bull definitively asserted that Natives were human beings with rational souls, asserting that the contrary idea was the work of Satan, and condemned the enslavement of Natives in the strongest terms.

But if all agreed the Natives were human, what kind of humans were they? In the sixteenth century, the category of "race" did not have the centrality for European thought about differences between human populations that it attained later. The term was not in common use, and when used to refer to a people it could refer to the social class of the European elite (a usage that continued into the nineteenth century) rather than a race in the modern sense. Religion remained the most important way of categorizing the world's peoples to most early modern European people. A roughly fourfold division of the world into Christians, Jews, Muslims, and "Idolaters" was common. A simpler division was twofold, between the "civil" European elite and everyone else. This division was unstable, as some viewed non-European and non-Christian peoples dwelling in urbanized societies such as the Chinese, Japanese, and Muslims as civil. The uncivil could include European peasants as well as non-Europeans, and comparisons between the Natives of the

Americas and the European lower classes were quite common. Another common way of categorizing differences was the climatic theory that the character of different societies was determined by their natural environments, a theory with classical roots. Thus the darker pigmentation of Africans and Americans was due to their exposure to the heat of the sun, although some objected to this theory by pointing out that children retained their parents' coloration, no matter where they were born. The dominant planet and astrological sign of a given area could also determine or influence the nature of its people.

The central question for Spanish intellectuals by the mid-sixteenth century was whether the Native American population were "naturally" slaves. The idea that some populations were naturally servile went back to Aristotle, who had applied the category to people who did not live in the civilized Greek way. The major figures in the debate were the Dominican friar Bartolomé de las Casas (1484–1566) in the Americas, an opponent of natural servitude, and Juan Ginés de Sepúlveda (1489–1573), a leading Spanish humanist Aristotelian and supporter of natural servitude. Although las Casas was widely regarded as having emerged from the controversy victorious, his victory had little effect on Spanish treatment of American Natives.

THE PROJECT OF AN ENGLISH EMPIRE OF KNOWLEDGE

In conscious or unconscious emulation of Spain, late-sixteenth-century England began to build its own empire of knowledge. The Elizabethan mathematician and Hermeticist John Dee (1527–1608) combined efforts to promote applied mathematics in English culture with the project of an English empire based on knowledge following Spanish models. Although Dee is often remembered as an astrologer and magus who claimed to be having conversations with angels via a crystal ball, he was also one of the foremost champions of a practical mathematical education in Tudor England. He was involved in the publication of some of the earliest English mathematical textbooks to employ Arabic numerals, and his "Mathematical Preface" to the first English translation of Euclid's *Elements* set forth a range of activities that employed geometric and arithmetical knowledge. His *General and Rare Memorials Pertayning to the Perfect Arte of Navigation* (1577) combines instruction aimed at navigators with a call for the establishment of a powerful navy and a transoceanic British empire.

The Casa de Contratación was a government institution, but private schools aimed at teaching useful astronomy and mathematics also appeared in many parts of Europe. One was Gresham College, the London college founded in 1596 under the will of the financier Sir Thomas Gresham (1519–1579). The college, with seven endowed professorships, offered public lectures in English rather than granting degrees. Its first few decades were its most successful. Gresham College's leading personality was Henry Briggs (1561–1630), who was the professor of geometry until 1620, when he left to be the first Savilian Professor of Geometry at Oxford. Briggs and his colleagues and successors emphasized useful knowledge for navigators and businessmen, served as advisers and promoters of voyages of exploration, and made the college an early center for disseminating the use of logarithms, a seventeenth-century mathematical innovation, for astronomical and navigational calculations.

The earliest English attempts to plant a colony in North America involved a scientist and friend of Dee, Thomas Harriot (1560–1621). Harriot had been involved in the study of navigation under the patronage of the sea captain Walter Raleigh (1554–1621). His *A Briefe and True Report of the New Found Land of Virginia*, initially meant as the introduction to a larger project, discussed the natural history, geography, and Native peoples of the region where Raleigh had attempted to plant a colony in 1585. (This was in the present-day state of North Carolina rather than Virginia.) It was one of the few works available in the late sixteenth century on the Americas north of the Spanish colonies and attracted Europe-wide interest. Like much English colonial science, it was designed to promote colonization. The fertility of the land and the mildness of the climate were emphasized. The tradition of promotional science continued into the eighteenth century, but it came from the colonists themselves as well as promoters.

TRADE AND COMMODIFIED KNOWLEDGE IN THE DUTCH EMPIRE

The Dutch Empire of the seventeenth century was based on trade, including trade in knowledge. Rather than acquiring great territorial kingdoms like those Spain possessed in the Americas, the Dutch concentrated on the key strategic points from which to gather and distribute commodities, becoming the single greatest trading force on the global scene. Thus Beverwijk, literally "beaver town" and re-named Albany by the English, and New Amsterdam, now New York, served the fur trade. Batavia, the modern Jakarta, was the center of the spice trade. Dutch colonialism was also less dominated by the state than was the Iberian model. Many of the commodities common in the Indian Ocean, whose trade the Dutch grew to dominate, were previously unknown to Europeans, and to make them profitable, Dutch traders needed to gather and disseminate the knowledge of their uses. Since Amsterdam was a center of the printing industry, much of this knowledge spread widely. Some of these works were quite voluminous. The culture of information in the Dutch Empire was more decentralized and more driven by the market, as opposed to government commands, than in the Spanish Empire.

Medical personnel, including ship's surgeons as well as physicians, played an important role in Dutch colonialism. A Dutch merchant, Robert Padtbrugge (1638–1703), who became governor of Malacca, was also a physician and encouraged investigation of Asian plants for their medical use. As had earlier been the case with tobacco, several Asian plants were promoted as cure-alls. The seventeenth-century Dutch "chemical physician" Cornelis Bontekoe (1647–1685) avidly promoted tea as a wonder drug, advancing the financial interests of the Dutch importers. (Bontekoe was a great booster of the medical virtues of the exotic substances being imported into Europe in the seventeenth century generally: He also endorsed the health-giving properties of chocolate and tobacco from the Americas and opium and coffee from the East.) Bontekoe's *Treatise on the Excellence of Tea* (1678) invoked his own personal experiences by claiming that tea had cured him of kidney stones and bloody urine. Bontekoe used both the traditional language of Galenic medicine and the new language of seventeenth-century medical alchemy to explain tea's helpful virtues. Tea "thinned" blood that had grown thick and cold, but it was also an alkali, which counteracted harmful acids. Tea fought dysentery by counteracting damaging acids introduced into the stomach by overindulgence in fats, vinegar, and wine.

Amsterdam also became the center of a market in natural curiosities—living and dead plants and animals from many parts of the world, brought by Dutch ships and bought by collectors from all over Europe. The collector's market could even finance scientific expeditions like the Amsterdam-based entomologist Maria Sibilla Merian's travels in South America. The spread of these items, not just to institutions but to private collectors, acquainted more and more Europeans with the diversity of Earth's living things and aided those botanists and natural historians who lacked direct access to exotic plants. The foundation of botany and comparative anatomy as disciplines that covered the Earth's flora and fauna, rather than being restricted to that of Europe and its immediate surroundings, owed much to the Dutch global trade network.

WAS THE NEW KNOWLEDGE "REVOLUTIONARY"?

The idea that European expansion was related to the Scientific Revolution is rela-tively new. Traditional pictures of the Scientific Revolution, emphasizing astron-omy, physics, and theoretical issues, had little room for navigational astronomy and less for pharmacology and natural history. But the new knowledge coming from the Americas, Africa, and Asia did provoke revolutionary changes in European thought. Navigation began to replace astrology as a motivation for state sponsor-ship of astronomy, leading to the creation of new institutions such as the Casa de Contratación and Gresham College, and eventually observatories like the ones at Paris and Greenwich. Knowledge of mathematics and astronomy became more widespread as more young men learned these disciplines in the hopes of nautical careers. Mathematical and astronomical skills occupied a growing place in European culture.

The new knowledge in natural history also had revolutionary impact. It added to the general disquiet with the ancients by demonstrating the existence of a whole world of plants and animals of which the ancients knew nothing. Programs for gathering, systematizing, and eventually publishing this knowledge were the "big science" of the early modern period, creating a tradition of organization and a methodical approach to nature. The empirical attitude that Europeans had to take to this new knowledge contrasted with the text-based and culturally freighted attitude taken to many traditionally known plants, animals, and other natural phenomena.

FOUR

ASTRONOMY AND PHYSICS FROM COPERNICUS TO NEWTON

During the Scientific Revolution, a planet's path in space changed from a perfect circle around the Earth, in which the planet was embedded in an enormous transparent sphere or orb that traveled at a constant speed, to an ellipse with one focus on the sun derived from the gravitational relation of the planet and the sun, in traversing which it slowed down and speeded up. This change involved nearly every prominent astronomer and physicist of the sixteenth and seventeenth centuries but began with a Polish cleric and astronomer named Nicolaus Copernicus. The "Copernican Revolution" became the paradigm of a scientific revolution. But the change was not limited to astronomy—the Copernican revolution had implications that utterly transformed physics as well, eventually leading to the "Newtonian synthesis" that would dominate Western physical thought for two centuries.

COPERNICUS

Copernicus, educated at Polish and Italian universities, spent most of his adult life as a canon of the cathedral at the remote East Prussian city of Frauensberg (now the Polish city of Frombork). He used one of the towers of the wall surrounding the cathedral for astronomical observations, although he was not a particularly skilled observer. Despite his lack of publications or university teaching, Copernicus acquired a reputation as an astronomer and in 1514 was invited to Rome to help reform the calendar. He refused on the grounds that astronomical theory was not advanced enough for effective reform. *On the Revolutions of the Celestial Spheres*, his masterpiece, was originally presented as an aid to calendrical reform.

Copernicus, unlike many of his contemporaries and successors during the Scientific Revolution, had little interest in making his ideas more generally known. He may have wanted to perfect his system before making it public, or he may have been influenced by Platonic or Hermetic traditions claiming that wisdom should not be shared with the vulgar. Georg Rheticus (1514–1574), a mathematics professor at the Lutheran University of Wittenberg, first made Copernicus's work widely known. (Copernicus seems to have had an easier time dealing with Protestants than many of his clerical contemporaries. Luther himself condemned Copernicus and his theories, but this seems to have had little impact in the Lutheran world.) Visiting Copernicus in 1539, Rheticus urged the publication of the manuscript. Rheticus published his own work, *Narratio Prima*, in 1540, giving an account of the motions of the Earth in the Copernican system. This was the first publication of Copernicus's ideas and was a kind of market test to see if there was a receptive audience. The audience was receptive enough that there was a second edition the next year. Copernicus entrusted the Latin treatise *On the Revolutions of the Celestial Spheres* to Rheticus to publish, but the young German was called to a university position in Sweden and left the manuscript to the Lutheran clergyman Andreas Osiander (1498–1552) to see through the press.

On the Revolutions of the Celestial Spheres, dedicated to the pope and published in 1543, the same year Copernicus died, argued that the Earth, far from remaining motionless at the center of the universe, rotates on its own axis once a day and circles the sun once a year. A third motion, a "wobble" of the axis itself, accounts for the precession of the equinoxes. A sun-centered universe had ancient Greek precedents, both in the mystical tradition of the Pythagoreans, who put the sun at the center to honor it as the central "hearth of the cosmos," and in the astronomy of Aristarchus of Samos. Copernicus himself was referred to in the sixteenth century as a Pythagorean. Some medieval scientists had also broached the idea, if only to refute it. Osiander blunted Copernicus's radicalism by adding a preface suggesting that his theories were only aids to mathematical calculation rather than descriptions of physical reality. Rheticus was enraged and would deface Osiander's preface in every copy of *On the Revolutions of the Celestial Spheres* that passed through his hands.

Copernicus's innovation was not the sun-centered cosmos but the mathematical explanation of how it worked. (Technically, Copernicus's system is not heliocentric, in that the planets are conceived as rotating around a hypothetical point at the center of the Earth's orbit that roughly coincides with the position of the sun rather than the physical sun itself. It is referred to as "heliostatic" in that the sun does not move.) Copernicus's theory had to retain the epicycles and deferents of Ptolemaic astronomy to match the observed motions of the planets, but it did explain certain celestial phenomena better than Ptolemy had. The fact that Mercury and Venus are never seen far from the sun is easy to explain on the principle that they orbit the sun more closely than does the Earth. The retrograde motion of the planets, when they appear to be moving backward, is also easier to explain in the Copernican system, where this phenomenon is identified as the Earth's passing them in orbit around the sun. However, Copernicus's system also seemed less elegant in that while everything revolved around the Earth for Ptolemy, for Copernicus the moon continued to revolve around the Earth while the planets revolved around the sun, and some denied that the universe could have two centers of motion.

Despite this break with the past, Copernicus's system was shaped in many ways by the Ptolemaic astronomy he was intimately familiar with. The structure of *On the Revolutions of the Celestial Spheres* was modeled closely on that of Ptolemy's *Almagest*. The Copernican system also used, at least as an explanatory device, solid crystalline spheres in which the planets are embedded and adhered to the established Aristotelian and Ptolemaic principle that heavenly motion was circular and uniform. By eliminating the equant—a mathematical device of Ptolemaic astronomy whereby the planet is considered to rotate uniformly around a point other than the center of its orbit—Copernicus proclaimed that he was actually more faithful to the principle of uniform circular motion than was Ptolemy, presenting this as the great advantage of his system.

One of the major questions of Copernicus scholarship is whether he was directly influenced by a group of Islamic astronomers led by Nasir al-Din al-Tusi (1201–1274) associated with the Maragha Observatory in Persia in the Middle Ages and their successors in the Islamic world. He does not explicitly refer to Islamic astronomers after the twelfth century in his writings, but he uses the mathematical theory of planetary motion devised by Muslim astronomers who had also identified serious flaws in the Ptolemaic system. However, it is possible that Copernicus came up with his ideas independently, and, like other astronomers in the Islamic tradition, the Maragha astronomers and their successors never went as far as rejecting geocentrism. Since Copernicus left no surviving scientific papers, it is impossible to fully reconstruct the development of his thought or be certain as to his influences, but it is possible that he was exposed to the information from the Islamic world in Italy, possibly through Byzantine Greek versions of the Arabic writings or through Jewish astronomers exposed to the Islamic astronomical tradition.

ASTRONOMY AFTER COPERNICUS

The decades following the publication of *On the Revolutions of the Celestial Spheres* saw the very slow spread of Copernicanism, its alteration into something very different from what Copernicus envisioned, the rise of a new alternative, the Tychonic system, the introduction of the telescope, and the continuance of a vigorous Ptolemaic tradition into the early seventeenth century.

Copernicanism in the Sixteenth Century

Few astronomers—perhaps under a dozen—accepted Copernicanism as an accurate description of the universe in the sixteenth century, although many more were willing to use Copernican tables as an aid to calculation or adopt specific Copernican ideas adapted to a geocentric cosmos. The principal objections to the new astronomy were not religious but were based on commonsense, Aristotelian physics, and astronomy itself. A moving Earth, not just revolving around the sun but also rotating, defied the evidence of the senses. Copernicus handled the Earth's rotation by asserting that it was the natural motion of a spherical body to rotate, and that everything on Earth is carried along in the Earth's rotation. He argued that it was more economical to rotate the relatively tiny Earth than the vast heavens, while Aristotelians claimed it was easier to move the perfect matter of the celestial heavens than the heavy Earth, and that the Earth's multiple motions violated the principle that objects had only a single motion.

Copernicus accepted the idea of Aristotelian physics that things were attracted to the center of the Earth, but displacing the Earth from the center of the universe also threatened a basic Aristotelian tenet, the idea that heavy objects fell to Earth because they sought their natural place at the center of the universe. The fact that the apparent positions of the stars did not move when the Earth moved—the lack of "stellar parallax"—also forced Copernicus and subsequent Copernicans to posit a much larger universe with the stars at a much greater distance from Earth than was accepted in Ptolemaic astronomy.

Copernicanism also made astronomy harder to do conceptually, as it substituted a platform away from the center of the cosmos and moving in three different ways in a cosmos with at least two centers of motion for a stationary platform at the center of the cosmos. Copernicanism also presented religious problems as the Bible's view of the universe was Earth-centered. For example, at the battle of Jericho Joshua was described as lengthening the day by making the sun stand still, not the Earth. As early as 1540, one of Copernicus's followers dealt with this objection by arguing that the Bible was adapted to the scientific understanding of its time, but little of the opposition to Copernicanism in the sixteenth century, whether by Catholics or Protestants, was based on its incompatibility with the Bible.

However, many astronomers accepted Copernicanism as a valid system for making astronomical calculations. Making calculations, rather than speculating on the structure of the universe, was considered by many to be the true task of astronomy anyway. This computational use of Copernicanism on the example of Osiander was particularly influential at the Lutheran University of Wittenberg, and it is sometimes called the "Wittenberg interpretation," a term coined by historian of science Robert Westman. Few accepted Copernicanism as a true picture of physical reality. Even among them interpretations varied. Some, closely following Copernicus himself, kept the crystalline spheres of traditional astronomy and simply shifted the center of the finite universe from the Earth to the sun. The more intellectually radical Italian friar and magician Giordano Bruno (1548–1600) put a sun-centered planetary system in an infinite universe with an infinite number of other stars and planets following the same arrangement. However, Bruno's cosmological vision had little impact on the development of astronomy—and even when he was burned at the stake in Rome, it was not for his cosmological beliefs.

Tycho and the Tychonic System

These changes were not just internal developments in European thought; they were influenced by celestial events themselves. A star bright enough to be seen in the daytime appeared in the constellation of Cassiopeia in early November 1572.

It steadily dimmed in brightness, disappearing from sight by March 1574, but it generated an extensive literature. Some astronomers and cosmologists claimed that it was a comet and debated whether it was above or below the sphere of the moon, the boundary, in Aristotelian cosmology, between the corruptible Earth and the perfect and unchanging heavens. Were the heavens truly incorruptible? The astronomer who published most extensively on the star was a Danish nobleman named Tycho Brahe (1546–1601). Tycho's first publication, *On the New Star* (1573), combined a record of his observations, a demonstration of the new star's position in or near the sphere of the fixed stars, and an astrological interpretation of its meaning. Although not widely distributed, this work contributed to making Tycho's reputation among astronomers, and he returned to the subject throughout his career. Tycho became the greatest astronomical observer of the pre-telescope era, as well as an influential astronomical theorist.

Tycho was granted the island of Hven by the Danish King Frederick II (r. 1559–1588) in 1576. There he established an observatory, Uraniborg, in the city of Urania, the muse of astronomy. At Uraniborg Tycho made the best and most systematic observations ever made with the naked eye, using improved instruments, many of which he designed himself and had built in the instrument shop that was part of the Uraniborg complex. Tycho's observations provided astronomers with the best data to date on the position of the celestial bodies, and Uraniborg itself became famous, the greatest center for astronomical research in Europe and an attraction for many visitors to Denmark, including royalty. Tycho received extensive financing from the Crown, and Denmark set the standard in terms of state support for scientific research at the time. However, when a new king unsympathetic to the high nobility of which Tycho was a member succeeded to the throne, the observatory was shut down and Tycho made his way to Prague, capital of the Holy Roman Empire. Tycho's greatest contribution to astronomy was the Tychonic model of the solar system, based on a stationary Earth, the moon and sun orbiting it, and the other planets orbiting the sun. Tycho rejected the Copernican model, as he saw no reason to accept the radical idea of the moving Earth. His new system offered several of the advantages of Copernicanism—the two systems are mathematically equivalent— without the physical and religious absurdities introduced by the moving Earth. He published his system in *Of More Recent Phenomena of the Ethereal World* (1588). The Tychonic model was quite influential in the seventeenth century, eventually displacing Ptolemaicism and becoming the chief rival to Copernicanism.

The New Ptolemaicism and the Gregorian Reform

Ptolemaicism was not standing still while Copernicus and Tycho were coming up with alternatives. In its last century, stimulated by Copernicus's theoretical challenge and Tycho's new data, it developed a refinement of technique and mathematical rigor that was unprecedented, the highest point in the long development of geocentric astronomy. The continuing vitality of earth-centered astronomy in the sixteenth century can be seen in the construction of the Gregorian calendar still in use today.

One of the most complex scientific problems faced by any civilization is coming up with a calendar. The fact that the days do not go evenly into the solar year means that any solar calendar with pretensions to accuracy will have to be irregular in terms of days. The construction of an accurate calendar, which went beyond merely assigning days to the year and often involved calculating the times of eclipses and major conjunctions, was a major responsibility of government in many early modern societies. The basic approach used in the Christian world of inserting an extra day every four years into the solar year had been developed by the ancient Egyptians, then refined by the Romans into the Julian calendar used in sixteenth-century Europe. However, by the late sixteenth century irregularities in the Julian calendar had piled up to the degree that it was off by ten days, and there was a widespread call for a new calendar. This was in the jurisdiction of the Church, which had a very long involvement with the calendar. The leading astronomer in Rome at the time was a young German, Christoph Clavius (1583–1612), a member of the recently founded Jesuit order who would become the head of the Vatican Observatory. Work on the calendrical reform began sometime between 1572 and 1575, and the new calendar was announced by its namesake and the sponsor of the calendar project, Pope Gregory XIII, in the papal bull *Inter Gravissimas* in 1582. Despite the superiority of the new Gregorian calendar, its origins in a papal commission made it suspect to Protestants and Orthodox Christians, and it was not adopted in some Protestant countries until the mid-eighteenth century, and not in Orthodox Russia until after the Russian Revolution. The fact that different countries were on different calendars sometimes led to confusion in comparing astronomical observations made in different places.

After the Gregorian reform, Clavius remained the leading Ptolemiac astronomer, producing a stream of astronomical and mathematical textbooks into the seventeenth century. He was impressed by some of Copernicus's technical innovations, which he adopted into the Ptolemaic mainstream by transferring the motions Copernicus ascribed to the Earth to new celestial spheres. The reach of Jesuit astronomers and calendar-makers trained in the Clavian Ptolemaic tradition would in just a few decades after the Gregorian reform extend as far as China.

The Coming of the Telescope

Ironically, Tycho's meticulous methods of naked-eye observation became obsolete just a few years after his death with the invention and dissemination of the telescope. The origins of the telescope are obscure, and arrangements of lenses and mirrors appear to have been used in late-sixteenth-century England and Italy to look at distant objects. The earliest recorded telescope combining a convex and concave lens in a tube, however, was in 1608 in the Dutch Republic, when a man named Hans Lipperhey applied for a patent. The principle of the telescope was so simple that much of its early spread was not caused by the physical introduction of telescopes, but people hearing about telescopes and constructing their own. The most notable example is Galileo Galilei, who built his own telescope after hearing about a Dutch model. Galileo's telescopes, with a magnification of 30 diameters, were the most powerful of their time, so powerful that they made his observations difficult to duplicate. The greatest technical innovator of the early telescope, however, was Kepler, who devised the so-called astronomical telescope, combining two convex lenses and obtaining greater accuracy of observation at the price of turning the image upside down. This is one of the few innovations in telescope design in this period based on optical theory rather than craft technique, and despite its greater accuracy, the upside-down image kept it from being widely adopted until the 1640s. By that time, telescopes were being designed and made for specifically astronomical uses and were revolutionizing the study of the skies for Copernicans and non-Copernicans alike.

The telescope made a great impression on European culture, as it was the first radical extension of human senses. Like the microscope, which appeared shortly afterward, it raised epistemological questions as to whether things "seen" through instruments belonged in the same category as the traditional "evidence of the senses." It made the hitherto neglected study of lenses a vital part of optics and brought home to astronomers the relative closeness of the planets in space and their relative similarity to the Earth as opposed to the unimaginable distance and difference of the stars. It enabled Galileo to discover the four largest satellites of Jupiter and the phases of Venus, and for astronomers to identify sunspots and the geography of the moon as well as hundreds of stars and other celestial objects that had previously been invisible to the naked eye.

Galileo, Kepler, and the New Copernicanism

The two most important astronomers of the generation after Tycho were the Copernican telescope makers Kepler and Galileo. Galileo was the son of the music theorist Vincenzo Galilei (1520-1591), from whom he may have picked up his bent for the application of mathematics. From an early age Galileo was discontented with Aristotelian physics, and his adoption of Copernicanism was part of his lifelong struggle against Aristotelianism more than a move motivated by purely astronomical interests. Galileo represents a major change in astronomy. He was not an astronomer at all in the classic sense, and despite his mathematical ability the laborious continued observation and painstaking construction of charts and tables that was the work of the traditional astronomer had no appeal for him. But by pointing a telescope at the sky, Galileo fundamentally changed the notion of what astronomy was about. His spectacular discoveries both provided powerful evidence in favor of Copernicanism, or at least against the Ptolemaic system, and revealed how much had been previously unknown about the skies. Galileo introduced the idea of discovery, which had already been established with the European exploration of the Americas, into astronomy. The universe revealed by his telescope was also incomparably more vast than that of Ptolemy, Tycho, or Copernicus. As Galileo pointed out, the telescope did not resolve the stars from points of light to small disks, as they did the planets.

He concluded from this that the stars were much smaller than had been thought, although the real reason was that they were much farther away.

Kepler created the most mathematically powerful and physically accurate system of planetary astronomy to date by adopting Copernicanism but questioning Copernicus's insistence on uniform circular motion. The last major astronomer to seriously practice astrology, Kepler was deeply influenced by neo-Platonic and magical traditions of cosmic harmony as well as quantitative astronomy. Kepler attended the Lutheran University of Tubingen, where Michael Maestlin (1550–1631), one of the rare Copernicans in academia, seems to have converted him to Copernicanism. Kepler's first book, *The Cosmographical Mystery* (1596), defended Copernicanism as an accurate picture of the heavens and set forth his theory of the relation of the spacing of the planets to the geometric relation of the regular solid, including calculations of the Copernican planetary orbits by Maestlin. (Regular, or "Platonic," solids are those all of whose faces and angles are equal and parallel. They are the tetrahedron, cube, octahedron, dodecahedron, and icosahedron.) As a Protestant, he was forced to leave Graz in 1598. Fortunately, his work had attracted the attention of Tycho, then the mathematician and astronomer to the Holy Roman Emperor Rudolf II in Prague. Tycho invited Kepler to Prague. Kepler worked closely with Tycho, inherited his astronomical data, and on his death succeeded him as Imperial Mathematician in 1601.

Kepler viewed science as an attempt to understand the mind of God. As God's creation, the universe had to be rationally structured and ordered rather than created by chance. The infinite and unordered universe of Giordano Bruno filled him with horror. This rational structure and order was mathematical and geometric. As God's creation, the universe was imbued with religious meaning. For example, the universe was fundamentally triadic, reflecting the Christian Trinity. The relation between the Father, Son, and Holy Spirit was analogous to the relation of the sun, the outer heaven of the stars, and the space between them. But unlike many who approached the universe in a mystical or magical way, Kepler was obsessed with numerical precision, and even a slight deviation of the position of Mars from that theoretically predicted led him to change his entire theory. He was obsessed with showing that his astronomical theories did not merely accurately predict planetary motions, but that they were physically true. He abandoned Copernicus's use of the center of the Earth's orbit, the "mean sun," as the center of the solar system, in favor of the actual sun, from which a force that governed the motions of the planets emanated. Influenced by William Gilbert's *On the Magnet*, Kepler identified this force as magnetic. Despite his belief in cosmic harmony, he detested the imprecision of many magical writers.

Kepler used Tycho's data to revolutionize astronomy. Unlike Ptolemy, Copernicus, Tycho, or his correspondent Galileo, he broke the tyranny of the idea that heavenly motion was perfect, and therefore circular. He reduced planetary motion to three laws, although he did not state them in that form. The first two laws appear in *The New Astronomy* in 1609 and the third appears in the 1619 *Harmonies of the World*, a work explicating the universe as a structure organized by geometric and musical harmonies. The three laws are (1) Planets move around the sun not in circles, but in ellipses with the sun at one focus; (2) A line drawn between the planet and the sun will always sweep the same area in the same amount of time. Therefore, planets accelerate as they approach the sun and decelerate as they move away from it; (3) The squares of the times the planets take to go around the sun are proportional to the cubes of their average distances from the sun. Kepler's theories of planetary motion, not immediately accepted, grew increasingly influential in the course of the century. However, the physical theories that emerged differed sharply from Kepler's picture of a harmonious universe. Instead of harmony, they were based on mechanism.

THE DEVELOPMENT OF NON-ARISTOTELIAN MECHANICS

The principal scientific problem Copernicanism presented was not the need to rethink astronomy but the need for a non-Aristotelian physics. Such fundamental Aristotelian tenets as geocentrism, the stability of the Earth, and the difference between the heavens and the Earth had to be abandoned. This was particularly wrenching because astronomy, as a branch of mathematics, ranked lower on the disciplinary hierarchy than did physics, a branch of natural philosophy. The science of mechanics was one of the most intellectually active during the Scientific Revolution. During its early phases, mechanicists built on the achievements of medieval scholastics, as well as revived material from antiquity such as, among others, the works of Archimedes and the treatise on *Mechanics* falsely ascribed to Aristotle. Mechanics as a science had been developed extensively in the Middle Ages, although more on a theoretical than an experimental basis. Medieval mechanics was the principal influence on the Italian engineer Leonardo da Vinci (1452–1519), whose ingenious mechanical ideas exerted little influence during the Scientific Revolution because they were not published or circulated. The science of mechanics also suffered from the lack of a standardized vocabulary, and many mechanical terms were used to denote different things, even by the same author.

The mechanics of bodies that are not in motion—statics—were studied by the Dutch engineer Simon Stevin (1548–1620), the early promoter of decimals. Stevin demonstrated the conditions that hold for equilibrium on an inclined plane, and in hydrostatics, a matter of great concern for the Dutch, he provided the first demonstration of the hydrostatic paradox—the fact that the pressure exerted by a column of water depends on its height and not the total weight of the water.

Galileo's greatest contribution to the new worldview was not his telescopic discoveries, which could have been made by any skilled observer with a good telescope, but the creation of a non-Aristotelian terrestrial physics. Mechanics, not astronomy, was Galileo's central intellectual project. Even his support of Copernicanism was less directed against Ptolemaic astronomy than it was against

Aristotelian geocentric physics. (The adoption of the modified geocentric cosmos of Tycho, which offered the mathematical advantages of Copernicanism and was adopted by many European astronomers, held no interest for Galileo.) Galileo advanced a quantitative physics rather than the predominantly qualitative physics of the dominant scholastic tradition. He believed strongly that natural philosophy needed to be mathematical. This raised professional as well as epistemological issues. Many believed that a mathematician such as Galileo was not equipped to comment on natural philosophy, a different—and higher—discipline. There were some precedents for a quantitative approach to mechanics in the Middle Ages, and one of the enduring controversies in Galileo studies has been over whether medieval quantitative mechanicians were an influence on him.

Galileo's greatest achievement in mechanics was working out the properties of uniformly accelerated motion, such as that of a falling body. In Galileo's new physics, things had no natural place as they did for Aristotelians. Objects fell at the same rate, whereas for Aristotelians heavier objects fell more quickly. Galileo was aware that in actual experiments, heavier objects often fell more quickly due to the resistance of the air, but he claimed that isolated from this factor, they would fall at the same rate. The distance fallen would be proportional to the square of the time elapsed during the fall—"Galileo's Law of Falling Bodies." The inability of scientists to produce a vacuum at this time meant that his theory could not be fully tested experimentally. Unlike the scholastics, Galileo adopted an experimental approach, rolling balls down inclined planes and measuring the distance they traveled over time. Galileo established that the increase in motion was continuous, rather than proceeding in spurts as had been commonly believed by scholastic physicists, and proportional to the square of the time. He extended the study of falling bodies to pendulums, particularly important because of their relation to clocks, and projectiles, important due to cannon. He also demonstrated the parabolic motion of projectiles. Although Galileo flaunted his departures from Aristotle, the most famous being the fact that falling bodies fell at the same rate rather than Aristotle's belief that massier bodies fell more rapidly, he kept the traditional Aristotelian distinction between natural and violent motion.

THE MECHANICAL PHILOSOPHY

The most successful attempt to replace Aristotelian natural philosophy as a whole rather than, as Galileo had, challenge particular Aristotelian propositions, was the mechanical philosophy. The mechanical philosophy viewed matter and motion as sufficient to explain all natural occurrences. This made it distinct from Aristotelianism, which treated qualities as existing independently from substances and substances as endowed with "virtues" such as gravity, and magical philosophies, which relied on attractive and repulsive occult forces acting at a distance, as astrologers believed the forces of the stars affected things on Earth. For strict mechanical philosophers, matter itself was "dead," or inert, acting only as motion was impressed upon it. Bits of matter interacted only by direct contact or impact. There was no distinction between "natural" and "violent" motion— motion was motion. Mechanical philosophy became the dominant, although never exclusive, approach to natural philosophy in the seventeenth century.

The most influential mechanical philosophers were two Frenchmen—René Descartes and Pierre Gassendi. Their mechanical philosophies took different forms and sprung from different sources. Descartes emphasized his own originality and saw the universe as a plenum, full of different kinds of matter. He also saw matter as infinitely divisible. Like Aristotle's, Descartes' natural philosophy denied the existence of a void. Gassendi was a classical atomist who explicitly drew from the Epicurean tradition of "atoms and a void." (Not all atomists believed in a void, but it was essential to Epicureanism, the dominant school of atomistic thought.)

According to Descartes' own account, in 1619 he had a vision of a philosophy that would be completely new. His 1638 *Discourse on Method* set forth his program, and three associated treatises exemplified his method as applied to geometry, optics, and meteorology, including matter theory. These works were in French rather than Latin, aimed at educated men and women generally rather than university scholars. Descartes was the first European male intellectual to think of women as an important part of his audience. Despite his early interest in the work of Francis Bacon, he was a rationalist who valued logical consistency over empirical observation. Descartes' picture of matter in motion was dominated by vortices, whirlpools of matter. Large circular vortices—Descartes knew Kepler's work in optics but ignored his theory of elliptical orbits—carried the planets around the sun.

Life, which seemed to defy mechanical explanations, was a major problem for Descartes as well as other mechanists. However, Descartes, who conducted dissections, claimed that he had never seen anything in a body that could not be explained mechanically. He hoped his philosophy would culminate in a vast reform of European medicine and devoted much work, particularly in the last years of his life, to physiology and psychology, publishing *The Passions of the Soul* in 1649. Generations of Cartesians wrestled with the link between the mind, which Descartes claimed was not reducible to matter (the so-called Cartesian dualism), and the body. Descartes speculated that the link was located in the pineal gland. Animals, lacking souls, could be treated solely as machines. He accepted the circulation of the blood but rejected the explanation given by its discoverer, William Harvey, that the heart functioned as a pump. Descartes thought blood was instead driven by heat.

Pierre Gassendi and the Revival of Classical Atomism

The great rival of Descartes, Pierre Gassendi, presented Epicureanism in terms of seventeenth-century mechanical philosophy, reviving the ancient doctrine of atomism, and asserting the existence of a void. Influenced by humanists and skeptics, he conceived a dislike for Aristotle while studying his philosophy at the College of Aix-en-Provence.

Gassendi's natural philosophy combined astronomical observations with humanist allegiance to ancient texts. His most notable astronomical achievement was the only accurate observation of the transit of Mercury in 1631, which he believed confirmed Copernicanism. Gassendi, combining the roles of Catholic priest and zealous Copernican, was shocked by the condemnation of Galileo and afterward publicly advocated the Tychonic system. His intellectual project, beginning in 1624, was the creation of a Christian Epicureanism to supplant scholastic Aristotelianism. This was a difficult challenge since Epicurus was identified with materialism, atheism, and immorality. Gassendi emphasized God's power to create the universe any way he pleased, but despite his claims that Epicureanism was compatible with Christianity, the Church viewed his philosophy with grave suspicion. Gassendi also asserted that empirical examination of sense-data and construction of probable explanations were superior to Aristotelian dogmatism and claims to know the inner essences of things.

Like other mechanical philosophers, Gassendi opposed magical and Platonic philosophies. He also opposed Cartesianism, contributing skeptical objections to Descartes' *Meditations*. Although much of Gassendi's work was not published in his lifetime, his complete works, including many of his surviving manuscripts, were printed in 1658. Gassendism, mostly expressed in difficult Latin rather than Descartes' elegant French, would be eclipsed in France by Cartesianism in the second half of the seventeenth century but had a great influence in England, particularly after the publication of Walter Charleton's *Physiologia Epicuro-Gassendo-Charletoniana* in 1654.

Although many natural phenomena could be explained by mechanical interaction, some presented difficult problems. Magnetism, which had assumed a more central place in the scientific agenda since the publication of Gilbert's *De Magnete* in 1600, was a favorite phenomenon of natural magicians, who saw in it indisputable evidence of occult forces acting at a distance, and it was therefore incumbent on mechanical philosophers to find a mechanical explanation. Descartes came up with a complicated explanation of magnetism based on a "subtle" matter, not immediately apparent to the senses. Screw-shaped particles were emitted by the sun and channeled through the Earth. The opposite polarities were accounted for by the fact that some of the particles have a left-hand thread and others a right-hand thread. Gassendi and other atomists also explained many physical phenomena in terms of the interactions of particles of various shapes. The phenomena that mechanical philosophers explained by matter and motion also included living things. This mechanistic biology was taken farther by Giovanni Alfonso Borelli (1608–1679) and the "iatromechanists," mechanical physicians, of the late seventeenth century.

France, the home of Descartes and Gassendi, was the center of the mechanical philosophy, from which it spread throughout Europe to varying degrees. It was successful in the Dutch Republic but less so in Germany, where alchemically influenced theories of a matter that was active, not passive in the way of the mechanical philosophy, dominated many people's thinking.

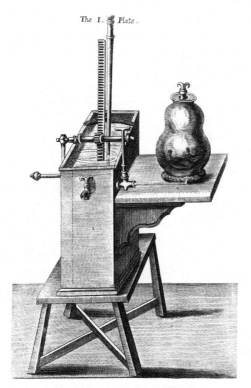

The I. Plate.

Figure 4-1.   Air Pump with Dead Animal. The air pump, by creating a space free of air, seemed to endorse the reality of the void. Animal experimentation was common during the later phases of the Scientific Revolution. A popular scientific activity was putting animals in chambers that had been emptied of air by the air pump and observing how long they lived. This illustration from English scientist Robert Boyle's *A continuation of New experiments, physico-mechanical, touching the spring and weight of the air, and their effects* shows an air pump with an asphyxiated animal.

Eclectic Mechanical Philosophy in England

Mechanical philosophy in both its Cartesian and Gassendist forms was introduced to England in the 1650s, a time when English intellectual life was in turmoil. The English Civil War from 1642 to 1649 had resulted in a greater openness to Continental ideas and major disruptions in English university life, challenging the Aristotelian dominance and leading to a plethora of projects for new curriculums. The English reception of mechanical philosophy was eclectic, in that ideas were drawn from both the Cartesian and atomist traditions, and nonexclusive, in that mechanical philosophy was combined with ideas taken from other traditions such as alchemy and Aristotelianism. Strict mechanical philosophy, with its insistence on mechanical and only mechanical explanations, was not congenial to the antidogmatic late-seventeenth-century English scientists who drew from the Baconian tradition. Interest in medicine in the vitalistic—and, ultimately, Aristotelian—tradition of Harvey and in alchemy meant that English mechanical philosophers were willing to consider the possibility of an active, non-inert matter, as long as it acted mechanically. Margaret Cavendish (1623–1673), the first English woman to publish a book on natural philosophy, combined atomism with self-acting matter, while Thomas Hobbes (1588–1679) attacked Cartesian dualism, arguing that the mind is as material as the brain. The chemistry of Robert Boyle combined mechanical and alchemical ideas, although later historians with an interest in "purifying" Boyle's chemistry of any taint of alchemy minimized the alchemical elements of his thought. Boyle was also a practioner of experiments using an air-pump, which by emptying a container of air was held to demonstrate the existence of a void and was thus evidence against the Cartesian belief in a plenum. Physicists and cosmological theorists such as Christopher Wren (1632–1723) and Robert Hooke (1635–1703) combined mechanical theories with the "magnetical philosophy" stemming from William Gilbert. Strict mechanical philosophy was held to lead to materialism and atheism by English Platonic philosophers such as Henry More (1614–1687), initially an enthusiast for Cartesianism who turned against it for religious reasons. The culmination of these tendencies was the natural philosophy of Isaac Newton, which combined mechanical explanations with universal gravitation, which many mechanical philosophers, particularly the Cartesians dominant on the European continent, saw as an intellectually illegitimate revival of occult and magical forces.

Cartesianism After Descartes

In the fifty years after the death of Descartes in 1650, Cartesianism became the predominant school of natural philosophy in France and most of Europe. It has been said that in the late seventeenth century every philosophical book published in France was either for or against Descartes. However, Cartesianism adopted many features that have little root in the work of Descartes himself and split into different traditions.

Methodologically, Cartesians also viewed experimentation as secondary to logical deduction as a mode of scientific enquiry, although they did not deny the usefulness of experimentation and many Cartesians, including Descartes himself, experimented. Experimental philosophy, as it was called, played a growing role in Cartesianism as well as other schools of natural philosophy by the late seventeenth century. Since Cartesian explanations of physical phenomena often turned on the properties of tiny bits of matter that could not be perceived directly, even after the invention of the microscope, the idea of a certain explanation demanded a lot of confidence. Many Cartesians deviated from Descartes by abandoning his belief in certain knowledge and making ingenious explanations for natural phenomena with the goal of plausibility rather than certainty. What came to define Cartesianism was less a strict adherence to Descartes' physics, as some Cartesians eventually came to accept the idea of a void, but a strict adherence to mechanical explanations.

A small band of dedicated Cartesians edited and published Descartes' letters and unpublished works, organized conferences, and finally orchestrated the dramatic return of Descartes' body from Sweden and its burial in Paris in 1667, keeping Descartes in the public eye. Cartesianism prospered at the expense of the Aristotelianism of the universities—although the struggle was prolonged—and Gassendi's rival philosophy.

In addition to the Copernican problem, Descartes also suggested the existence of an uncentered universe, with the solar system not occupying a central place—since while a central place was essential to Aristotelian physics, and even Keplerian astronomy, it was of no importance to Cartesian physics. Like atomism, Cartesianism was also theologically suspect as materialist. This was not just true in the Catholic world: There was religiously based resistance to Cartesianism in the Protestant universities of the Dutch Republic, Germany, and Sweden as well as Catholic France. However, some individual Jesuits adopted Cartesianism, and by the early eighteenth century Catholic university professors in some areas were allowed to teach Cartesianism, like Copernicanism, as a "hypothesis." However, unlike other challengers to Aristotelianism, Cartesianism, with its emphasis on deduction from first principles, was ideal for pedagogical purposes, and it was being taught in French universities by the 1690s. The logical organization of Cartesianism also made it ideal for presentation in textbook form. Cartesianism dominated the late-seventeenth-century market for textbooks in natural philosophy, both in France and outside it. Cartesianism did not require a great deal of mathematical or technical knowledge to understand, and so it was an ideal philosophy for scientific popularizers like Bernard de Fontenelle (1657–1757), whose *Conversations on the Plurality of Worlds* (1686) was one of the most commonly translated and republished works of the entire Scientific Revolution, carrying the Cartesian gospel well into the eighteenth century, a period often thought to be dominated by Cartesianism's rival Newtonianism.

Within France, the Catholic religious of the Oratorians, founded in 1611, became strongly Cartesian. Cartesianism helped the Oratory to establish a separate and modern intellectual identity at a time when the Church was still dominated intellectually by Aristotelianism. Outside France, Cartesianism benefited from the leading role played by French elite culture in Europe during the *grand siècle*, the age of Louis XIV (r. 1643–1715), when the French language was the language of educated and cultivated Europeans. Cartesianism's Copernican emphasis on the sun as the center of the system of vortexes also fit in well with the absolute monarchy of Louis XIV, the "Sun King." In the Protestant world, Cartesianism spread from the Dutch universities, where it was already influential during Descartes' lifetime, to those of Geneva, Scotland, Scandinavia, and to a lesser extent Germany, although the conservative English universities remained Aristotelian, as did most universities in the Catholic world. Cartesian natural philosophy influenced the most radical thinker of the seventeenth century, the Dutch-Portuguese Jew Baruch Spinoza (1632–1677), who took it in the direction of pantheism and determinism. It also shaped the natural philosophical thinking of Gottfried Wilhelm Leibniz (1646–1716), the leading natural philosopher and mathematician of late-seventeenth-century Germany.

By the early eighteenth century, Cartesianism faced a new rival, Newtonianism (although Newton himself had originally been a Cartesian). The struggle between the two would last until Newtonianism's ultimate victory well into the eighteenth century, but Cartesianism's emphasis on logic and deduction from first principles remains influential in French science and culture.

ISAAC NEWTON AND NEWTONIANISM

The Scientific Revolution in astronomy and physics culminated in the work of English scientist Isaac Newton, which set the frame for the sciences until the emergence of quantum physics and relativity in the dawn of the twentieth century (Fig. 4-2). Newton's *annus mirabilis*, a period in 1665–66 when he discovered

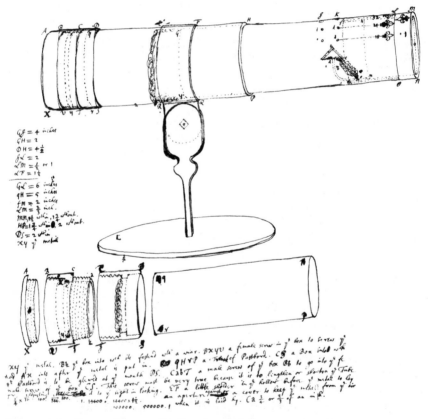

Figure 4-2. Isaac Newton Reflecting Telescope Sketch. Isaac Newton had less interest in technology than did most of the leading figures of the Scientific Revolution. One exception was his invention of a reflecting telescope.

the binomial theorem, laid the foundations of differential and integral calculus, analyzed the refraction of light, and began his work on universal gravitation, has a strong claim to be the most remarkable epoch for a single mind in the history of human thought. Newton's main work brought together the traditions of mathematics and natural philosophy far more successfully than had Galileo, as can be observed by its title, *Mathematical Principles of Natural Philosophy* (1687).

Inspiration for the publication of the work came from Newton's friend Edmond Halley. In 1684 Halley inquired of Newton on a visit to Cambridge, where Newton was a professor, about his opinion of an attraction between celestial bodies based on an inverse-square law. On discovering that Newton had already calculated that such orbits would be elliptical, Halley encouraged him to publish the results. *Mathematical Principles of Natural Philosophy* set forth a system of physics uniting celestial and terrestrial phenomena. Building on the work of Galileo and Kepler, Newton established a system where a broad range of motions in both the heavens and the Earth could be viewed as determined by three laws, canonized as "Newton's laws of motion." These are that objects at rest tend to stay at rest while bodies in motion tend to stay in motion (the principle of "inertia"), that the acceleration of a body is directly proportional to the force acting on it and inversely proportional to its mass, and that every action produces an opposite and equal reaction. Like Galileo's laws of falling bodies, these laws applied to idealized bodies. Newton also demonstrated that Kepler's laws of planetary motion could be derived from his laws of motion plus the inverse-square law of gravitation—that two objects attracted each other proportionately to their mass and inversely in proportion to the square of their distance. Although Newton was not the first to attribute the elliptical orbits of the planets to gravitation operating on the inverse-square principle, he demonstrated the connection with unprecedented mathematical rigor and sophistication. Newton himself never left England, but he drew on observations from a wide area—from New England, Maryland, and Brazil across the Atlantic to the island of Goree off the coast of West Africa. The unusual, once-a-day tides of the Gulf of Tonkin in distant Vietnam attracted the interest of not just Newton but many Europe-based scientific investigators.

Newton was open to a wide range of beliefs and systems of thought, all of which he thought of as diverse ways of getting at the one truth. He did not reject the mechanical philosophy and was originally influenced by the vortices of Descartes and the atomism of Gassendi. However, he was also interested in alchemy, which has a matter-theory based on altogether different principles. Newton was a believer in the *prisca sapientia*, the ancient wisdom, held at the beginning of human society and then lost. Much of his work was an attempt to recover the ancient wisdom. This position had become unusual in late-seventeenth-century science. The magical tradition, with its emphasis on secrecy, may also have been congenial to Newton's somewhat paranoid temperament: Many of his discoveries he made public very reluctantly.

Gravity, like magnetism, presented a problem to the mechanical philosophy. It seemed to require action at a distance, and one of the prime tenets of the mechanical philosophy was that bodies could affect other bodies only when they are touching. Cartesians and other mechanical philosophers argued that recognizing the ability of one body to affect another at a distance would lead to the return of occult qualities such as the celestial influences of the astrologers. Newton, by contrast, invoked the idea of a nonmaterial force permeating the universe, which had affinities with the worldviews of the alchemists and some of the ancient philosophers. The fact that Newton's equations worked became generally accepted, the Aristotelian and Cartesian explanations of gravity were increasingly discredited, but nobody, including Newton, knew why Newton's equations worked. The idea that science is about figuring out what happens rather than why it happens is an expansion of Newton's experiences with the theory of gravity. Newton claimed not to make "hypotheses" to explain gravity without direct evidence, although he did speculate as to its causes and hoped to find a mechanical explanation.

The final struggle between Newtonianism and Cartesianism would extend outside the chronological boundaries of the Scientific Revolution itself, only being resolved well into the eighteenth century. The philosophy of Descartes remained strongest in Descartes' own country, France. But by the end of the seventeenth century, it was apparent to most of Europe's educated elite that not only were Aristotelianism and Ptolemaic astronomy wrong, what was going to replace them was not an alternative ancient philosophy like Epicurean atomism or neo-Platonism but one of the two leading forms of "new philosophy." There had been a revolution in intellectual affairs.

FIVE

RELIGION IN THE SCIENTIFIC REVOLUTION

The Europe of the Scientific Revolution was also undergoing its most dramatic religious changes since the Christianization of the Roman Empire. The Protestant and Catholic Reformations and the subsequent era of religious conflict had an immense impact on both ordinary believers and religious leaders. These changes had direct and indirect effects on science.

THE HISTORIOGRAPHY OF RELIGION AND SCIENCE

Few issues in the history of the Scientific Revolution are more thorny and complex than the relation of science and religion. The trial of Galileo by the Roman Inquisition and the Roman Church's hostility toward Copernicanism generally have shaped the way the issues have been thought about for centuries. The trial became the key piece of evidence for supporters of the idea of science and religion as perpetually at war, as expressed in such classic nineteenth-century works as John William Draper's *History of the Conflict between Science and Religion* (1874) and Andrew Dickson White's *A History of the Warfare of Science with Theology in Christendom* (1896). This idea has become known as the "conflict thesis" and is still influential in how people think about science and religion. But other historians have pointed out that much scientific research and discovery went on in religious institutions—the university itself was a religious institution—and was carried out by devout scientists who believed that their work was part of their duty to God. From anatomists to natural philosophers, many scientists saw what they were doing as revealing the glory of God through his creation. Some historians have gone so far as to see the Scientific Revolution as an essentially religious movement, or have argued that Christianity had certain characteristics that have made it more receptive to scientific development than other religions. Few serious historians of science now support the "warfare" thesis, but the issue of religion and science remains lively.

The situation is further complicated by the division between Catholic and Protestant Europe. Both produced major contributions to the new science, but liberal historians like Draper, intellectually dominant in many Protestant environments, have suggested that Protestantism was more congenial to scientific innovation. There is no Protestant equivalent to the trial of Galileo as a high-profile confrontation of religious authority and scientific freedom, but is this because Protestantism supported scientific progress, or is it simply that Protestant churches did not have the kind of authority the Catholic Church had? Anti-Catholicism remained a potent force in the Protestant intellectual world, including the academic world, well into the twentieth century, and the charge that Catholicism was antiscientific was one of the most potent weapons in the Protestant armory. Historians sympathetic to the Catholic Church—Catholic, Protestant and non-theist—have pointed out that the Church was the greatest institutional patron of science until the late seventeenth century, and that many scientists were also Catholic priests and members of religious orders who saw their work as part of a religious vocation.

THE PROTESTANT REFORMATION

The Protestant Reformation is traditionally considered to have begun with the 95 Theses of German theologian and contemporary of Copernicus Martin Luther (1483–1546) in 1517, attacking certain Catholic practices and doctrines. Although Luther initially hoped to reform the Catholic Church, the differences soon led to a split and the establishment of a new "Protestant" church. Protestantism split into a bewildering array of factions, while establishing dominance in northern Europe and the British Isles, with a substantial Protestant minority in France and Switzerland.

Protestant theologians asserted that the Bible was the sole source of religious truth, although they were not always entirely sure about which books belonged in the Bible. This does not mean that they interpreted every word of the Bible literally—a hermeneutic that would not emerge until the rise of modern fundamentalism. Many Protestants believed that the Bible's text had been "accommodated" to the cultural and intellectual limitations of its original readers. What Protestant Biblicism meant was that Protestants denied that the tradition of the Church or the Church hierarchy had the power to define doctrine. Protestantism developed a heavily biblicist style of religious argument that influenced its approach to science.

Lutheranism and "Reformed" Christianity, based on the theology of French cleric John Calvin (1509–1564), were the major Protestant movements of the sixteenth century, but others existed as well. The most important for the history of science was rationalism, the belief in analyzing the dogmas of religion through the use of human reason. Rationalism was not as large or as influential in the sixteenth century as it would become later, but it was established among some intellectual circles, particularly in Italy, where it was influenced by Aristotelianism. Sixteenth-century Christian rationalism mostly played out around the issue of the Trinity and the divinity of Christ. Rationalists denied the Christian doctrine of the Trinity in favor of the unity of God. Some rationalists also denied the innate immortality of the soul, arguing that the soul slept after death until it was reawakened for the Last Judgment. These beliefs, particularly anti-trinitarianism, aroused the same horror in mainstream Protestants that they did in Catholics but would influence the theology of Isaac Newton, among others.

Protestantism appealed to those discontented with the established order in education and got mixed up with other projects for university reform. Although Protestantism originally rejected school divinity, Aristotle, particularly in a humanist form with emphasis on the original Greek text, was too influential to be banned. Scholastic Aristotelianism could be adapted to Protestant needs, and Protestant schools continued to teach Aristotelian natural philosophy.

The Protestant Reformation had resulted in a religiously divided Europe. However, the barriers to scientific communication were not insuperable. Although in the age of Galileo and Descartes high-level scientific writing was increasingly published in vernacular languages, much was still published in Latin and could be read internationally. There was a great deal of translation across cultural and linguistic borders, particularly from Catholic writers. Protestants and Catholics corresponded on scientific topics, a practice growing in the seventeenth century as the importance of religious divisions waned. Although Protestantism covered a relatively small part of Europe, greater intellectual and commercial freedom meant that Protestant cities like Amsterdam were overrepresented among the centers of European printing. Catholic writers such as Galileo were able to take advantage of this by publishing works that may have been too religiously controversial for Catholic publishers in Protestant cities.

THE CATHOLIC REFORMATION AND AUTHORITARIANISM

The Catholic Church did not stand passively by as Protestants remade the religious map of Europe. Catholics launched a vigorous reform program of their own, in part a response to Protestant gains and in part a work of reform tendencies in the Church that predated Protestantism—the "Catholic Reformation." A key element of the Catholic Reformation was an insistence on authority. From the relatively open and intellectually pluralistic church of the Middle Ages and the Renaissance, the Catholic Church became a much more centralized and dogmatic institution in the sixteenth century. A permanent Inquisition, the Roman Inquisition, was established in 1542, with jurisdiction over Italy. The new Inquisition accompanied other new controls on intellectual and religious life such as the Index, a list of books Catholics were forbidden to own, print, or read, established in 1559. The Index included Protestant and other works viewed as threatening to Catholic orthodoxy and morality.

The effects of the Index in science and medicine should not be exaggerated. The focus of the Index remained those books that challenged Catholicism on a religious basis, not a scientific one. The power of the Inquisition and Index varied greatly between Catholic countries, particularly in France, which did not even allow the Inquisition to enter the country. Even in Italy, where the Index was strongest, wealthy people had fairly easy access to many banned books in nonreligious fields. The power of the Index and Inquisition waned in the seventeenth century, although the Index was not formally abolished until 1966.

THEOLOGY AND SCIENCE

The new science raised many theological issues for both Catholics and Protestants. Both considered theology the "queen of the sciences," the highest branch of human knowledge. The relation of theological truth to the truths arrived at in other disciplines, including natural philosophy, had been a central issue in intellectual life since the Middle Ages.

Natural Theology

The Scientific Revolution was connected to changes in the way theologians described the relation of God and the natural world. The idea of a "natural theology," in contrast to the "revealed theology" of the Bible, had a long history. While specifically Christian "revealed" doctrine such as Christ's divinity could only be known through Scripture, many aspects of God's being could be known through study of the natural world. Nature and Scripture were frequently linked as the "two books" authored by God and revealing his divine qualities.

Isaac Newton's science was closely related to his natural theology. Newtonian natural theology was based on the idea of a God as a lawgiver. Although Newton did not invent the concept of a scientific law, he made far heavier use of it in constructing his system than had his predecessors like Descartes. For Newton, laws were given by a lawgiver, a God who continued to be involved in the working of the cosmos. The debate between the Newtonian Samuel Clarke (1675–1729) and Newton's great Continental rival Leibniz in 1715 turned on the distinction between Newton's God, directing the universe, and Leibniz's idea of a universe created by God to be so perfect it would run of itself. Newton's theology ascribed the great regularities of the universe to God rather than the wonders, prodigies, and miracles that many ordinary and elite Europeans saw as the most obvious evidence of God's existence and intentions for the world.

By the late seventeenth century, Newtonian natural theology was attracting interest across a broad religious spectrum, a process that would continue into the eighteenth-century Enlightenment. Newton himself was a rather unorthodox Christian, but Newtonian natural theology was adaptable to Deists, Protestants, Liberal Catholics, and even Jews, and sometimes even preceded the full acceptance of Newtonian physics.

In the early eighteenth century, natural theology based on Newtonian physics was joined by natural theology based on natural history. A pacesetter here was the English natural historian John Ray (1627–1705), author of *The Wisdom of God Manifest in the Works of Creation* (1691), a work of "physico-theology," applying the argument from design to the details of living things. William Derham (1657–1735), Boyle Lecturer and author of the Newtonian *Astro-Theology* (1714), was also the author of *Physico-Theology* (1713) (Fig. 5-1). On the Continent Derham and Ray were joined by authors such as Friedrich Christian Lesser (1692–1754), author of works showing the power and goodness of God from the study of stones, insects, and seashells.

PHYSICO-THEOLOGY:
O R, A
DEMONSTRATION
O F T H E
BEING and ,ATTRIBUTES of GOD, from His *Works* of *Creation*.

Being the Subſtance of Sixteen SERMONS Preached in St. *Mary le Bow-Church, London,* at the Honourable Mr. *BOYLE*'s Lectures, in the Year 1711 and 1712.

With large NOTES, *and many curious* OBSERVATIONS.

By W. DERHAM, Rector of *Upminſter* in *ESSEX,* and F. R. S.

Mala & impia conſuetudo eſt contra Deos diſputare, ſive animo id fit, ſive ſimulatè. Cicer. de Nat. Deor. L. 2. ſine.

The Fourth Edition, Corrected.

LONDON: Printed for W. INNYS, at the *Prince's Arms* in St. *Paul's Church-Yard.* M DCCXVI.

Figure 5-1. Title Page of *Physico-Theology* by William Derham. The title page of the collection of the Reverend William Derham's Boyle Lectures sets forth his intellectual program.

The Bible and Science

The growing tendency of both Catholics and Protestants to appeal to the Bible in religious controversy spread to other fields, and the Bible began to be treated as a source of scientific knowledge to a far greater extent than it had been in the Middle Ages. The Bible made many statements that were relevant to science about the nature of the cosmos and specific phenomena. One way of organizing natural information was "hexaemeral," according to the days of creation different things came into being. The hexaemeral tradition had flourished in the Middle Ages and was by no means extinct in the early modern period. The Bible was also a source of data that could be integrated into science. The worldwide flood described in the book of Genesis was widely accepted as part of the history of the Earth and used as an explanation for such otherwise mysterious phenomena as fossil seashells found on mountaintops.

One principle for bringing the Bible into harmony with natural philosophy was the "accommodation," which was also used in other areas of biblical interpretation. This was the idea that scriptural language was "accommodated" so as to be understandable to its first hearers, who were unlearned. Thus references to "God's right arm" did not mean that God had a literal right arm, but referred to God's power in a way that was easily understandable. Accommodationists could extend this argument to deal with scientifically problematic passages in the Bible. Since Joshua's contemporaries and the early readers of the Bible would have been geocentrists and would have perceived the sun as standing still, that was how the miracle was described in the Bible even if, in reality, God had temporarily stopped the Earth from rotating. However, many people viewed accommodationism with suspicion as a way of evading the Bible's plain meaning.

Biblically based natural philosophies could also be put forth as religiously superior alternatives to Aristotelianism. In late-seventeenth-century England, there was a strong interest on the part of many natural philosophers in a "Mosaic Cosmology," adapted from the Bible and named after Moses. However, the Bible was simply not a treatise on natural philosophy, and trying to extract one from it was impossible without assistance, acknowledged or unacknowledged, from natural philosophers. In practice, the Mosaic Cosmology turned out to be a version of Cartesianism rather than a strict deduction from the Bible.

The Copernican Problem

The most famous problem that this greater interest in the Bible and science created was the Bible's incompatibility with Copernican astronomy. Although the principal objections to Copernicanism in the sixteenth century were based on the commonsense perception of the stable Earth and the incompatibility of heliocentrism with Aristotelian physics, the Bible, read as a geocentric document, also played an increasingly important role. The passage in the book of

Judges in which God made the sun stand still for Joshua to vanquish his ene-mies was adduced as evidence that the sun, not the Earth, moved. This affected the reception of Copernicanism as early as the first publication of *On the Revo-lutions of the Celestial Spheres* in 1543 when Osiander suggested that Coperni-cus's new world picture be treated as an aid to calculation rather than a literal description of the cosmos. The idea of using Copernicanism for calculation was not controversial—during the reorganization of the calendar that created the current Gregorian calendar, the Vatican's chief astronomical expert, Christoph Clavius, used Copernican tables while firmly supporting geocentric astronomy, but portraying it as a picture of physical reality ran into trouble with the Bible as well as with Aristotelian physics.

Copernicanism became more of a religious issue in the early seventeenth century as the Catholic Church, interested in reasserting its authority in post-Reformation Europe, was moving toward proclaiming a monopoly of biblical in-terpretation while more astronomers, led by Kepler and Galileo, were adopting heliocentric astronomy. Catholic authorities feared that a diversity of views on scriptural meaning would lead to individuals and groups with differing views splitting from the Church, going so far as to forbid vernacular Bible translations in Italy. The right of "individual interpretation" was considered characteristic of Protestantism (although Protestant Churches could be quite authoritarian themselves). Although Church authorities were sometimes open to different ap-proaches to natural philosophy, they were not open to interpretations of the Bible that contradicted the official interpretation.

Galileo's famous distinction, that the Bible tells us how to go to heaven but not how the heavens go, was not acceptable to Catholic leaders even though it was consistent with the Council of Trent's claim of the Church's infallibility on issues of faith and morals. By asserting that natural philosophers such as himself were better equipped than theologians and Church leaders to interpret the Bible on scientific issues, Galileo was violating the Church's monopoly on interpretation. In 1616, Cardinal Robert Bellarmine, one of the Church's leading theologians, worked out an arrangement whereby Galileo would be allowed to continue to teach Copernicanism as a way of facilitating computation but not as a true pic-ture of the universe (a Catholic version of Osiander's "Wittenberg Interpreta-tion"), but this settlement proved impermanent.

Protestants, who lacked an institution with the authority of the Catholic Church or the bureaucratic reach of the Inquisition, also sometimes resisted Co-pernicanism on scriptural grounds, but Protestant astronomical experts who adopted it faced little institutional opposition. The Lutheran Kepler gave a scrip-tural defense of Copernicanism in the foreword to his *The New Astronomy*, and by the late seventeenth century heliocentric astronomy was widely adopted by educated Protestants, including virtually all Protestant natural philosophers. The trial of Galileo, which associated Copernicanism with resistance to the In-quisition and the authority of the Pope, may have actually boosted heliocentrism among anti-Catholic Protestant intellectuals.

The Eucharist and the Mechanical Philosophy

One issue where religion and science interacted and the Bible offered little guidance was the Eucharist. It was a longstanding dogma of the Catholic Church that the bread and wine consecrated during the Mass were literally transformed into the flesh and blood of Jesus Christ, while continuing to appear to human senses as bread and wine—"transubstantiation." The phrase "This is my body," as uttered by Jesus at the Last Supper, was interpreted in a literal sense, but the main religious basis for upholding transubstantiation was not the Bible but the tradition of the Church, which Catholics but not Protestants viewed as a source of authority on a par with Scripture. Not content simply to view the process as a miracle, the Church had developed a philosophical explanation for the apparent paradox of flesh that tasted like bread. Scholastic Aristotelians in the Middle Ages had interpreted this paradox as an example of the distinction between "substance," the inner essence of a thing, and its "qualities" that were discernible through the senses: The "substance" of the bread became flesh, while its "qualities" remained those of bread.

Protestants broke with this tradition, asserting that the substance of the bread and wine were not changed. Protestants differed among themselves on Eucharistic doctrines, but all declared that the bread and wine remained physically bread and wine. The Eucharistic issue was widely identified as the principal theological difference between Catholics and Protestants by the end of the sixteenth century.

As long as explanations of transubstantiation were couched in Aristotelian terms, new theories of matter faced a theological barrier in the Catholic world. The mechanical matter theories of Cartesians and atomists could not accommodate the distinction between substance and qualities, and without that distinction the dominant physical theory of transubstantiation fell apart. Catholic matter theorists like Descartes tried to come up with alternative explanations, but these were never as appealing to Catholic authorities as the Aristotelian theory, and Descartes' works were put on the Index in 1663. Pierre Gassendi argued that since the Eucharist was a miracle, it was unnecessary to come up with a material explanation at all, but this failed to mollify Catholic authorities. Since Protestant theories of the Eucharist were not conceived in materialistic terms, they did not create the same problems.

DOING SCIENCE IN CATHOLIC SOCIETIES

Religion, along with other factors, affected who did science and how it was done in different European societies. Scientists in Catholic and Protestant societies faced different challenges and opportunities. Ever since the Middle Ages, the Catholic Church had been the leading supporter of scientific studies in Europe through the church-affiliated university system, religious orders, and the court patronage of Church dignitaries, culminating in that of the papal court itself. One area where the Church played a particularly important role was astronomy, driven by its responsibility for the Christian religious calendar, which culminated in the Gregorian calendar reform.

Church patronage of science extended to many other fields. In addition to the medical schools of universities, the Church employed numerous physicians and other healers. The position of papal physician was particularly prized, and occupied by, among others, Marcello Malpighi (1628–1694), the discoverer of the capillaries, the tiny blood vessels between the veins and the arteries. Advances in medicine were particularly important to the Church's aging, and frequently ailing, leadership.

The Catholic Religious Orders and Science

The impact of religion on science was not merely intellectual, but also institutional. A central institution of the Christian Church in the Middle Ages was the religious order, a dedicated body of men or women under special vows, sometimes priests and sometimes not. Protestants, however, quickly abandoned the idea of a special religious vocation beyond or other than the ministry itself, and the convents, monasteries, and priories that had dotted the landscape of Europe since the late Roman Empire disappeared from the newly Protestant territories along with the religious orders that had maintained and inhabited them. The case was quite different in Catholic Europe, where many of the old religious orders flourished and new ones were created. Since much of the scientific and educational effort in medieval Europe had been carried out by members of religious orders, this distinction had a profound impact on the development of Protestant and Catholic science.

Much of the intellectual burden of the new Catholicism was carried by a new religious order, the Society of Jesus or Jesuits, founded in 1540 and very successful, with about 8,500 members by the end of the sixteenth century. The Jesuits emphasized action, including the cultivation of intellectual excellence, over contemplation. They became an educational leader within the church, running an excellent network of schools and colleges for any boy who wanted to attend them, whether or not destined for a clerical career. Jesuit schools appealed to the nobility and to the smartest boys, including some from Protestant families, increasing the Society's association with the intellectual elite. Jesuit schools were particularly well known for their teaching of mathematics. Many leading scientists, including Cristoph Clavius and José de Acosta, were Jesuits, and Jesuit schools trained many important natural philosophers and mathematicians in the Catholic world, such as Descartes. Jesuit institutions were leaders in mathematically based sciences such as optics and astronomy. Natural philosophy, on an Aristotelian basis, was also taught as part of the philosophical curriculum.

Jesuits always subordinated natural philosophy to religious ends, and their science was dominated by the search for the signs and emblems of God that he had left everywhere in the created universe. The leading Jesuit scientist in mid-seventeenth century Rome, Athanasius Kircher (1601?–1680), for example, was as fascinated by stones formed in the shape of the cross or of various religious symbols and personalities as he was by the properties of magnets, and he built one of the seventeenth century's greatest museums. Kircher's massive treatises on such disparate subjects as the Earth, music, light and shadow, China, and ancient Egypt traveled with Jesuit missionaries to many parts of the world, earning him the title of the natural philosopher read over more of the world than any of his rivals.

One of Kircher's most influential works was his decoding of Egyptian hiero-glyphics, treated as complex symbols with deep philosophical and religious meaning. (Kircher's interpretation was later shown to be wrong.) This emblem-atic approach to nature as a repository of symbols, as much as the defense of Aristotelianism, required the rejection of mechanical philosophies. The idea of a world full of divinely created emblems did not fit with the world of clashing bits of matter put forth by Descartes and Gassendi. This rejection of mechanical philosophy did not necessarily imply a last-ditch defense of Aristotelianism. By the second half of the seventeenth century, Jesuit natural philosophy was moving away from general assertions. Rather than broadening their individual discover-ies and experiments into theoretical claims, Jesuits put forth and analyzed mul-tiple explanations for phenomena without necessarily picking one out as the truth. Jesuits were also leaders in experimentation, contributing to the develop-ment of optics, electrical science, and magnetism. The Jesuit Francesco Maria Grimaldi (1618–1663) performed important experiments on the diffraction of light and gave one of the first accurate accounts of it. Kircher and another Jesuit, the Italian Niccolo Cabeo (1586–1650), were leading students of magnetism. Cabeo was the first scientist to describe electrical repulsion. This experimental philosophy was open to non-Aristotelian explanations, and Jesuit physics as actually practiced grew more eclectic, although Aristotelianism was not formally abandoned until well into the eighteenth century. Jesuits regarded their science and their religion as part of the same intellectual endeavor: Francis Xavier (1506–1552), the first Christian missionary to Japan, claimed Japanese people had a poor understanding of the motions of the stars and planets because they did not believe in a creator; lacking knowledge of a creator, the Japanese had no chance to understand creation.

The Church put limits on Jesuit intellectual endeavors, as they did on all Cath-olics. Jesuits were required not just to defend Catholic doctrine in matters scien-tific (as in all other areas) but to believe it. Although there was some intellectual pluralism among the early Jesuits, in 1611 a decree by the General of the Order, Claudio Aquaviva (1543–1615), required all Jesuits to defend the authority of Aristotle in philosophy, including natural philosophy. (This decree was precipi-tated by a theological controversy over grace and predestination, but it applied to natural philosophy as well.) Galileo had good relations with Jesuit scientists, who dominated the Roman scientific community, for much of his career, but Jesuits such as the astronomer and sunspot expert Christoph Scheiner (1575–1650) led the opposition to his Copernicanism. In the seventeenth century, Jesuits, like other Catholic scientists, adopted the cosmology of Tycho, which combined the mathematical advantages of Copernicanism with the natural philosophical and biblical advantages of the moving Earth. (Ironically, the heliocentrism of Copernicus, a Catholic cleric, dominated the Protestant astronomical world in the final decades of the Scientific Revolution, while Catholics followed the Protestant Tycho.)

Although the Jesuits were preeminent in the sciences among Catholic religious orders, not all followed the same Aristotelian path. The Franciscan Minims produced only a small number of scientific savants, but they were much more willing to adopt new ideas in physics than were the Jesuits. The French Minim Marin Mersenne (1588–1648) was a leading champion of the mechanical philosophy and a correspondent of both Descartes and Gassendi. The French Oratorians took advantage of the reluctance of the Jesuits to fully embrace the new science to be the first Catholic order identified with Cartesianism. The leading Cartesian philosopher and mathematician of the late seventeenth century, Nicolas Malebranche (1638–1715), was an Oratorian. However, in 1678 even the Oratorians were forced to nominally accept Aristotelianism.

The Institutional Limits of Science in the Catholic World—Galileo and Van Helmont

The institutional power of the Catholic Church, far exceeding that of any Protestant Church, gave it the ability to directly oppose scientific ideas by going after their champions. The mobilization of the Bible and Catholic authority against heliocentrism culminated with the trial of Galileo before the Roman Inquisition in 1633 and the subsequent enforcement of the ban on the teaching of Copernicanism throughout the Catholic world (Fig. 5-2). Although some Catholic Aristotelian natural philosophers were involved in the campaign against Galileo, the issue turned on the essentially religious issue of whether Galileo had violated the Church's ban on teaching Copernicanism as a physically true description of the universe. Bellarmine himself had died in 1621, and the arrangement had broken down as Galileo's Copernicanism had become more open and a new generation of Catholic theologians were less likely to sympathize with Galileo's position than Bellarmine had been. After the publication of *Dialogue on the Two Chief Systems of the World*, there was very little doubt of Galileo's guilt. He was forced to recant and sentenced to spend the rest of his life under house arrest at his country home near Florence. Galileo was warned that if he treated of Copernicanism again, he would be considered a relapsed heretic, and the penalty for relapsed heretics was death. He avoided the subject of Copernicanism in his publications for the rest of his life, but even so, he published his books in the Protestant city of Amsterdam.

Galileo was not the only Catholic scientist put on trial by the Church. His contemporary, the Spanish Netherlands Paracelsian chemist Johannes Baptista Van Helmont (1579–1644), was also judged and condemned by the Inquisition in 1625. The charges against him, based on his writings, were those of magic and

Figure 5-2.   Galileo Portrait. This portrait, dating about a decade before his famous trial in 1633, identifies Galileo as both a member of the Academy of the Lincei, an early scientific society, and as Mathematician and Philosopher to the Duke of Tuscany.

diabolical arts, charges far more grave than those against Galileo. He was sentenced to house arrest and also spent some time in prison. Van Helmont's writings were suppressed for many years.

One of the result of the trials of Galileo and Van Helmont was a greater insistence on conformity within the Catholic scientific world. Catholic astronomers were obliged to defend the Church's position on heliocentrism, sometimes introducing biblical and other religious arguments into astronomical treatises, as in the Jesuit Giovanni Battista Riccioli's massive *New Almagest* (1651). The impact of the decision was particularly marked in Italy, under the jurisdiction of the Roman Inquisition that had condemned Galileo. Van Helmont's condemnation had a similar but even harsher chilling effect on Catholic studies of chemistry than Galileo's condemnation had on astronomy, in effect ruling out chemical studies altogether for the Catholic scientist. Faced with monolithic Church opposition, chemistry became heavily dominated by Protestants in the seventeenth century.

National Differences in Catholic Science

Not all Catholic countries reacted to the condemnation of Copernicanism and chemistry and the assertion of Church authority over science in the same way. France, a Catholic kingdom, followed an exceptional developmental path throughout the Catholic Reformation. It did not formally accept the decrees of the Council of Trent, and there was no Inquisition and little enforcement of the Index. A Protestant Church was legally tolerated for most of the seventeenth century. The French Catholic Church was also the home of the "Gallican" party, which emphasized the historical rights of the national Church and the limitations on the power of the papacy. The French episcopate, dominated by noblemen, looked to the king as much as or more than to the pope for leadership. As a result, scientific life was freer in France than in other Catholic countries. Partially due to this unique stance, France would displace Italy to become the scientific leader of the Catholic world in the later seventeenth century. Another reason was the wealth and power of the French monarchy, which would enable it to replace the papacy as the leading institutional patron of European science with the founding of the Royal Academy of Sciences (1666) and the Paris Observatory (1667).

Despite the relative freedom of French scientific life, Church constraints did play a role. French Cartesianism, compromised by its association with both Copernicanism and Eucharistic heresy, shifted from Descartes' own quest to find the absolute and demonstrable truth about nature to a set of conventions used to provide plausible, but not certain, explanations for natural phenomena. Catholic suspicion of Cartesianism was one reason why French savants were reluctant to take as strong a stand for its truth as Descartes himself had been. On the other hand, Catholic authorities' greater hostility to Gassendist atomism, with its Epicurean and "atheist" associations, was one reason why Cartesianism came to dominate French scientific thought in the late seventeenth century. As elsewhere after the trial of Van Helmont, chemistry in France was a Protestant-dominated discipline that declined after the crackdown on French Protestantism in the late seventeenth century, although it revived in the eighteenth century.

Italy maintained a vigorous scientific life after the trial of Galileo, but one that operated within severe constraints. Italian scientists like Galileo's disciple Evangelista

Torricelli (1608–1647) were leading experimenters, but their experimental results could not be interpreted in a theoretical way that would challenge Aristotelianism or geocentric astronomy. One exception was medicine, an area in which the Church laid down few rules and one in which Italian scientists such as Malpighi continued to play a central role.

At the opposite extreme to France were the Iberian countries, Spain and Portugal. Although these countries had been leaders in European science in the sixteenth century due to their roles in European contacts with the outside world, they became increasingly insular in the seventeenth century due to the close alliance between the government and a repressive Catholic Church. As early as 1559, Spanish students were forbidden to study at foreign universities, although this prohibition was not always strictly enforced. Aristotelianism still dominated the teaching of natural philosophy in Spain in the early eighteenth century, as Catholic universities elsewhere were moving to more eclectic approaches emphasizing experimentation and incorporating elements of the mechanical philosophy and Newtonianism.

DOING SCIENCE IN PROTESTANT SOCIETIES

Although churches could exert a great deal of power in Protestant societies, they did not have the controlling authority of the Catholic Church. There were also far weaker connections between Protestant churches in different countries, even ones that shared the same doctrines and church organization, than there were between Catholic churches. Although Protestant ministers were sometimes active in the scientific community, there was no equivalent of the Jesuits or any other religious order devoted to intellectual concerns. Protestant scientists had to find other ways to support themselves, and until the founding of the Royal Society in England in 1660 they had no formal organization outside the universities remotely comparable to the Catholic religious orders.

Protestants were also faced with the problem that the French and Italian universities, the most prestigious in Europe, remained in Catholic hands. This did not completely bar Protestant students—Padua admitted Protestants, including some outstanding ones, like William Harvey—but it did mean Protestants could not serve on their faculties. Some universities in Protestant territories rose to the occasion. Luther's Wittenberg, founded only a few years before the Reformation, became the intellectual center of the Lutheran world, and several German and Scandinavian universities remodeled their curricula after Wittenberg's example. Luther's humanist disciple Phillip Melancthon (1497–1560) had great influence over curricula in Germany, insisting on maintaining the Latin-based university culture. For Reformed Christians, the city of Geneva in modern Switzerland was an academic as well as a religious center, while England's "ancient universities," Oxford and Cambridge, adapted with some difficulty to the new religious order. The University of Leyden, in the Dutch Republic, became a major center of science in the seventeenth century.

Lutheranism and the Early-Sixteenth-Century German Botanical Community

In the early sixteenth century, amid the turmoil of the early Lutheran reformation, a group of innovative botanists emerged in Germany including Otto Brunfels (c. 1489–1534), Leonhard Fuchs (1501–1566), Jerome or Hieronymus Bock (1498–1554), and Valerius Cordus (1515–1544). Claiming to restore the classical tradition of botanists such as Dioscorides, these scientists pioneered the incorporation of the plants of Germany and northern Europe, as well as some of the species recently introduced from the Americas, into the classical botanical tradition. The members of the new school of German botanists were all converts from Catholicism to the new Lutheran church. Like most botanists in the sixteenth century, they were physicians. As physicians, they were connected to the new German universities founded or reformed in this period to suit the new needs of the Lutheran Church. Fuchs in particular was associated with Melanchthon and his humanist and Protestant reformation of German universities. The idea of reform strongly influenced the work of the German botanists, as they saw themselves redeeming a corrupted botany and thus a corrupted medicine as Luther and Melanchthon were redeeming a corrupted religion. The "true" Greek medicine and botany needed to be recovered from centuries of errors by Muslims, whom Fuchs wished to eliminate from the medical school curriculum. The turmoil that the German Church and universities went through in the Reformation opened up opportunities for men like Fuchs and the new ideas they carried with them. Brunfels, a monk in the tough Carthusian order before he converted to Lutheranism, even expected writing on botanical subjects to support him outside the monastery.

Although Fuchs maintained intellectual connections across confessional lines to Catholic botanists and even dedicated some of his books to Catholic rulers, he viewed his work in a Protestant religious context. At Wittenberg, botany was taught as part of the arts curriculum in natural philosophy rather than in a separate medical school (although the teacher was a physician). As in other areas of science in the Lutheran university, there was a heavy emphasis on God's providential design. Like Luther, Fuchs, who published a translation of his major herbal into German, saw himself as addressing the common man. He encouraged nonphysicians to study plants, not solely for their medicinal uses but also to draw closer to God through the study of his noble creation.

Millenarianism and the "Hartlib Circle"

Much science in the Protestant world was associated with a variety of apocalyptic belief known as "millenarianism." Millenarians believed in a "millennium," a thousand-year reign by Christ and his saints on earth, and many in the seventeenth century believed the millennium was coming soon. The millennium was associated with increased human power over nature, sometimes viewed as the restoration of the power of Adam before the Fall, and it was one source of the belief in intellectual progress. Not all Protestants were millenarians—millenarianism was more common among Reformed Protestants than Lutherans—but millenarians often cultivated relationships across national and confessional boundaries.

One international grouping of Protestant millenarians was the "Hartlib circle," a group of correspondents interested in scientific, religious, and political reform. Samuel Hartlib (c. 1600–1662), born in Prussian Poland of mixed German and English descent, was at the center of a network of scientific correspondence and joint projects extending throughout Protestant Europe as far as the English colonies in North America. In England, he became involved in projects to restore learning and unite the Protestant Churches in a millenarian context, preparing for the second coming of Jesus Christ and his reign on earth. He saw himself and his associates as an international brotherhood to advance true learning and godly religion. Hartlib was also inspired by Bacon and the Czech educator Jan Comenius (1592–1670), seeking to improve human technological ability in areas such as mining and agriculture. Some foreigners interested in the sciences and in educational reform, such as Comenius, came to England hoping to influence the direction of its development.

Revolution, Millenarianism, and Science in Seventeenth-Century England

England, only a marginal factor in sixteenth-century science, had become a leader by the late seventeenth century. Many historians have tried to relate that fact to its religious conflicts. The "Merton thesis," named after its originator, American sociologist Robert K. Merton (1910–2003), credited the rise of English science largely to Puritanism, a particularly strict and biblicist form of Protestantism. Although the Merton thesis in its original form has been rejected by scholars, many have found other connections between England's complex seventeenth-century religious history and its science. One connection is through millenarianism: Many of the important English scientists or persons prominently involved in the sciences in the later seventeenth century were millenarians.

The English Civil War in the 1640s pitted a largely Puritan Parliamentary party against a religiously conservative Royalist party, which supported the established order of the Church of England as well as the monarchy. The victorious Puritans ruled England in the 1650s and had several projects for intellectual and academic reform. The mostly Aristotelian and religiously conservative English universities had supported the Royalists during the Civil War, and many of their faculty had retired, gone into exile, or been expelled by the victorious Puritans. In this fluid postwar situation, the Puritans promoted projects for educational reform and the broadening of the educational base by teaching natural philosophy, medicine, and natural magic at the universities on a non-Aristotelian basis. Many of these reform projects were explicitly Baconian, emphasizing pragmatic and technological applications over abstract theorizing. There was also widespread interest in the mechanical philosophies of Descartes and Gassendi.

The rise of the "new philosophy" at Oxford can be dated from the arrival of John Wilkins (1614–1672) as Master of Wadham College in 1649. Wilkins's informal group of experimental philosophers included Robert Boyle, the mathematician John Wallis (1616–1703), and Christopher Wren, all of whom became leaders of English science. Many left Oxford after the Restoration of Charles II in 1660 to form the nucleus of the Royal Society, the first enduring scientific society.

The English Civil War and Interregnum was Hartlib's heyday. He sought government backing for new educational and scientific institutions and the reform of old ones emphasizing natural and religious knowledge over humanist studies, and other projects for social and intellectual reform. His *A Description of the Famous Kingdome of Macaria* (1641) described an ideal state where applied natural knowledge led to a better and more prosperous life for its citizens, in the tradition of scientific utopias such as Bacon's *The New Atlantis*. The Hartlib circle of the 1640s and 1650s included such natural philosophers as the alchemist George Starkey (1628–1665), the first scientist of note to be born in the British colonies of America, Boyle, and William Petty (1623–1687), the pioneer in applying quantitative methods to the study of society—"political arithmetic." Hartlib himself was appointed to superintend an "Office of Address" for the advancement of learning at Oxford, although this was never actually instituted.

After Charles II was restored to the English and Scottish thrones with widespread popular support in 1660, natural philosophers such as Wilkins and Boyle conformed to the restored Church of England, indicating their shallow commitment to Puritanism. Members of the Hartlib circle such as Boyle and the German Henry Oldenburg (1619–1677), who began his career as a premier scientific networker by writing letters to Hartlib, were instrumental in the new Royal Society, which was given a royal charter in 1662 as a mark of the new alliance of the Crown and natural studies. In the new atmosphere, where millenarian hopes were frequently identified with the "enthusiasm" or religious fanaticism blamed for the Revolution, natural philosophy needed a new justification. The champions of science in the Restoration claimed it contributed to religious and political stability by diverting people's interest from controversies in those fields, as well as fostering economic development. Hartlib himself proved less ideologically flexible, dying in obscurity shortly after the Restoration. Moderate millenarians like Boyle involved themselves in scientific and technological projects, hoping to contribute to the improvement of life in the millennium.

THE SCIENTIFIC REVOLUTION IN THE JEWISH WORLD

Not only Christians had to concern themselves with the religious implications of the new science. Jewish communities existed throughout Christian Europe, and many Jews were aware of the Scientific Revolution or even participants in it. The European Jewish community was the first non-Western Christian community to have to come to terms with the Scientific Revolution that had originated among

Catholics and Protestants. As in the Christian world, a class of religious profes-
sionals, the rabbinate, occupied a strong position in Jewish intellectual life, and
much of its authority was based on the study of ancient texts whose teachings
could not always be reconciled with the new science. The basic authoritative documents were the Torah, the five books of Moses, the Hebrew Scriptures, and the
Talmud, a body of Jewish laws and commentaries. These documents were as authoritative in natural philosophy as in everything else, but in practice they were
subject to flexible interpretations. The philosopher Moses Maimonides (1138–1204)
had adapted Aristotelian natural philosophy and Ptolemaic astronomy to Jewish
use in the Middle Ages, as the scholastics had adapted them to Christian use. Although many rabbis respected the wisdom of ancient and modern non-Jewish, or
"Gentile," sages, they claimed that Jewish sources should be followed when they
conflicted with Gentile authorities.

In addition to practicing Jewish communities, themselves divided into northern and eastern European Ashkenazi Jews and Sephardic Jews of Iberian descent
as well as smaller groups, Europe was also home to a population of *conversos*,
Spanish and Portuguese Jews who had converted to Christianity, often under
duress, and their descendants. Although many *conversos* and their descendants
were sincere Christians, some secretly practiced Judaism or sought to move to
areas, such as in the Islamic world or the Dutch Republic, where they could
openly return to the Jewish faith.

The main discipline in which Jews engaged with the Scientific Revolution was
medicine, in which both Jews and *conversos* had a long history. Physicians were
leaders in Italian and Sephardic Jewish communities, and many were rabbis as
well as medical practitioners. Europe's premier medical university in the sixteenth century, Padua, even admitted Jews, although they were charged twice the
tuition of Christians. However, Jews were not admitted to teach on medical faculties and played a less prominent role in medical theorizing than in medical practice. Jewish and *converso* doctors published collections of case histories but made
few contributions to the theoretical understanding of the human body. One exception was the role of the Portuguese *converso* physician Amatus Lusitanus
(1511–1568) as one of the early discoverers of the valves of the veins. Jews and
conversos such as Lusitanus who engaged in scientific controversies with Christians were also subject to anti-Semitic attacks, limiting their participation in the
public life of science and medicine. When permanent scientific societies began in
the late seventeenth century, Jews were also barred from membership, as they
were from most organizations in Christian Europe. The first Jew was not admitted to a Western scientific society until the eighteenth century.

Science raised religious issues for Judaism as well as Christianity. Astronomy
was as important for determining the Jewish calendar as it was for the Christian
and Muslim calendars. Jewish religious authorities had similar problems with
the incompatibility of the new science with literal readings of the Bible that
Christian churches had, and Copernicanism penetrated the Jewish community
only slowly. The first allusion to Copernicus in Jewish literature, the Prague rabbi

Judah Loew's *The Paths of the World* (1595), uses the difference between the un-named Copernicus and Ptolemy to contrast the conflicting words of the Gentile sages with the unchanging wisdom of the Jews who had received knowledge directly from God at Mt. Sinai.

The first known Jewish writer to endorse the new astronomy, although not Copernicanism, was the Prague rabbi and astronomer David Gans (1541–1613), an acquaintance of Tycho's and Kepler's. Unlike many other Jewish writers, Gans had little interest in demonstrating the superiority of Jewish knowledge to modern Gentile science, and in fact viewed astronomical knowledge among his fellow Jews as extremely weak. Although he praised both Copernicus and Ptolemy, he came down on the side of the Tychonic system.

The Italian Jewish community, one of Europe's oldest, was particularly affected by the work of their fellow countryman Galileo. Rabbi Joseph Delmedigo (1591–1655), the first known Jewish Copernican, was born in Crete, then a part of the Venetian Empire. He became a student of Galileo's at the University of Padua, from which Delmedigo graduated with a medical degree in 1613, although at this time Galileo does not seem to have taught Copernicanism in his lectures. Like many Jewish scholars, Delmedigo wandered through much of Europe and the Ottoman Empire, eventually settling in Prague. Delmedigo was possessed of a mission to explain the new science to his Jewish contemporaries. His work *Sefer Elim* (1628), one of only two of Delmedigo's books published during his lifetime, is the first Jewish book to endorse the superiority of the Copernican model, although it does not discuss the question at length.

The Jewish intellectual community at Prague, the home of Gans and, for much of his life, Delmedigo, was destroyed along with much else in eastern European Jewry by the Thirty Years' War from 1618 to 1648. Copernicanism did not spread far in the Jewish community after Delmedigo's work, although it was denounced by Jewish thinkers Isaac Cardoso (1603?–1683) and Tobias Cohn (1652–1729), who described Copernicus as the "First-Born Son of Satan" (although this was a Talmudic expression referring to intellectual creativity and acuteness). Both Cardoso and Cohen made a mixture of religious, natural philosophical, and empirical arguments resembling those of Christian anti-Copernicans. Rabbinical authorities continued to be suspicious of Copernicanism as contradicting the Bible well into the eighteenth century. An alternative Jewish strategy for dealing with Copernicanism was exhibited by the Mantua rabbi Judah Briel (1643–1722), who argued that ancient rabbis were heliocentrists, and modern Gentile scientists were only vindicating their position. Therefore, argued Briel, the authority of the rabbis should always be followed even when contradicted by non-Jewish scientists.

A leader in the adaptation of the new science to Jewish purposes was the London Sephardic rabbi David Nieto (1654–1728). Nieto was the leader of the Jewish community in England during the height of English Newtonianism. He never became a full-fledged Newtonian—in fact he was at best ambivalent about Copernican astronomy—but he incorporated elements of the mechanical philosophy as it had developed in England into Jewish apologetic and drew from the natural theology of British Newtonians such as Samuel Clarke.

New discoveries in science also had potential implications for Jewish law of which Jewish leaders were increasingly aware. Jewish law permitted the killing of lice on the Sabbath, as they were believed to be "spontaneously generated" out of decaying matter, while forbidding the killing of fleas, which were the products of sexual reproduction. This question was the subject of a debate in the Italian city of Ferrara in the early eighteenth century, as Isaac Lampronti (1679–1756), a rabbi and Padua-trained physician and medical educator, argued that lice too were grown from eggs, adducing the observations of non-Jewish scientists using the relatively new instrument, the microscope. Therefore killing lice on the Sabbath should not be permitted. Other authorities, however, argued that centuries of Jewish interpretation and the authority of the wisest and holiest rabbis could not be overruled by Gentile scientists.

SIX

Cultures and Institutions of the Scientific Revolution

The Scientific Revolution was a revolution not merely in the content of science—scientific theories and information—but also in the culture and institutions surrounding scientific activity. It saw the fundamental alteration of old institutions like the university and the creation of new ones like the scientific society. Changes occurred both in state- and church-sponsored institutions and in ones developed in the private sector, such as the periodical.

Many of these new institutions, like the periodical, were adaptations of institutions that were developed outside science. The Scientific Revolution also saw fundamental transformations in European culture as science became more central. Methods associated with the new science—in particular quantification—were applied to social and political issues.

THE NEW SCIENCE AND THE UNIVERSITY

Although the university was a conservative institution, many universities were altered by the Scientific Revolution. The rise of new branches of knowledge was reflected in the founding of new university chairs, and eventually the guiding philosophy of higher education was replaced.

The grip of Aristotelianism on the curriculum was reinforced by the fact that the new philosophies did not produce as powerful a synthesis over as many branches of knowledge. Cartesianism was the first philosophy to successfully challenge Aristotelianism in the university, although its success was highly geographically limited. Like Aristotelianism, it could claim to be a "complete" philosophy that could be applied throughout the curriculum. Cartesianism's emphasis on deductions from first principles was also well suited for pedagogy, including the writing of textbooks. Although the Church's hostility meant that Cartesianism could not initially challenge Aristotelianism in Catholic universities, it was adopted in Protestant Dutch universities in the mid-seventeenth century and was taught in French universities by the end of the century.

One strategy for accommodating the new science without formally accepting it or teaching the new philosophies was shifting to an emphasis on experimentalism. In universities that followed this strategy, the teaching of physics was less oriented to the examination of texts and more to the demonstration of experiments. Acquiring a strong collection of experimental equipment, including mercury barometers and air pumps, was a necessity for schools wanting prestige in physics. This approach was particularly congenial to Jesuit schools, which shifted to a more experimental approach to physics in the eighteenth century. The wonders shown with experimental equipment fit with a religious emphasis on the wonders of God's creation and did not have to be presented with a theoretical explanation, useful at a time when Aristotelian explanations were unconvincing yet adopting any others was fraught with danger.

The defeat of Aristotelianism in the early modern university was not complete. It continued to dominate the universities of Spain and Portugal well into the eighteenth century due to the intellectual isolation of these countries. The dominance of a very conservative Catholicism in Iberia meant that Copernicanism was forbidden, and barring Copernicanism meant barring the natural philosophy of the Scientific Revolution in either its Cartesian or Newtonian versions. Spain, which had been a leader in science and technology following the Colombian encounter with the Americas, slipped even further behind the rest of Europe.

Medical Schools and the Revolution in Medicine

Among the first areas to be reshaped by new scientific discoveries was the medical faculty, the most active center of research in the early modern university. Medical professors, beginning with the Padua professor Andreas Vesalius, had made many of the discoveries that were challenging the traditional authorities' beliefs concerning the human body. The dynamism of the Italian medical departments in the following decades is memorialized in the names of many of the human organs, from the Fallopian and Eustachian tubes (named after the Professors Gabriele Fallopio [1523–1562] and Bartolomé Eustachius [1500?–1574]) to the pancreas of Aselli (named after Professor Gasparo Aselli [1581–1625]). This anatomical revolution in medicine culminated in the Padua graduate William Harvey's discovery of the circulation of the blood through the heart, lungs, veins, and arteries and Marcello Malpighi's subsequent discovery of the capillaries.

However, the new anatomical knowledge did not immediately overthrow the dominant Galenic system, as the system could simply absorb the new information, as it had absorbed the ideas of the medieval Arab physicians, without changing its fundamental therapeutic assumptions. The relevance of the new information for medical treatment was not always clear, while Galenism offered a system of diagnostics and remedies to suit a wide variety of conditions. (The most important new remedy discovered in the early modern period was quinine, which was found in South America and brought to Europe by the Jesuits as a cure for malaria, but the new drug had little theoretical importance.) A more fundamental challenge to Galenism than the new anatomy was Paracelsianism, which Paracelsus himself presented as a complete rejection of university medicine. However, university medical schools proved able to absorb much of the new medicine. In the second half of the sixteenth century, some medical professors became advocates of "chemical medicine," whether as strict Paracelsians or as "syncretic" physicians believing in a blend of chemical and Galenic medicine. The first university chair of chemical medicine was founded at the University of Marburg in 1609.

What eventually overthrew Galenic medicine was not Paracelsianism but the mechanical philosophy. By the late seventeenth century, some professors were applying Cartesianism and mechanical philosophy generally to medicine. The leading light of this effort was the Leiden professor Herman Boerhaave (1668–1738). These "iatromechanists" sought to understand the body as a mechanical entity. Physicians in the chemical tradition that ultimately derived from Paracelsus, such as Boerhaave's contemporary the German professor Georg Ernst Stahl (1660–1734), saw the body as driven by processes unique to living things—"vitalism"—rather than the mechanical or chemical processes characteristic of inanimate matter.

SCIENCE IN THE COURT

The courts of many monarchs, princes, and prelates were important centers of science. Although early modern courts varied in the approaches they took to science, there are some common features of courtly science. Courtly science was based on patronage, with the ideal the patronage of the ruler him- or herself. The higher the status of the patron, however, the more demands he or she would place on the "client"—the best patrons were interested in patronizing only the best clients. More institutionally fluid than universities, courts were more open to new ideas and valued originality and innovation. For example, Paracelsian physicians were prominent in many European courts in the late sixteenth century even while largely shut out of the universities. The traditional disciplinary hierarchy mattered less; one reason Galileo left the University of Padua for the court of the Duke of Tuscany was that as a mathematician he was considered incompetent to pronounce on natural philosophy in a university but could do so in a court. Astronomers also found their status higher in courts than universities, particularly if they could give the ruler astrological advice. Courtly science often presented itself not as a matter of simply understanding nature, but as exerting power over nature. Technical expertise, to carry out the prince's military and engineering projects, was highly valued. For example, many mathematicians were recipients of court patronage. Alchemists, with their claims to enhance a prince's wealth through the making of gold or by some other means, were also very common in courts.

Court culture was international, and many scientists found patronage outside their native land, as Tycho Brahe did at the court of the Holy Roman Emperor after leaving Denmark. Courtly science valued discourse and conversation, as opposed to the authoritarianism of the university lecture format. Conversation was not meant to be conclusive, and the ingenious explanations and theories of natural philosophers were likely to be evaluated in terms of entertaining versus tedious rather than true versus false. Court science emphasized the individuality of "curious" and "marvelous" phenomena rather than looking for universally valid generalizations. It was uncourtly to be overly loyal to a philosophical system, and university Aristotelians—"dogmatists"—were frequent targets of court mockery. Courtier-scientists liked to contrast their "free" intellects to the "slavery" of the Aristotelians to their master.

Gifts were fundamental to the court patronage economy, and both client and patron made them. The most famous courtly scientific gift of the Scientific Revolution was intangible, Galileo's gift of the moons of Jupiter, the "Medicean stars," to the Medici Duke of Tuscany to serve as emblems of the family. The dedication of a book to a prince or great noble was a form of gift and was usually done in the hope of patronage. Princes gave, received, and collected exotic and rare objects as tangible manifestations of their power. Organized into "cabinets of curiosities," these courtly collections were among the ancestors of the museum and often included exotic animals, plants, and gems along with antiquities.

Of course, the scientific interest of courts varied according to the interest and circumstances of the prince, and courtly science changed over time. A minor European prince, Duke René II of Lorraine (1451–1508), made his modest capital of St. Die a European center of geography through his patronage of a new edition of Ptolemy's *Geography*. It was from St. Die, in 1507, that the first map referring to the newly discovered continents to the west as "America" was printed. Some princes were keen scientists themselves: Prince Wilhelm IV of Hesse-Cassel (1532–1592) was a skilled astronomer who made his court a leading scientific center. The Holy Roman Emperor Rudolf II's occultism made him a major scientific patron. Others, such as Elizabeth I of England (1533–1603), simply gathered scientists as part of an overall program of patronage including writers, artists, musicians, and many others. Wealthy princes such as the king of France or the pope were able to create massive patronage empires, whereas small German and Italian courts had to be much more selective about whom they could patronize and often were treated by ambitious clients as stepping stones to more prestigious courts.

The Decline of the Court as a Place for Science

By the late seventeenth century courtly science was in decline, eclipsed by the revived university and the new scientific society, as well as the growing culture of popular science.

The reasons for the decline of courtly science have to do with the growing expense of science and the general retreat of courts from a central cultural position throughout much but not all of Europe. Some of the most active scientific cultures, such as those of the Dutch Republic and post-Civil War England, existed in societies where courts did not play a central role. In other societies where courts continued to be central, such as France, a lack of personal interest in science on the part of the ruler contributed to the location of science outside the court milieu in societies. One of the most "courtly" societies, that of Italy, was becoming marginalized within European science by the late seventeenth century, eclipsed by the wealthier and less Church-dominated societies north of the Alps. Court science continued in the Holy Roman Empire with its numerous small courts, where scientific societies were slow to start.

THE CREATION OF THE SCIENTIFIC SOCIETY

The most important institutional innovation of the Scientific Revolution was the scientific society. Societies brought together people interested in advancing natural knowledge outside the institutional structure of the university and were generally oriented to creating new knowledge rather than preserving old knowledge (Fig. 6-1). Although loose gatherings of people interested in natural questions emerged sporadically from the late sixteenth century, sometimes with some form of state sponsorship, the first permanent scientific societies, the Royal Society in England and the Royal Academy of Sciences in France, did not emerge until the 1660s.

The Italian Origins of the Scientific Society

The idea of a structured intellectual gathering place outside the university can be traced to the Italian Renaissance and its creation of the "academy," a gathering of intellectuals usually under the patronage of a sponsor. Academies were frequently linked to the court and dependent on the patronage of the ruler. The earliest academies devoted to the natural sciences appeared in the southern Italian city of Naples. A "Secret Academy" devoted to the testing of medical formulas and experimenting led a shadowy existence in Naples from around 1542 to 1548. Better documented is the second Neapolitan academy, natural magician Giambattista Della Porta's Academy of Secrets in the 1550s. Both Della Porta and Galileo were members of the Academy of Lynxes in Rome in the early seventeenth century. All of these early academies ran into trouble with the political authorities or the Inquisition, to which they were particularly vulnerable due to their lack of a reigning prince as a sponsor. More successful was the Academy of Experiment based on the ducal court of Florence, which lasted from 1657 to 1667. This academy broke up when its principal patron, the Duke's brother Leopold, became a cardinal. The Academy of Experiment was a transitional institution between courtly science and the permanent scientific society. One of its practices that pointed toward the future was its publication of a collection of its experiments.

The weakness of the academy model was its dependence on individual leaders and patrons. Even the most successful of the Italian academies, the Academy of

Figure 6-1.   Microscopic View of a Fly. This view of a fly appeared in Robert Hooke's *Micrographia*, a publication sponsored by the Royal Society.

Experiment, lacked any kind of corporate existence—it was simply a gathering of like-minded individuals under princely patronage, meeting at Leopold's convenience. These types of academies could never really compete with the massive institutional presence of the university, which in some cases could trace its history for centuries and often possessed an impressive set of buildings and other properties and a legal personality as a corporation that enabled it to own property. Nor were the kind of minor Italian princes who sponsored the earliest academies in a position to finance really big projects.

THE NEW, STATE-SPONSORED SOCIETIES OF THE LATE SEVENTEENTH CENTURY

The coming together of the academy with the greater financial and cultural resources of the great European monarchs produced a new kind of society. The first example of the new kind of society had nothing to with the sciences; it was the French Academy, founded in 1635 by Cardinal Richelieu to promote the French language. The French Academy was a great success (it is still in existence today) and provided a precedent for several academies founded in the reign of Louis XIV (r. 1643–1715). Academies reflected the glory of Louis, the "Sun King," and helped centralize European intellectual and cultural life in Paris. Among the new academies was the Royal Academy of Sciences, founded in 1666, which became Europe's leading scientific organization in the eighteenth century.

The Royal Academy of Sciences represented an important step in the professionalization of science. Its core membership of sixteen consisted of elite French and European scientists who were paid for what they did. The Royal Academy was connected with the Paris Observatory, founded in 1667, which had the mission of preparing a new map of France as well as assisting in navigation. The earliest publications of the members of the Academy were anonymous, associating its work with the collectivity and the king rather than with individual savants. To maximize its authority, the Academy did not take a side one way or the other on the issue that dominated French intellectual and scientific life, Cartesianism, although several Academicians, including the star of its early days, the Dutch physicist Christiaan Huygens, were themselves discreet Cartesians. Even when Cartesian theories were discussed in the Academy's publications, the name of Descartes was rarely invoked. Jesuits, the premier defenders of Aristotelianism, were also not admitted, contributing to their marginalization in later-seventeenth-century science. The Academy's position shifted in 1699, when as part of a reorganization explicit Cartesians were allowed to become members, including Father Nicolas Malebranche of the Oratorians, the leader of the Cartesian movement in France.

The Academy was closely allied with the French state. In addition to the new map of France, Academicians took on tasks such as the testing of new weapons and planning the aqueducts and fountains of the king's splendid new palace at Versailles. Leading officials of the French state oversaw the Academy's operation, including Jean-Baptiste Colbert (1619–1683), the chief minister, and ministers of war and finance. The Royal Academy's dependence on state funding was a vulnerability, given the fact that subsequent ministers of Louis XIV were less positive to the Academy. The ever-increasing financial demands of Louis' wars caused the Academy's budget to be cut, but its existence was never threatened.

The Royal Academy's principal rival, England's Royal Society, adopted a very different model. The Royal Society was built on informal gatherings of men interested in the sciences who met at Oxford and London. The few paid Fellows, although vital to the Society's workings, were of lower status than its unpaid leaders. The most notable of the paid workers were the secretary, Henry Oldenburg (although he did not actually receive a salary until 1669), who continued his international scientific correspondence begun with the Hartlib circle, and the curator of experiments, Robert Hooke. The Royal Society was full of curious gentlemen with a moderate interest in natural philosophy as well as leading natural philosophers such as Robert Boyle and Sir Kenelm Digby. The President of the Royal Society was usually chosen for his social and political connections and status rather than for skill in science, although this changed with the ascension of Isaac Newton to the presidency in 1703. Although the Royal Society was founded as part of the larger project of establishing a stable, if repressive, political and religious order after the turmoil of the British Civil Wars, its founder, Charles II, was chronically short of money and could devote little to the new institution. By giving it a charter, however, Charles ensured that the Society, unlike the Academy of Experiment, had a legal existence and could own property and enter into contracts, greatly contributing to its permanence. The Society existed on the dues it collected (meaning that a considerable portion of the Society's meetings were devoted to exhorting Fellows to pay their dues) rather than on a government subsidy like the Royal Academy of Sciences. While the Academy actively recruited scientists like Huygens to come to Paris, the Royal Society made no effort to lure foreign scientists to London, although some foreigners became Fellows. The Society also lacked the elaborate institutional hierarchy of the Royal Academy, and Fellows were expected to treat each other as equals.

One similarity between the Royal Society and the Royal Academy was that both avoided taking a corporate position on the clashes between schools of thought. The Royal Society included practitioners of the mechanical philosophy, such as Boyle, alongside Aristotelians and even an astrologer, Elias Ashmole (1617–1692). Early Royal Society writers such as Hooke frequently referred to the inspiration of Francis Bacon, but Baconianism was more identified as a collaborative and empirical approach to science that it was a school of natural philosophy. The Royal Society's motto, *Nullius in Verba*, "nothing in words," was meant to appeal to a Baconian skepticism about intellectual authority and a preference for "facts" over rhetoric. Baconianism also helped the Society identify as English at a time when the major schools of the new natural philosophy, such as Cartesianism and Gassendism, were based on the European continent. Another similarity was that their memberships were not restricted religiously among Christians—both included Protestant and Catholic scientists, although developments in Louis' foreign policy in the 1670s made the Royal

Academy increasingly unfriendly to Protestant scientists. The Royal Society was also, in the Baconian tradition, involved in projects for economic development, which represented a great deal of the Society's effort to demonstrate its practical uses. One was the compilation of the knowledge of artisans and craftspeople that would have been called "histories of trades," but this was never carried out.

By bringing together persons interested in different aspects of the sciences—from natural philosophy to botany—scientific societies played an important role in defining the sciences as a field. The Royal Academy's famous *eloges*, orations given at the death of a member, whether one of the core members or a corresponding one, helped define the model of the scientist as a disinterested seeker of truth.

The Berlin Academy

The leading scientific societies founded in the subsequent decades followed the French model of professionalism rather than the British model of amateurism. Gottfried Wilhelm Leibniz was a major promoter of scientific societies in central and eastern Europe. The first German scientific society on the French model was the Berlin Academy of Sciences, founded by the Prussian ruler Elector Frederick III (r. 1688–1713) under Leibniz's guidance in 1700. Prussia was rising among German states, and the founding of a new academy when none of the other German princes had one was a way to further the Prussian claim to preeminence. The new academy combined the functions of the French Academy and the Royal Academy of Sciences, with sections devoted to language and literature as well as physical and mathematical sciences, to put the Prussian capital of Berlin, hitherto a cultural backwater, on the European intellectual map. The Berlin Academy was financed by a monopoly on almanac printing, an innovation avoiding either the Paris Academy's dependence on government funding or the Royal Society's dependence on irregularly paid dues, and was followed by other European academies founded in the eighteenth century. The establishment of a permanent academy enabled the Berlin scientific community to weather lack of interest and on occasion outright hostility from subsequent military-minded Prussian rulers, one of whom insisted on classifying the savants of the Academy as "royal buffoons."

GOVERNMENT- AND UNIVERSITY-RUN OBSERVATORIES

The greatest astronomical observatory of the sixteenth century, Tycho Brahe's Uraniborg, had been the work of one individual, albeit a very wealthy one working with royal patronage, and when Tycho abandoned it in 1597, it ceased to exist. Tycho had never planned for the observatory to be a permanent institution, but a place to gather a set of accurate astronomical observations to form a new planetary theory. The seventeenth century was marked by the creation of observatories attached to an institution rather than an individual and envisioned as permanent institutions. (The last private household observatory to make significant contributions to astronomy was Hevelius's.)

The first university with an observatory was Leiden, the leading scientific university of the Dutch Republic. Leiden established its observatory in 1633. In the Catholic world, the Jesuit University of Ingolstadt followed four years later. The rise of the telescope made observatories larger and more expensive, and founding a new large-scale observatory began to require the resources of a state. (Hevelius's observatory was the last major observatory not to use instruments with telescopic sights.) The two most important observatories founded in the seventeenth century were the state observatories of France and England, the Paris Observatory, founded in 1667, and the Greenwich Observatory, founded in 1675. Both were founded with pragmatic needs in mind. The Paris Observatory was created as part of a complex of scientific and cultural institutions, including the Royal Academy of Sciences, which joined the previously existing Royal Botanical Gardens to make Paris the center of European science. Although individual astronomers were free to carry on their own projects, the director, Gian Domenico Cassini (1625–1712), an Italian astronomer recruited to relocate to Paris, was involved in a project to produce the first mathematically accurate map of France. Like the Royal Academy, the Paris Observatory also demonstrated the glory of the French king. Discoveries in its early years included the satellites of Saturn and the divisions of its rings (Cassini is memorialized in the "Cassini Division" of Saturn's rings) and the discovery of zodiacal light. The Observatory was at the center of a network of geodesic observers that enabled the mapping of the Earth with unparalleled precision.

The needs of navigation were paramount at the Greenwich Observatory, which was founded to create more accurate and complete tables of stellar and planetary positions that could be used by English seafarers. (Greenwich's position as the zero point of the world time system inaugurated in the nineteenth century is testimony to its continuing importance for navigation and timekeeping.) However, in contrast to the palatial Paris Observatory, Greenwich faced the classic problem of English government scientific institutions in the Restoration—underfunding. Both observatories were loosely affiliated with the dominant scientific society of their nation. The Royal Society's authority over Greenwich, obtained in 1710, was not well defined, contributing to the conflict between its head, the Royal Astronomer John Flamsteed (1646–1719) and Newton, who sought to control Greenwich in his capacity as president of the Royal Society. Such was the relative poverty of Greenwich that Flamsteed had to buy many of the instruments out of his own pocket. The connection between the Royal Academy and the Paris Observatory was much tighter and the Observatory ran much more smoothly, possibly due to the French state's more consistent funding, with some Academicians actually living in apartments in the Observatory.

European, along with Asian and North American, observatories had a serious limitation—they could not be platforms for observing the increasingly important southern sky. However, most of the Southern Hemisphere lacked the infrastructure for establishing permanent observatories. The solution was to establish temporary observing stations to compile southern data. The first systematic observer of the southern sky was Georg Markgraf, who established a temporary observatory on the island of Recife in 1638.

THE CULTURE OF COLLECTING

The building of collections, a practice that could be traced to the Renaissance, was an important part of scientific culture, particularly in natural history. All kinds of things could be collected, natural and manmade objects, gems, plants, and scientific instruments. Some collectors specialized in a narrow field; others embraced a huge variety of objects to represent the world in a cabinet.

The possession of a rich collection was an important part of the self-presentation of many scientists and natural historians. The authority of a collection backed up the assertions of a natural historian. Athanasius Kircher retained his position at the center of the Jesuit scientific world in large part through his extensive collection, the Musaeum Kircherianum, which was a must-see for visitors to Rome. Sir Hans Sloane (1660–1753) built the greatest collection in early-eighteenth-century England, the foundation of the British Museum, and became president of the Royal College of Physicians and the Royal Society largely on the strength of his prestige as a collector (Fig. 6-2). This type of collecting was only possible for persons of wealth, like Sloane, or those occupying a privileged

Figure 6-2. Dried Plants from the Herbarium of Sir Hans Sloane. Dried plants from the herbarium of Sir Hans Sloane, the greatest collector of the Scientific Revolution.

position as Kircher did at the center of the Jesuit order. Both of their collections became institutionalized after their deaths rather than being broken up by being sold piecemeal to other collectors or passing to their heirs.

Botanical Gardens

One of the most prestigious types of collection was the living collection. Collections of exotic animals had as yet little relevance for science, except for occasionally producing specimens for dissection, but living collections of plants, known as botanical gardens, were impressive research-oriented institutions. Large botanical gardens were supposed to contain a huge variety of species from diverse geographical locations, in the most extreme cases representing the world. The earliest botanical gardens were associated with medical schools and focused on plants with medical uses.

The deluge of new plants coming into the knowledge of European botanists led to an expansion of the size and number of botanical gardens. Two of the earliest incorporating recently encountered plants were those of the Universities of Pisa (1543) and Padua (1545). The leading example, and a pioneer in the establishment of botanical gardens outside the medical school world, was France's Royal Botanical Garden, which would be the center of European botany into the eighteenth century. Established in 1640, the Royal Botanical Garden kept the connection with medicine as its supervisor was the King's Physician. The global reach of the garden was enhanced by its leaders Guy Crescent Fagon (1638–1718) and Joseph Pitton de Tournefort (1656–1708), who collected over a thousand plants in a visit to the Ottoman lands from 1700 to 1702.

The desire of garden operators to represent the world was often reinforced by the layout, which in some gardens was divided into quarters representing Europe, Asia, Africa, and the Americas. Botanical gardens were also among the earliest scientific institutions to be established in European colonies, where governments hoped to develop exploitable crops.

SCIENTIFIC PERIODICALS

The periodical press was a creation of the seventeenth century. Most early periodicals were devoted to news, and the first periodicals devoted to science did not appear until after the founding of scientific societies, to which they were closely allied. The earliest example was *Philosophical Transactions*, founded in 1665, the pet project of Royal Society secretary Henry Oldenburg, who held the widest scientific correspondence in the late seventeenth century. Since Oldenburg did not receive a salary from the Royal Society until 1669, *Philosophical Transactions* was an important financial resource for him. Although *Philosophical Transactions* was not formally associated with the Royal Society, it drew from its prestige and much of its material was derived from Society meetings. Readers outside London viewed it as a way of keeping up with the Society's activities. The publication was a grab-bag, in English, French, and Latin, of reports of experiments, letters from correspondents on a diverse range of subjects, including mines and monstrous births, and book reviews. By including publications from a diverse range of foreign writers, including Huygens, Hevelius, and the Dutch microscopist Antoni van Leeuwenhoek, as well as many obscure correspondents, *Philosophical Transactions* gave an overview of science throughout Europe rather than just England. Observations from the English colonies in America were also published and the journal circulated there as well. Even foreign Jesuits, viewed with great suspicion by most English Protestants, could publish in the journal. *Philosophical Transactions* published natural historical reports from the distant Philippines sent by the Czech Jesuit Georg Joseph Kamel (1661–1706).

Despite *Philosophical Transactions'* multilingual publication, it was still limited by language in its audience, as few people on the European continent read English. Its French rival was the *Journal des Scavans*, founded in 1665, a few months before the English journal, by the lawyer Denis de Sallo (1626–1699). Like *Philosophical Transactions*, some of whose material it reprinted (*Philosophical Transactions* reciprocated by publishing material from the French periodical), the *Journal des Scavans* was aimed at a Europe-wide audience, but because it was in French rather than English it was better suited for this role. It had a less narrow focus on science and was a lively champion of the new philosophy in its Cartesian and Copernican form. Both journals started out as ventures independent of their countries' scientific academies but were absorbed into the Royal Academy of Sciences and the Royal Society over the ensuing years.

SCIENTIFIC POPULARIZATION

By the late seventeenth century, new scientific knowledge was available in a variety of forms, including periodicals, letters, tracts, textbooks, and public demonstrations. The alchemical and Hermetic tradition of keeping knowledge secret had been marginalized in favor of an ideal of knowledge as open, although the difficulty of the mathematics in a text like Newton's *Mathematical Principles of Natural Philosophy* in some ways kept its meaning as hidden as did the old allegorical language of alchemy. "Newtonians," however, could give the basic ideas of the text in a form that ordinary educated people could understand. The potential audience for the new scientific knowledge extended to a wide range of society's elite of both genders.

Unlike some early scientific works written for a popular audience, such as the books of secrets, the new popularization assumed that readers and spectators had a fundamentally passive relation to the new knowledge, absorbing rather than creating it. The ability to follow scientific developments and converse knowledgeably about them was becoming essential to the polished gentleman or lady, particularly in England and France, the most active centers of the new science in the late seventeenth century.

One classic French popularizing text, which provided the model for many others, was Bernard de Fontenelle's *Conversations on the Plurality of Worlds*. The format of

the work, a dialogue in which a male savant enlightened an intelligent but unin-
formed noblewoman, mirrored the work of popularization itself, in which the re-
ceivers of natural knowledge were conceived of as fundamentally passive. The "male
savant explaining things to intelligent upper-class woman" model would become
quite popular, followed by such eighteenth-century classics of scientific popularization as Francesco Algarotti's *Newtonianism for Women* (1737), actually dedicated to
Fontenelle, and Leonhart Euler's *Letters to a German Princess* (1768–1774).

A key role in the popularization of Newtonian physics was played by the
French Protestant, or Huguenot, exiles who operated in the Dutch Republic,
which had the freest printing industry in Europe. Since few on the Continent
could read English, and Newton's Latin works were famously difficult, it was necessary that Newtonianism be presented in an acceptable French to reach a European
audience of the educated, particularly given the popularity and wide availability of
Newtonianism's rival Cartesianism. French-language periodicals published in the
Dutch Republic and edited by Huguenots filled that need.

The new science was most impressive, however, not when described but when
publicly demonstrated. Lecturers and demonstrators appeared throughout the
cities of western Europe. Public exhibitions of experiments could now provide a
career for scientists like the Cartesian Pierre Polinière (1671–1734) in France or
the Huguenot exile and Newtonian Jean Desaguliers (1683–1744) in England.
The most advanced equipment, such as air pumps, was necessary for effective
display. By the late seventeenth century, electrical equipment was becoming more
in vogue, particularly due to its ability to generate dramatic sparks and shocks.

Experimental demonstrations were not merely a matter of dramatic effects.
Demonstrators also explained the effects using Cartesian (in France and elsewhere on the Continent) or Newtonian (in Britain, its Empire, and the Dutch
Republic) language. Desaguliers, a Huguenot Church of England minister who
shunned preaching for a career as a scientific demonstrator, was a particularly
able advocate of Newtonian physics. Popularization was also frequently put forward in a religious context, as preachers and demonstrators presented science as
a way of understanding the ways of God and creation. The "Boyle Lectures,"
founded in the will of Robert Boyle to justify Christianity against atheism and
deism without engaging in the disputes among Christians, were a particularly
popular venue for natural theological preaching. The Reverend William Derham's Boyle Lectures on "Physico-Theology" and "Astro-Theology" were bestsell-
ers in printed form, demonstrating a Newtonian God's providential design of the
universe. From the macro to the micro scale, writers on insects exalted the exqui-
site care with which God had formed these tiny organisms.

The production of scientific equipment for an amateur market also enabled
persons interested in the sciences to duplicate at home some of what they read
about or saw at public demonstrations. Telescopes and microscopes were produced for home users. Microscopy, ironically, flourished as a hobby in the
eighteenth century, a time when, particularly after the death of Leeuwenhoek
in 1729, it had nearly completely stalled as a scientific project.

Despite the large audience for popularizations, however, excessive interest in things scientific, particularly natural history, could provoke satirical ridicule. "Sir Nicholas Gimcrack," the title character of the English playwright Thomas Shadwell's *The Virtuoso* (1676), was a parody of the gentleman of the Royal Society, with his ambitious plans for "improvement" and his claim to have turned a bull-dog into a spaniel and vice versa by transposing their blood. The French drama-tist Molière's *The Learned Ladies* (1672) mocked the Cartesian women of French salon culture, as Susanna Centlivre's *The Basset-Table* (1705) ridiculed—much more affectionately—female English amateurs of natural philosophy.

Philosophical Transactions and the *Journal des Scavans* had a lay readership and helped popularize science, but the 1690s saw the coverage of science in peri-odicals not aimed at a scientific but a general audience, including women. Eng-land, where the Censorship Act had lapsed in 1695, had a remarkable flowering of periodicals in the next decade, several of which dealt with science. John Dunton's *Athenian Mercury*, based on answering questions sent in by readers, dealt with several scientific topics. Dunton employed Richard Sault (d. 1702), a contributor to *Philosophical Transactions*, to answer questions on mathematics and natural philosophy. John Tipper's *The Ladies' Diary* won some celebrity for the difficult mathematical problems it featured.

Science and Salon Culture

The salon was a French innovation of the early seventeenth century. Salons origi-nated as weekly gatherings hosted by aristocratic women in special rooms dedi-cated to the purpose. Their original mission was the refinement of manners, speech, and literature, and science did not originally play a large role in salon culture. But by midcentury, many salon hostesses became interested in natural philosophy, particularly Cartesianism. Cartesianism dominated the salons for several reasons. Many of Descartes' most central works were written in elegant French, accessible to salon hostesses who could not read the learned (and male) language of Latin. (Descartes chose French partly because it could be read by women. His rival Gassendi, who wrote a difficult Latin, had much less impact on salon culture.) Cartesianism provided a platform to oppose the Latin Aristotelianism of the exclusively male French universities, which salon culture stigmatized as "pe-dantic." Occultism was also considered intellectually suspect and somewhat de-grading in comparison with a mechanist Cartesianism. Victory in the salons was important for the overall triumph of Cartesianism in France, despite opposition by powerful forces in the Church, state, and university.

Salons were places for conversation and valued interesting and entertaining natural phenomena, such as the pair of chameleons from Egypt the salon hostess Madame Madeline du Scudery (1607–1701) kept in a heated cage. (Although she believed, or claimed to believe, that chameleons fed on air and light rather than gross physical food, she still managed to keep her chameleons alive for longer than the Royal Academy of Sciences had kept an Egyptian chameleon they had received a few years earlier.) They also valued ingenious explanations for puzzling phenomena, although it was considered rude to insist too strongly that one possessed the only correct explanation and thus shut off the possibilities for further conversation. Acceptability in leading salons was an important qualification for aspiring Parisian natural philosophers such as Huygens or Fontenelle, both of whom used salon contacts to build their careers. Salons also served to introduce science into the polite culture of upper-class Parisian men and women.

Science and the Marketplace—Maria Sibilla Merian and William Whiston

The culture of science also enabled scientists to support themselves financially and keep themselves in the public eye outside the institutions of the university, court patronage, and the scientific society by participating in the market. Two examples are the German-Dutch entomologist Maria Sibilla Merian (1647–1717) and the English natural philosopher William Whiston (1667–1752). Although widely admired for her research and her skills in illustration, Merian was barred from participating in scientific institutions because of her gender, while Whiston was a defiant anti-trinitarian heretic excluded from the institutions of early-eighteenth-century English science. Although his views on the nature of God were similar to those of his early mentor Isaac Newton, he was not discreet as Newton was, and as a result lost his position as Lucasian Professor of Mathematics at Cambridge University (to which he had succeeded Newton) in 1708. Even the supposedly religiously tolerant Royal Society refused to admit Whiston.

Merian supported herself as a writer and a vendor in the international market for scientific specimens. Her position in Amsterdam, the center of the international trade in specimens and scientific novelties, was ideal for this purpose. Like other early modern businesspeople, she worked with members of her family. Merian and her daughter Dorothea went on a lengthy trip from 1699 to 1701 to the Dutch colony of Surinam in northern South America, a region of which European scientists knew little as yet, to collect specimens for resale. On her return to Amsterdam, she corresponded with other family members dispersed across the Dutch Empire whom she expected to send specimens for her to sell.

Merian's participation in the scientific market was not restricted to specimens; she was also a highly adept student of insects and an illustrator. The knowledge she had gained on her trip was embodied in the form of a lavishly illustrated book, *Metamorphoses of the Insects of Surinam* (1705), which she sold herself along with her botanical and entomological watercolors. This commercial strategy was not successful in the long run, as she seems to have died in poverty after a stroke that partially paralyzed her, but it did enable her to support herself and produce scientific work for many years (Fig. 6-3).

After losing his academic position, Whiston plunged into the voracious London science market, giving popular lectures and demonstrations in coffeehouses and exhibition halls while publishing numerous short pamphlets on the

Figure 6-3.   Maria Sibilla Merian Bookplate. This plate from Merian's book on the insects of Surinam showcases her ability to combine multiple images in a single illustration.

astronomical events of the day. (A typical title is *An Account of a Surprizing Meteor, Seen in the Air, March the 6th, 1715/16.*) He also published explications of mathematics and Newtonian physics for the textbook market and tutored young men of means in mathematics. Whiston spent many years in the quest of the biggest financial prize available to early-eighteenth-century English scientists, Parliament's Longitude Prize, but failed, like many others, although the Board of Longitude gave him £500 to survey Britain's coasts. Whiston's finances were not completely free of patronage—he received a pension from Queen Caroline of £40 a year, and some leading figures of the Whig party attended his lectures and encouraged others to as well—but he was in no way a "court" figure.

The Scientist as Servant of Global Empire—Edmond Halley and his Contemporaries

While Merian and Whiston operated on the private market to support themselves as scientific experts, their contemporary Edmond Halley (1656–1742) operated with a combination of scientific society patronage and state employment. Unlike his friend Newton, who spent his whole life in England without apparently the faintest interest in going anywhere else, Halley's career was intimately linked with British global expansion and its connections to the European continent, making him a pioneer of international and global science. He took no real side in the vicious partisan struggles of Britain in his time: He approached the ideal of the apolitical civil servant that would be the model that many later "government scientists" would follow. Like many apolitical civil servants, however, this meant a stance in favor of the government of the day and against its enemies, foreign or domestic. Halley differed from his friend Newton, his fellow Newtonian Whiston, and many other leaders of the Scientific Revolution in that he seems to have lacked strong religious views. Given the strong connection between religion and politics in early modern Europe, his religious and political indifference were connected. He was often considered to be irreligious by his contemporaries, but there does not seem to be much evidence for that either. His encounters with scientists who followed other models of a scientific career illuminate the emerging role of professionalized science in the final phases of the Scientific Revolution.

Halley was born into a wealthy London business family. He submitted the first of his many papers to the Royal Society at the age of nineteen, a discussion of methods of computing planetary orbits. During his life, a great deal of the British Empire was being built, and Britain was attaining global power. This meant that navigation was rising on the British agenda, just as it had risen on the Spanish agenda during the sixteenth century. Halley served this agenda both as a theorist and as a captain and explorer. He also held several Royal Society positions, serving on the Council and being elected Clerk in 1686.

Halley's first major achievement was the establishment of an observatory on the island of St. Helena in the southern Atlantic in 1677. The expedition was financed by the Treasury, with passage provided by the East India Company, the British company that controlled trade with India and would provide the nucleus for British conquest there, at the behest of Charles II. Its purpose was the creation of a star chart for the Southern Hemisphere to improve navigation. Halley made the best chart of the southern sky available to that point. It was also the first stellar chart based on telescopic observation.

Shortly after Halley's return to England he was sent as an unofficial emissary of the Royal Society to the Danzig astronomer Johannes Hevelius. This was a particularly interesting confrontation, as the new scientist Halley met one of the last holdouts of the old household astronomy. Hevelius was also the last major astronomer to use instruments without telescopic sights and to work at his own private observatory, largely independently of governments. He set up an observatory in his hometown called Stellaeburg and began making observations with the help of his wife, Catherina Elisabeth. Although he was not a government employee like the astronomers of Paris and Greenwich, he received the patronage of Louis XIV and three successive kings of Poland. Hevelius discovered several comets and was the first astronomer to describe a variable star, which he called Mira. He had a long association with the Royal Society. Hevelius had been admitted as a Fellow in 1664, one of the first foreigners admitted, and published frequently in *Philosophical Transactions*. The reason Halley was sent to Danzig was Hevelius's dispute with Robert Hooke over telescopic sights for astronomical instruments, which Hooke supported and Hevelius refused to use. Halley examined Hevelius's instruments and make observations alongside Hevelius and his staff. Halley found Hevelius's observations highly accurate, but two months after his departure, Hevelius's instruments were destroyed by fire. Halley returned to England, setting out for Paris shortly thereafter. There he did observations alongside Cassini, a very different astronomer than Hevelius. It seems this was when Halley got seriously interested in comets, as there was a spectacular one that year.

Halley's friendship and intellectual alliance with Isaac Newton would be essential to his scientific career. In addition to inspiring Newton to publish *Mathematical Principles of Natural Philosophy*, Halley, as Clerk to the Royal Society, saw the finished work through the press, personally bore the financial responsibility, and contributed a Latin ode to Newton. Newton also drew on observations Halley had made and those he had gathered from others during his European trips. Halley's interest in comets was related to his work with Newton on celestial dynamics. It had not been clear that comets orbited the sun in ellipses, like planets, or even that they orbited at all. The periodicity of comets had not been established in Europe (even though the Chinese had already figured it out). Halley's *Synopsis of the Astronomy of Comets* (1705) described comets orbiting the sun in elliptical paths like those Kepler had described for the planets. Halley predicted the return of the comet of 1682, "Halley's Comet," in 1758. Halley suggested that there be coordinated observations of the comet, even though he knew he would not be alive to see it, partly as a way of providing experimental evidence for Newtonian gravitation.

Much of Halley's work was concerned directly or indirectly with navigation and sailing, particularly the longitude problem. Halley's three Atlantic voyages as captain of the *Paramore* from 1698 to 1701 to map the variations of the Earth's magnetic field were the first ocean voyages dedicated primarily to scientific purposes. The Royal Navy was extremely doubtful about having a scientist with no seafaring experience captain a vessel, and there would be no similar voyages until the nineteenth century. Halley's map of the magnetic variations, published in 1701, employed the new technique of "isogonic" lines connecting positions that had the same variation. Halley also charted trade winds and tidal patterns. In 1703 Halley was sent by the English government to scout out and map a naval base for a fleet to be based in the Adriatic, then a theater of the war of the Spanish succession, although the naval base never materialized.

Halley's astronomical achievements spanned a number of fields. He discovered the acceleration of the moon over long periods of time—the "secular acceleration." His discovery of lunar acceleration began with an effort to restore the text of the Arab astronomer Abu Abdallah Mohammad ibn Jabir Al-Battani (c. 850–929), whose accuracy Halley admired, although he did not know Arabic and worked from Latin translations. Al-Battani's observations were particularly useful in that they were chronologically midway between Ptolemy's and Halley's own time. Halley invented a method of using the transits of Venus across the sun as a means of determining the distance from the Earth to the sun, although the next transit was in 1761 and he did not live long enough to actually apply them. He also discovered the movement of the stars relative to each other.

Halley's relationship with the other major English astronomer, the Royal Astronomer John Flamsteed, was contentious. In the beginning the two worked together, but they quarreled beginning in the early 1680s, and the division grew irreconcilable after Halley's publication of Flamsteed's star chart in 1712. Although both Flamsteed and Halley were government employees, testifying to the increasing professionalization of science by the last phase of the Scientific Revolution, Flamsteed's career was very different. He believed the highest task of astronomy was the painstaking accumulation of precise observations rather than creating cosmological theories or astrological predictions. His hero was Tycho, not Copernicus or Kepler. In this he was very different from Halley, who was primarily interested in the theoretical implications of observations. Halley and Newton were impatient for Flamsteed to publish his data, which they regarded as valuable evidence for the theory of universal gravitation and perhaps a basis for further refinements to the theory. However, Flamsteed wanted the catalogue to be as perfect as possible, whatever the time it took, and since he had spent his own money to acquire the instruments he used to make the observations, he regarded the data as his own property. Newton, one of the Royal Society's Visitors to the Observatory, and Halley regarded Flamsteed as a civil servant whose observations were public property. As President of the Royal Society, Newton had Flamsteed, a Fellow since 1677, kicked out for nonpayment of dues in 1709. (Although Newton was technically justified in doing so, in practice it was rare for a Fellow to be dismissed for nonpayment.)

Halley's publication of a pirated edition of the Flamsteed observations in 1712 provoked Flamsteed's wrath. (Flamsteed referred to Halley as "Ursus," after an opponent of Tycho, in his correspondence.) Flamsteed bought up and burned three hundred of the four hundred copies printed, but the affair motivated him to prepare his own edition of the observations, *Historia Coelestis Britannica* (1725). It was posthumously published in three volumes by his widow, Margaret Flamsteed (1670?–1730), who had assisted his work, and two of his former associates. It was the finest star catalogue to that time.

Halley's conflict with Flamsteed did not adversely affect his career; he was appointed Savilian Professor of Geometry at Oxford in 1703. His best-known mathematical accomplishment as professor was his contribution to a new edition of the surviving Greek text and Latin translation of the *Conics* by Apollonius of Perga, a work on the geometry of conic sections. Of the surviving seven books of the *Conics*, the last three do not survive in the original Greek but only in Arabic translation. Halley's role was mathematical rather than philological. A new edition of Apollonius was a classical product of humanist science, which would have been perfectly comprehensible in the fifteenth century. However, the era when scientists and mathematicians would do these types of editions was passing. In the future, this kind of work would be done by classical and Arabic scholars rather than scientists.

In 1715 Halley provided an interesting example of how science could be used for propaganda with a popular appeal. Unsurprisingly, Halley was attempting to dissuade people from rising against the government. A spectacular solar eclipse could be interpreted as expressing God's disapproval of the recent accession of the House of Hanover to the British throne, replacing the House of Stuart. Since there was actually an armed rising by "Jacobite" defenders of the Stuarts, this was an issue of great importance. Halley authored a broadside providing a technical interpretation of eclipses with a drawing of the geometry of this particular eclipse, discouraging readers from viewing the eclipse as a sign of disapproval of the new dynasty.

The new dynasty's appreciation of Halley can be seen by the fact that in 1720, after Flamsteed's death, Halley succeeded his old enemy as Royal Astronomer. Although he replaced the instruments Flamsteed's heirs had removed from the Observatory with more modern ones, his tenure as Astronomer was not distinguished. Halley continued to pursue his scientific interests throughout his long life. In 1729, Halley's role not just in English but in world science was recognized by admission as a corresponding member of the Royal Academy of Sciences.

SEVEN

SCIENCE AND SOCIETY

The seventeenth century was a time of great social change and turmoil. European empire-building and contacts with other parts of the world continued, raising a host of new issues related to the differences between groups of humans. The question of the proper relation of men and women was contentious, as women and a few male allies exploited access to the printing press to challenge traditional gender roles. The wars of religion and revolutionary uprisings of the first half of the century, culminating in the English Revolution, which saw the public trial, conviction, and decapitation of the king, put issues of political authority and the right way to order society on the agenda as well. It is a mark of the growing confidence of the natural philosophers and scientists that they thought they had something to contribute to all of these debates.

SEXUAL DIFFERENCE

The idea that differences between males and females and their respective roles in reproduction were capable of scientific and medical explanation went back to the ancient world. The basic division was between theories emphasizing the similarities of males and females and those emphasizing their differences. Historian Thomas Laqueur has argued that early modern interpretations of sexual difference fall into two broad categories. The similarity or "one-sex" school, drawing on Aristotelian or Galenic theory, believed women to be incomplete men, whose organs had not been fully pushed out due to insufficient heat. Thus the vagina was an inside-out penis, and the ovaries were often referred to as female testes. Parallelism extended to many biological processes. Even menstruation could be seen as paralleled by hemorrhoidal bleeding. Many one-sex thinkers thought the female orgasm was as necessary for conception as the male one. So similar were male and female bodies that some females could change into males as a result of a sudden influx of heat, although the reverse process was impossible—a qualification that early modern men would have found reassuring. Most of the leaders of European anatomy, including Andreas Vesalius and William Harvey, supported the one-sex interpretation, although there were many nuances and points of difference within one-sex thinking. Strict Aristotelians believed that every human being could be classified as male or female; medical thinkers influenced by Galen or Hippocrates believed a few people were genuine "hermaphrodites," intermediate between the sexes. The medical discovery of the clitoris in the 1550s, disputed between the Italian physicians and medical professors Realdo Colombo (c. 1510–1559) and Gabriele Fallopio (1523–1562), further complicated the issue, challenging the similarity school by raising the question of whether the vagina or the clitoris was the female "equivalent" of the penis. However, many one-sex thinkers were able to treat both the vagina and the clitoris as "female penises," depending on the context, without acknowledging a contradiction. (The discovery of the clitoris also contributed to a rising concern with female homoeroticism, which led some male physicians to advocate clitoridectomy, either of unusually large clitorises or, more radically, of all clitorises.)

The difference, or "two-sex," school, which had less ancient textual authority than the similarity school and was less prominent in the sixteenth century, argued that males and females were fundamentally different and complementary, at least in their sexual and reproductive roles. Difference thinkers, such as the French anatomist and royal physician Andre Dulaurens (1558–1609), minimized the existence or importance of structural similarities. Two-sex thinkers claimed that since God created all things perfect, including women, women were equally perfect as men. (This does not mean that they claimed that women should receive more equal treatment in society, although some did, any more than the perfection of animals meant that they should be treated as equal to humans.) Sex changes were merely hermaphrodites whose male organs had been concealed, or possibly women with enlarged clitorises, or simply frauds. The difference thinkers were an increasing presence in European anatomy beginning in the late sixteenth century and painted themselves as challengers of ancient authority like other thinkers in the Scientific Revolution. (However, Hippocrates could be invoked against Galen and Aristotle as a supporter of the distinct differences of the sexes.) Paracelsus, the archetypal rebel against the ancients, also championed the idea that men and women were so different that different sciences of medicine were required to deal with their bodies. The growing number of medical specialists in "women's diseases," for whom women's distinctiveness underlay their own claims to professional authority, also emphasized the separateness of the sexes.

The similarity approach was linked to an Aristotelian hierarchical cosmology. Women, exhibiting the qualities of coldness and moistness as opposed to the heat and dryness of men, were hierarchically subordinate to them. Difference thinkers, however, often retained the categories of cold and heat to explain sexual difference, even though they were severed from the original Aristotelian and Galenic context in which they made sense. However, the mechanical philosophy with its severance from Aristotelianism was congenital to thinking about male and female difference. The full development of a biology based on the idea that male and female were radically opposed, however, would not take place until the mid-eighteenth century.

Seventeenth-century natural philosophers exhibited a range of attitudes on gender and science. Francis Bacon argued that true science was a masculine endeavor. However, this argument was aimed less at women than it was at Bacon's male intellectual rivals: For Baconians, ancient science, even though it was created by males like Aristotle, was "feminine"—passive in its relation to nature. Masculine science—the kind Bacon advocated—would take a more active and dominant role, ruling over nature. Cartesianism was the seventeenth-century natural philosophy most likely to lead to questioning male domination. This was not because Descartes was a believer in the equality of the sexes or even particularly interested in gender issues (although like many male natural philosophers he did have women friends and correspondents with whom he shared his ideas). Cartesianism ignored the Aristotelian categories of hot/cold and moist/dry on which so much thinking about sexual difference was based and assumed a disconnection between the mind and the body, making it congenial to assertions of the equality of the sexes. The assumption that "souls have no sex," common in Christian theology, meant that women and their advocates could now assert that whatever differences existed between the bodies of men and women were simply irrelevant to the spiritual and intellectual capacities of their souls. The French Cartesian François Poulain de la Barre (1647–1725) wrote an influential pro-equality tract, *The Equality of the Two Sexes* (1673), translated into English as *The Woman as Good as the Man* (1677). The natural philosophy of the English physician and Fellow of the Royal Society John Locke (1632–1704), another thinker with many women intellectual correspondents and friends, also placed little emphasis on differences of gender. As an educational writer, he advocated the same education for upper-class girls as for upper-class boys.

Women and Scientific Institutions—Maria Winkelmann and the Berlin Academy

In practice, however, male natural philosophers, whatever their philosophy, excluded women from scientific institutions, whether traditional ones like universities or new ones like scientific societies. This issue was faced by the Berlin Academy shortly after its foundation. Among the new academy's first tasks was the creation of an observatory, and the astronomer it hired, Gottfried Kirch (1639–1710), worked closely with his wife, Maria Winkelmann (1670–1720), a by no means unusual arrangement in German astronomy, still strongly influenced by the household tradition. (Both of Hevelius's wives had been full partners in his astronomical projects, and Hevelius had been Kirch's teacher.) After Kirch's death, Winkelmann sought, with Leibniz's support, to take his place, but the leaders of the Berlin Academy decided that it was unsuitable for a woman to have this position. Winkelmann's competence was never questioned, merely the appropriateness of an academy seeking to rival London and Paris having a woman astronomer, something that would never even have been considered in the Royal

Society or Royal Academy of Sciences. Eventually Winkelmann's son Christoph was appointed astronomer to the Academy, although she continued to do much of the work behind the scenes.

RACE, SLAVERY, AND SCIENCE

The nature of the differences among groups of human beings was one of the most important questions for many thinkers in seventeenth-century Europe and its expanding colonies. The increased contacts with the rest of the world that had begun with the era of Columbus and Vasco da Gama had continued and intensified. The increasing volume of the slave trade with the development of sugar and other "plantation" crops contributed to the fact that the differences between Europeans ("whites") and Africans ("blacks") assumed some of the importance that the differences between Europeans and Native Americans had had in the sixteenth century. (So dramatic was the growth of the slavery-based sugar economy in the mid-seventeenth century that sugar was often linked with gunpowder and printing as one of the technological wonders of the age.) Growing awareness of human cultural differences and the religious divisions of Europe itself meant that the old system of dividing humans principally by religion was losing much of its usefulness. The materialism of the mechanical philosophy—its lack of interest in souls or spirits—opened the door to a view of human beings as primarily differentiated by physical characteristics, but the causes of those differences remained a much-disputed question.

In the early Scientific Revolution, the dominant way of thinking about differences between large, geographically separate groups of human beings did not use the concept of "race" in the modern sense—strictly heritable qualities. Instead, environment, particularly climate, played a major role, to the extent that some feared that Europeans settling in the Americas would become physically like Native Americans. An alternative or supplemental theory ascribed physical differences to different conditions during infancy, as Native American women were believed to deliberately shape the heads of their children by squeezing them between boards. During the Scientific Revolution, European and colonial thinking would move much closer to the modern concept of race, although other traditions continued into the eighteenth century. The early modern creation of "race" as a category is a vast and historiographically contentious issue in which science was only one aspect, and seldom the most important.

A longstanding partial exception to the climatic theory of human difference was black Africans, who had a long history as the "other" of white Europeans, going back to the classical era. Although Africans' dark skin was frequently ascribed to the hot tropical sun, the persistence of blackness among Africans outside sub-Saharan Africa and their descendants was noted by scientists, including Robert Boyle. Growing experience with the diversity of non-European peoples made the theory of the climate as sole cause untenable.

One question that was often answered in racial terms was the high death rates from disease suffered by indigenous American populations who came into contact with colonists. This high mortality is nowadays explained as a "virgin-soil" epidemic, caused by the Natives' lack of immunity to diseases introduced by Europeans and Africans, and compounded by the violence and disruption of the European invasion. However, the theory of disease immunity was not an intellectual resource available to early modern European (or Native Americans) themselves, who still sought an explanation for this puzzling, if often welcome (to Europeans), phenomenon. Religiously, some Europeans explained the great dying as the providential design of God clearing a way for his favored children, Christian Europeans. However, as providential causes did not exclude natural ones, some still sought to explain the phenomenon's medical or other natural causes. One reason was the supposed fragility of Native bodies. Although Europeans respected what they perceived as the physical toughness and endurance of Natives, they also saw the Natives as fundamentally inferior on a biological level due to their susceptibility to disease, establishing a "biological" rather than cultural or religious gap between the two peoples.

Questions about human difference, both physical and cultural, figured prominently in the questionnaires sent out by scientific societies to travelers and officials journeying outside Europe. Skin color in particular was the object of scientific curiosity in the late seventeenth century, especially in England, which assumed the leading role in the Atlantic slave trade from around the 1670s. The year of the foundation of the Royal Society also saw the foundation of the Royal Company of Adventurers trading into Africa, England's first attempt at a slave-trading monopoly company, and the first historian of the Royal Society, Thomas Sprat, referred to the two organizations as "twin sisters." The Royal Society itself purchased stock in the Royal African Company, the much more successful successor to the defunct Royal Company of Adventurers, in 1682, and several Fellows were involved in the Royal African Company or in colonial ventures. (John Lord Carberry, president of the Royal Society from 1686 to 1689, had previously been governor of Jamaica.) The skin of a black African, or "Moor," was part of the Society's collection, while the skins of other peoples were not collected. The Society's project was not explaining white skin color, assumed to be the human norm even though in practice only displayed by a minority, but of explaining dark skin with a growing emphasis on black Africans. Theories of blacks' skin color included "black blood" or the presence of a layer of black skin over or under a layer of "natural" (i.e., white) skin. The growth of microscopial science in the late seventeenth century led to investigations of black skin by leaders in the field. Marcello Malpighi believed it was caused by a "black mucous" between two layers of skin, while Leeuwenhoek believed that black babies developed tiny black "scales" while white babies developed transparent ones. The question of whether black African babies were born with light skin, only darkening with exposure to the hot tropical sun, also received much attention. In a meeting in March 1690, the Society discussed "the Colours of Animals, and Particularly of the Negroes, whether it was the product of the climate or that they were a distinct race of Men," showing both the growing tendency to link black Africans with animals and the growth of the idea of race and inherited characteristics as an alternative to environmental explanations. Sir Hans Sloane, of all the leaders of the Royal Society, had the most direct experience with black people and the slave plantation economies, as he had served as a physician in Jamaica, treating both whites and blacks. His initial entrée into the scientific community was based on his Jamaican writings and the natural history and cultural specimens he brought back from the island, including a "manati whip" made from the skin of the Caribbean aquatic mammal, the manatee, and used to punish slaves. Sloane profited from slavery long after leaving Jamaica, importing slave-grown sugar and chocolate, of which he was one of the leading promoters in England. He was a firm supporter of the "race" as opposed to the environmental theory and linked the horrifying punishments of rebellious slaves that he had witnessed in Jamaica to the "perversity" of the black race.

The Royal Society's greatest rival, the Royal Academy of Sciences, was also involved with the slave trade. It relied on French slave-traders, such as the Senegal Company, to provide passage for the scientists the Academy sent out to gather specimens and observations, such as the expedition to the island of Goree and the Caribbean from 1681 to 1683. The differing agendas of scientists and slave-traders and the limited power of the Academy led to conflicts, but without the resources to mount its own expeditions the Academy had to adapt itself to slavers' concerns.

Francois Bernier and the Racial Classification of Humanity

Schemes for a global classification of human races by observed characteristics along the lines of classifications of plants and animals, rather than by religious affiliation or descent from the sons of Noah, emerged relatively late in the Scientific Revolution. One of the first was by the leading French champion of Gassendism, François Bernier (1620–1688). His *New Division of the World among the Different Species or Races of Men that Inhabit it* (1684), one of the earliest works to use "race" in the modern sense, divided humanity into a small number of groups based on skin color, physiognomy, and areas of habitation. Bernier largely ignored biblical theories to take a secular approach. He drew on his experience in India, where he had been a physician to the Mogul emperor Aurangzeb (r. 1658–1707), but generalized his analysis to parts of the world of which he had no direct experience. The group Bernier refers to as the "first race," emphasizing its primacy, included Native Americans, Middle Easterners, and Indians as well as Europeans, as the greater darkness of some of these peoples compared to the "whiteness" of Europeans was caused by exposure to the sun rather than being an innate characteristic. Africans, whom Bernier had mainly encountered in the slave markets of the Islamic world, were "Blacks" as their darkness was innate. Chinese, Japanese, and other East and Central Asians were another race, although closely related to the first race. Laplanders, for whom Bernier had contempt and little direct experience, were another group of their own. Each race had a series of characteristics that could be ranked hierarchically. In addition to the publication of his book in French, Bernier had English connections, including a friendship with Fellow of the Royal Society and philosopher John Locke, and he attended at least one Royal Society meeting.

Scientific authority also played a role in classifying anomalous individuals, as when the Royal Society was asked to examine the credentials of George Psalmanazar (1679–1763), a European impostor who claimed to be a native of Formosa (modern Taiwan), spinning an elaborate story of an entire civilization in the mountains away from the shore where Europeans had direct contact with the island. The incomplete "racialization" of European thought even in the early eighteenth century can be seen in the fact that Psalmanazar's typically "European" appearance was not considered proof of his fraudulence as an East Asian. Rather than examine his body Edmond Halley asked a series of questions about the astronomical characteristics of Formosa, which he knew the answers to not on the basis of direct experience but on the basis of astronomical calculation. Psalmanazar managed to dodge the questions, however, and the Society did not expose the fraud.

"Pre-Adamitism" and the Origins of Polygenism

The emphasis on racial difference characteristic of some thinkers during the Scientific Revolution was always limited both by the obvious close kinship between different peoples and by religion. As became apparent shortly after the arrival of Europeans in most of the world, different branches of humanity were interfertile. The dominance of Christianity, with its story of the creation of humanity from a single couple, meant that the mainstream position on humanity remained one of "common descent" from Adam and Eve, or "monogenesis," rather than treating different groups as having completely separate origins.

The position that challenged common descent was "pre-Adamitism," which attracted interest from some participants in the Scientific Revolution. This doctrine held that not all humans were descended from Adam, but that the Book of Genesis described the origin of only part of humanity. The implicit questioning of the authority of the biblical narrative meant that this position was always religiously suspect and therefore difficult to voice openly. The intellectual founder of the "pre-Adamite" theory was the French Protestant Isaac La Peyrère (1596–1676), who argued in *Prae-Adamitae* (1655, translated into English as *Men Before Adam* in 1656) that Genesis was not a history of the human race, but solely of the Jews. This established the intellectual possibility that different branches of the human race could have separate ancestry—"polygenism." La Peyrère's work was not primarily directed at the European encounter with Africans and Native Americans in the early modern period—they, like the Europeans, were equally the descendants of the non-Jewish, pre-Adamite creation. He believed that the theory of a pre-Adamite humanity solved certain biblical mysteries like the origin of Cain's wife. La Peyrère also denied that the flood of Noah had been universal. Since it had not drowned the whole world, the "pre-Adamite" peoples had survived to the present day. The theory also offered a way to reconcile the "short" six-thousand-year biblical narrative with the growing evidence from European contacts with China, Mesoamerica, Egypt, and other foreign civilizations that humans had been on Earth for much longer. The pre-Adamite theory was, however, incompatible with a literal reading of the biblical narrative and called into question the idea of humans inheriting original sin from Adam, an idea central to Christianity. It was vigorously condemned by Protestant and Catholic religious authorities and attracted numerous scholarly refutations.

Despite religious opposition Pre-Adamitism was the object of growing interest from some late-seventeenth-century scientists, who applied it to racial questions the original theory was not designed to address. The idea that the Jews were the sole legitimate descendants of Adam was quietly abandoned in favor of one that Europeans occupied that "favored" status. Material concerns drove some of this evolution. Some slave owners supported a non-Adamite origin for their slaves, on the grounds that this would justify their status as slaves. Robert Boyle, who had a strong Christian religious commitment, opposed the growth of pre-Adamitism on religious grounds, both as a challenge to the veracity and completeness of the biblical account and as a barrier to efforts to convert the slaves to Christianity, a project close to his heart. Pre-Adamitism was secularized into the doctrine of "polygenism," the belief that rather than springing from a single ancestor, different branches of humanity had different origins. (Polygenism was not a European monopoly; Native Americans in the seventeenth century seemed to have increasingly viewed themselves, the white invaders, and African Americans as having fundamentally different origins.) While polygenism was very frequently accompanied by claims of racial superiority, the creation of racial distinctions and the justification of slavery and colonialism on the basis of racial difference were not dependent on polygenism. Bernier himself was a monogenist with no interest in pre-Adamitism.

The growth of European racism would lead away from the idea of all humans, whatever their distinct qualities, as equally descendants of Adam and Eve to one that linked non-European peoples, particularly black Africans, to nonhuman apes. In many ways, black Africans and apes moved into the intellectual and cultural position that had previously been occupied by the "monstrous races" whose existence had been disproved over much of the world, that of intermediaries between humanity and the animals. The idea of a link between black Africans and monkeys had a long history predating the Scientific Revolution in European thought, partly because the two groups were associated with the same, "exotic" part of the world. Europeans had little direct experience with apes prior to the sixteenth century, as the only monkey or ape indigenous to Europe is the Barbary ape of Gibraltar, which was a Muslim possession until its conquest by Castile in 1462. However, apes appeared in classical literature and an occasional one made its way to Europe as an exotic pet. Awareness of monkeys and apes, African, Asian, and American, increased in the sixteenth century as the similarities of humans to these other primates raised questions of classification.

The struggle between environmentally determined theories of human difference and inherited "racial" theories and between monogenism and polygenism would not be resolved in the Scientific Revolution itself, as environmental theories would make a comeback in the eighteenth century. The full development of biological theories of the innate and immutable characteristics of different human groups and their arrangement in a hierarchy with Europeans and their descendants at the top—"scientific racism"—would occur in the eighteenth and nineteenth centuries, but it would build on the foundations laid during the Scientific Revolution.

Colonialism, European Superiority, and the "Baconian" Ideal

The idea of power or "empire" over nature, central to much of the scientific ideology of the seventeenth century and particularly identified with Francis Bacon, had colonial applications. One argument for the superiority of the colonizers' civilization was that only they had the power to fully exploit the resources of nature. The superiority of European-derived technology is a constant theme in colonial writings, many (but by no means all) of which dismissed the technology of the indigenous people (although much of it was adopted by the colonizers). Technological and economic superiority could even be applied between different empires, as in the late seventeenth century some English philosophers, including members of the Royal Society, argued that since the "backward" Spanish were not developing areas they claimed in Central America, the English had a right to them.

The idea that other societies could be ridiculed for their inferiority in natural knowledge extended beyond technology into the new natural philosophy of the Scientific Revolution itself. European travelers in the Ottoman Empire frequently spoke of the scientific barrenness of the Ottoman lands, although travelers in Persia, then under the rule of the Shia Muslim Safavid dynasty frequently seen as potential allies against the Sunni Muslim Turks, were more respectful of local science. In the British colonies of America, initial regard for Natives' astronomical skills was displaced by the late seventeenth century by the belief that Natives were completely ignorant of the subject. Fontenelle's *Conversations on the Plurality of Worlds*, a work that generally supported the superiority of "polite" European (and particularly French) civilization over all rivals, mocked the people of India for their alleged belief that the world was supported on the backs of elephants—a stereotypical image that would have a long career to the present. Fontenelle also credited the peoples of the East Indies and America with having ludicrous explanations of eclipses—that the sun and moon were temporarily devoured by demons during periods of eclipse, or that eclipses were the result of the sun and moon quarreling. These silly ideas were contrasted with the modern Cartesian and Copernican astronomy and physics Fontenelle endorsed. While for the missionary Francis Xavier the inferior science of the Japanese had been a consequence of their specifically religious ignorance, for Fontenelle the scientific ignorance of non-European populations was not a consequence of anything but their generalized inferiority. This contrast of scientific ideas was particularly powerful because it could be applied to all non-European societies. Europe was not technologically ahead of China, the Islamic world, and India in many respects—and certainly not able as yet to impose its will by force on them as it was on some Native Americans—but Europeans believed in the superiority of their science. Although the European belief that Europe possessed the one true religion was by no means diminishing or becoming marginalized, it was increasingly accompanied or even eclipsed by the belief that Europe possessed the one true science.

SCIENCE AND POLITICS

The growing prestige of natural philosophy and mathematics led to attempts to apply them to social and political problems. Political models were fiercely debated in the seventeenth century, with a high point being the English Revolution from 1642 to 1649, which led to an outburst of political debate. The English mechanical philosopher Thomas Hobbes, influenced by the failure of the monarchy during the revolution, believed that the humanist emphasis on rhetoric had corrupted political thought, and suggested that geometry offered a better model in politics as it did in other areas of thought. The self-seeking individuals who form the basis of Hobbes's view of society had much in common with the fundamental particles of mechanical philosophers, and society was determined by their interactions in a mechanical way. Another royalist natural philosopher, Margaret Cavendish, suggested that freedom of debate led to the overthrow of established political orders, and that it needed to be suppressed in the sciences as well as in politics and religion.

Other English natural philosophers, including Robert Boyle, emphasized the application of scientific and technical knowledge, in the Baconian tradition, which would make England prosperous while contributing to social stability. This was not the later ideology of unfettered, "capitalist" acquisitiveness, but one of the moderation of the passions in pursuit of a well-balanced while abundant life that would benefit both the individual and society at large.

The systematic application of mathematical and quantitative techniques to social issues flourished in England during the seventeenth century, inspired by the empiricist Baconian ideology that manifested itself in the early Royal Society. Practitioners included the close friends John Graunt (1620–1674) and William Petty (1623–1687), both Fellows of the Royal Society (Fig. 7-1). Graunt's *Natural and Political Observations Mentioned in a following Index, and made upon the Bills of Mortality* (1662) was very popular, even attracting the notice of Charles II. The book's impact was such that the Royal Society admitted him as a Fellow on the strength of it, even though his background as a London merchant was considered below that of the gentry and aristocracy who dominated the Society's ranks. The Society also published a second edition.

Petty, Graunt, and subsequent political arithmeticians were concerned with population, which was believed a key source of national strength. This idea went back to the sixteenth century and was expressed by such classic social theorists as the Frenchman Jean Bodin (1529/30–1596). The larger the population of a kingdom, the greater its wealth and potential power, if the population were deployed correctly. Concern with population led naturally to concern with birth, death, and disease. Even more than other branches of the new science, political arithmetic was meant to be an aid to government, enabling governments to make choices based on numbers rather than subjective impressions. The style of the work is terse, lacking long digressions, a choice that Graunt hoped would make it more readable to busy statesmen. It was also meant to enable individuals to make wiser choices—Graunt believed that the popular underestimation of the danger

DUBLIN, 1682.				
Parishes.	Houses.	Fire-places.	Baptiz'd.	Buri'd.
St. *Fames*,	272	836 ⎱	122	306
St. *Katharines*,	540	2198 ⎰		
St. *Nicholas* without, and St.*Patricks* ⎱	1064	4082	145	414
St. *Bridgets*	395	1903	68	149
St. *Audones*	276	1510	56	164
St. *Michael*	174	884	34	50
St. *Johns*	302	1636	74	101
St. *Nicholas* within, and Chirst-Church *Lib.* ⎱	153	902	26	52
St. *Warbors*	240	1638	45	105
St. *Michans*	938	3516	124	389
St. *Andrews*	864	3638 ⎱	131	300
St. *Kevans*	554	2120 ⎰		
Donabrook	253	506	87	233
	6025	25369	912	2263

Figure 7-1. **Demographic Tables by Sir William Petty.** One of the many demographic tables produced by Sir William Petty.

of syphilis (it was likened to such rare causes of death as snakebite) encouraged men to engage in risky sexual behavior. His dedication to the Royal Society paints the organization as a leader in the overall project of social improvement to which he hoped to contribute.

Graunt's work was based on the London Bills of Mortality, weekly tabulations of christenings and deaths based on information gathered by old women and reported to parish clerks that had been issued since the late sixteenth century. The Bills made some attempt made to distinguish causes of death, particularly plague, as information as to its early incidence was of particular concern. Graunt used this information and other sources against which he checked it to estimate the total population of London as around 380,000, debunking contemporary estimates that ran into the millions. He also attempted to aggregate and adjust the statistics to draw conclusions about the medical states and lifespans of the London populace, an early approach to "public health." Graunt's drawing of observations from state-gathered raw information was in the Baconian tradition, as was his contribution of his work as part of an ongoing project rather than a finished argument.

Petty, a physician, got his start in applying mathematics to social questions as Physician-General to the English Army occupying Ireland in 1654, when he proposed to take over the surveying of land seized from Irish rebels. Petty's work not only produced the Down Survey, the first accurate mapped survey of Ireland, but also made Petty a rich man. His first publication in political arithmetic, *A Treatise of Taxes and Contributions* (1662), was followed by a series of works attempting to estimate national wealth, including the posthumously published *Political Arithmetick* (1690), which gave the field its name. Petty's works were the first detailed quantitative efforts to estimate national capital, income, and expenditure. Petty was not just making estimates for its own sake, however; he used his data to make policy recommendations. Ireland, where he lived for much of his life, remained a concern. He was an early member of a long line of British and European thinkers reaching into the twentieth century who would see colonial territories, such as Ireland, as places to carry out vast projects of social engineering, often with a strong scientific and quantitative element, that could never be carried out in the "mother country" due to the resistance of powerful established institutions. Conquered territories, by contrast, could be treated as "blank slates" in which indigenous populations lacked the ability to resist imperial projects. The ravages of war and English oppression had produced a poverty-stricken population in Ireland, and various plans were put forth for reviving the Irish economy. Like his fellow imperial planners, Petty made suggestions that were often more feasible in theory than in practice. In his last years he put forth an ambitious plan, far beyond the reach of any seventeenth-century government, to depopulate Ireland, make it a huge cattle farm with a population of a few hundred thousand, and settle the excess population in England. Petty's interest in colonial space later extended to Pennsylvania, where he estimated that excessive Native mortality would open up space for further European colonization. Despite Petty's championing of colonization he was not a polygenist, but devoted considerable energy to refuting the "pre-Adamite" theory, pointing out that political arithmetic showed that the descendants of Adam and Eve through many generations were perfectly capable of populating the Earth.

In the next generation English political arithmetic was carried on by Charles Davenant (1656–1714) and Gregory King (1648–1712). Davenant was a political pamphleteer and eventually a member of Parliament. He used political arithmetic to figure out the best taxation scheme to pay for England's wars with France. His friend and collaborator King, a civil servant who served on several commissions related to public accounts but published nothing of his own, was a much more original political arithmetician. He divided the English population, of whose overall number his estimate is close to that of modern scholars, into five classes for purposes of analysis, setting forth in tabular form the income and expenditure of each. King also systematically compared the English economy with that of its principal rivals, France and the Dutch Republic, and estimated global population based on the distribution of people over land. Unlike Petty and Graunt, neither King nor Davenant ever became Fellows of the Royal Society, which under the presidency of Newton from 1703 to 1727 was moving away from social research. Despite his own economic knowledge, as demonstrated during his time as Master of the Mint, Newton believed that the Royal Society should restrict itself to natural science, particularly its mathematical branches.

Although English writers dominated political arithmetic they did not monopolize it. The eminent French military engineer Sebastien Vauban (1633–1707), a member of the Royal Academy of Sciences, published several works in the field in the late seventeenth and early eighteenth centuries. Like the English political arithmeticians, Vauban put forth his work to make policy recommendations. In the declining years of Louis XIV, Vauban argued for the abolition of the complex French tax code with its myriad exemptions, with a flat tax levied on all without exception. His book was condemned by the French government. Although "political arithmetic" as a separate discipline declined in the eighteenth century, it remained to influence the development of economics.

Science and Political Legitimation

Science also served to ideologically legitimate polities, although it took a back seat to religion, the primary context in which rule was justified and evaluated in the early modern period. By sponsoring scientific societies, monarchs put themselves forward as patrons of learning—it is no coincidence that the two leading scientific societies of the late seventeenth century, the Royal Society and the Royal Academy of Sciences, were both "royal." The Holy Roman Emperor Leopold I (1640–1705) went a step further in 1687, recognizing the Academy of the Curious into Nature, a small, informal physician-dominated group founded in 1652 that operated principally by correspondence, under the new name of the "Leopoldina."

The acceptance of Copernicanism in France might have been speeded by its harmony with the exaltation of Louis XIV, the "Sun King." In Britain, Desaguliers wrote a lengthy poem on the application of the Newtonian system to politics, *The Newtonian system of the world, the best model of government: an allegorical poem* (1728), which unsurprisingly backed the monarchy and Parliament of Great Britain as the most rational of political systems as the Newtonian was the most rational system of natural philosophy: "The limited Monarchy, whereby our Liberties, Rights and Privileges are so well secured to us, as to make us happier than all the Nations round about us, seems to be a lively Image of our System; and the Happiness we enjoy under His present Majesty's Government, makes us sensible, that ATTRACTION is now as universal in the Political, as the Philosophical World."

EIGHT

The Scientific Revolution in the Colonial World

Although the major developments in the Scientific Revolution, from the rediscovery of ancient natural philosophy to the rise of mechanism to the foundation of the world's leading scientific societies, took place in Europe, its impact was felt outside Europe as well. The impact was greatest in areas under European colonial domination. The theories, practices, institutions, and instruments of the Scientific Revolution were beginning to spread across the world.

THE SCIENTIFIC REVOLUTION IN THE COLONIAL AMERICAS

The impact of the Scientific Revolution in the colonial Americas varied greatly between the colonies of the various European powers. The two countries that had established the most populous and settled colonies were Spain and England, but there was also some scientific interest in the French colonies. Portugal, in contrast with the vivid institutional life of Spanish America, did not build educational or scientific institutions in Brazil.

As Europeans established permanent settlements in the New World, the institutions and practices of European intellectual life went with them. Institutions such as the University of Mexico City or Harvard University taught a mostly Aristotelian curriculum, adapting to new intellectual currents with some time lag relative to Europe. But colonial institutions and groups could never compete with European ones as generators of new knowledge. Although only a small percentage of Europeans had either a job conducive to carrying out scientific research or the leisure to pursue it as an avocation, the American percentage was even smaller, out of a much smaller population to start with. Conditions were also not ideal for the occasional American who did practice scientific research. Although telescopes, microscopes, and other instruments of the new science made their way to the colonies, they were not of the same quality and abundance as instruments in Europe itself. Nor did the most advanced books necessarily make their way quickly and in large numbers to American libraries. The problem with the lack of an American infrastructure for science can be seen in the career of the alchemist George Starkey, born in the English Caribbean and educated at Harvard, who had to leave the colonies for London partly because of the difficulty of acquiring the experimental equipment required for alchemical research in New England. Given these handicaps, it is unsurprising that no American attracted much notice from Europe as an original scientific thinker until Benjamin Franklin in the eighteenth century.

Where colonial institutions and individuals did have an advantage was in the science of the colonial world itself. The tradition of European investigation of the natural history of foreign lands continued throughout the early modern period, although the predominantly medical interest of many of the early naturalists faded by the late seventeenth century in favor of broader views that were somewhat less use-oriented. Both Spanish and English colonies saw the formation of natural history and science circles connected to Europe. In Spanish America, where intellectual life was dominated by the clergy, these were associated with religious orders, particularly the Jesuits. Athanasius Kircher, whose works were popular in Baroque Mexico, had several Mexican correspondents. In English America, a network of correspondents connected with the Royal Society carried on the work.

SCIENCE IN THE SPANISH COLONIAL WORLD

Although Spain was not a leading participant in European science in the seventeenth century, research and theorizing continued in the Spanish colonies in the Americas, particularly led by the Jesuits and other Catholic religious orders that dominated intellectual life there.

José de Acosta and Natural History in Colonial Spanish America

The leading sixteenth-century natural historian of Spanish America was the Jesuit priest José de Acosta (1539–1600), author of *Natural and Moral History of the Indies* (1590). De Acosta studied the natural and civil history of Peru, where he spent about fourteen years as a missionary before returning to Europe. Unlike many natural historians in the Americas, De Acosta was not a physician nor was he primarily interested in medical applications. He also found previous histories of the New World to be excessively focused on describing and marveling at its wonders rather than analyzing how they came to be.

De Acosta's natural history was revolutionary in questioning Aristotle and ancient authority generally. As a Jesuit, De Acosta was committed to Aristotelian philosophy and analyzed the world around him in fundamentally Aristotelian terms. He sought not to surpass but to emulate the ancients in describing a world that they had never known. However, he was aware that Aristotle had made mistakes in thinking that the tropic regions where De Acosta had lived and worked were too hot to be inhabitable. In fact, since all of the classical authors and even the Church fathers had lived in the temperate zone, their work was not well suited for the tropics. De Acosta also faced the problem of integrating the undoubted presence of humans and other species characteristic of Afro-Eurasia in the Americas, and was the first to speculate about humans arriving in the Americas via an overland journey from Asia in the far north. De Acosta's works were written in Spanish rather than Latin, aimed at an audience of middle—and upper-class Spaniards who may not have been Latin readers, and went through several editions. *Natural and Moral History of the Indies* was translated into several European languages (including Latin) and was one of the most popular sources of information about the Americas inside and outside of Spain.

A Scientific Community in Colonial Mexico

As in Spain itself, in its colonies Spain suppressed the astronomical and physical part of the Scientific Revolution. However, the isolation of Spanish-American intellectuals from the new astronomy and physics of the seventeenth century was never complete, particularly as the grip of the Inquisition began to weaken in the later part of the century. Diego Rodriguez, a member of the Mercedarian order, was appointed the first professor of mathematics and astrology at the University of Mexico in 1637. He was aware of the work of Galileo and Descartes, although his own work was highly colored by astrology and neo-Platonic interpretations of the cosmos. Another exception to the isolation of Mexico from the latest thinking was the cartographer and natural philosopher Carlos de Siguenza y Gongora (1645–1700). Siguenza y Gongora, a professor of mathematics and astrology at the University of Mexico City, had a complicated relationship with the Jesuit order, which he had hoped to join, finally achieving his ambition on his deathbed. However, his astronomy led him into conflict with another leading Mexican intellectual and Jesuit, Eusebio Kino (1645–1711). Kino, born in Italy, became the leading surveyor and cartographer of the northern frontier of seventeenth-century Mexico. His extensive work established the foundation for the cartography of the area, among other things determining that Baja California was a peninsula and not an island. The European-educated Kino operated in the same tradition of Catholic Jesuit learning as Siguenza y Gongora, but his astronomy and natural philosophy were much more conservative. The two clashed in a much-publicized controversy over the comet of 1680. Kino, who accepted the Jesuit belief in the geocentric cosmos, believed it was an omen, while Siguenza y Gongora believed it was a naturally occurring phenomenon with no meaning beyond natural philosophy. His first book on the comet, *Philosophical Manifesto against Comets, Deposed from their Empire over the Fearful* (1681), was opposed by other Mexicans even before Kino arrived from Europe. (Similar debates over the meaning of celestial events were going on in Europe at the time, as in the controversial work of the French Protestant intellectual Pierre Bayle published the year after Siguenza y Gongora's, *Various Thoughts on the Occasion of a Comet*). Kino also supported the traditional Aristotelian theory that comets were exhalations from the Earth, while Siguenza y Gongora upheld the "modern" theory that they were celestial phenomena. In the debate, Siguenza y Gongora invoked the astronomy and natural philosophy of Kircher, Descartes, Gassendi, and Galileo and suggested that scientific and other philosophical truths should be reached by reason rather than appeals to authority.

The natural philosophy of Siguenza y Gongora's contemporary and correspondent, the playwright and nun Sor Juana Inez de la Cruz (1651–1695), was an eclectic mixture of Aristotelianism, Hermeticism, Epicurean-Gassendist atomism, and Tychonic astronomy, resembling that of Kircher, whose work she was very familiar with. (She even coined the word *kircherize* to describe the practice recommended by Kircher of putting words in combinations.) She put forth this philosophy in an epic poem, *Primero Sueno* or *First Dream* (1692).

SCIENCE IN ENGLISH AMERICA

Initially, English science in the new world differed from French and Spanish in not being state-sponsored. Private colonization companies that worked in alliance with the state played a greater role. Much of the early scientific work related to America was done primarily for promotional purposes, to impress potential settlers with the bounty of the new lands. This tradition continued into the eighteenth century.

The founding of the Royal Society helped integrate colonial efforts into English science on a deeper level. The Royal Society's mission of promoting the English economy incorporated an interest in colonial economic development through greater knowledge of natural resources, and from the early days of the Society residents of the colonies participated in its work. The Society's leadership was frequently involved in colonization companies and other colonial ventures. The Royal Society sent lists of "queries" with persons journeying to the colonies or colonial correspondents in hopes of gathering information, emulating the actions of the sixteenth-century Spanish government in a much less systematic and not always effective way, as Fellows in England did not always have a good idea of what questions to ask. Other difficulties in communication could also lead to problems, as when the New England minister and Newtonian Cotton Mather (1663–1728) was wrongly accused of falsely passing himself off as a Fellow of the Royal Society because his name did not appear on printed lists of Fellows.

John Winthrop Jr., Governor of Connecticut and Alchemist

The first colonial resident admitted to the Royal Society was John Winthrop Jr. (1606–1676), who was visiting London at the time. The son of Massachusetts founder John Winthrop (1588–1549), Winthrop was a practitioner of medicine and alchemy and brought the first telescope to New England. He first became governor of Connecticut in 1657, holding the position with one brief interruption until his death in 1676. Like many colonials interested in the sciences, Winthrop was primarily motivated by their applications to economic development and defense against the Natives. He sponsored the development of ironworks and facilities for the manufacture of saltpeter, an essential ingredient in gunpowder.

Although not a significant original alchemical thinker like his American contemporary and associate George Starkey, Winthrop was a learned and skilled alchemical practitioner. Winthrop had traveled extensively when a youth in Italy and the Ottoman lands seeking alchemical knowledge, and even from New England he maintained a correspondence with many of Europe's alchemists and natural philosophers, including Samuel Hartlib and other members of the Hartlib circle. An avid admirer of John Dee, the prophet of a scientifically informed English empire, he collected books from Dee's library. (Such was Winthrop's identification with the Hermetic tradition that Cotton Mather, who admired him, called him "Hermes Christianus," the Christian Hermes.) In the mid-1640s, when the British civil wars coincided with the last phases of the Thirty Years' War on the European continent, Winthrop promoted the idea of a colony in New England for British and European alchemists. It came to nothing due to quarreling between Massachusetts and Connecticut and difficulties with local Natives. (The idea of America as providing a safe haven from a war-torn Europe for leading scientists, who would then contribute to American development, would have a long history extending into the Second World War.) However, Winthrop was able to attract some Americans interested in alchemy to the area of New London and foster the development of a small alchemical community that shared books and laboratory equipment, always difficult to obtain in New England.

A committed Puritan like his father, Winthrop went beyond interest in the practical aspects of alchemy to see it as playing an important religious role. Like other millenarians, he saw material improvements as hastening the thousand-year reign of Christ. Winthrop was also a supporter and practitioner of Paracelsian medicine. Although he lacked a medical degree, he had one of the most extensive practices in New England—credentials meant little so far from European centers of knowledge, and very few university-trained physicians emigrated during the seventeenth century. The absence of an organized medical faculty or college of physicians practicing Galenic medicine meant that alchemical practitioners like Winthrop did not face institutional opposition.

Winthrop applied his alchemical knowledge to a variety of New England projects, such as the creation of a works to refine salt from seawater, salt being necessary for the preservation of the fish that were one of New England's main industries, and the manufacture of saltpeter. He was the chief promoter and initially the manager of the ironworks founded at Braintree, Massachusetts, in 1644, which used an advanced process, and established mines for lead and silver.

The presence of alchemically oriented natural philosophers like Winthrop in the early Royal Society was not unusual. Winthrop's friend Sir Kenelm Digby was a founding member, as were Robert Boyle and Elias Ashmole. The connections Winthrop had won through alchemy, the Hartlib group, and the Royal Society circle were instrumental in his winning a royal charter for the Connecticut colony. This was a particular challenge as Winthrop, like other New Englanders, was associated with the Puritans who had supported the English Revolution at a time when the monarchy had been restored and many of the changes associated with the Revolution were being reversed. Winthrop was particularly valuable in the early years of the Society as a source of information on New England, an area most Fellows had little direct knowledge of. Winthrop's correspondence and connections with the Royal Society continued after his return to New England in 1663, and he attempted to use the Society to win backing for development projects such as the creation of a textile industry that would employ, and thus "civilize," local Natives. Winthrop had to walk a fine line, providing the Society with information that would be useful, or at least harmless, to Connecticut while warding off the centralizing agenda of the Restoration government, of which the Society, with its craving for information, was a part. Despite the implorings of Henry Oldenburg, the Society's secretary, he never produced a natural history of Connecticut that would have revealed natural resources suitable for exploitation, but he was happy to provide the Society with astronomical observations and stuffed rattlesnakes.

The Boston Philosophical Society and Cotton Mather

In the late seventeenth century, the English colonial city with the liveliest scientific culture was Boston, the metropolis of New England. The close proximity of the American colonies' leading educational institution, Harvard, was one factor making for Boston's preeminence, as was the emphasis on a learned ministry exhibited by New England Puritanism. Two groups prominently represented in Boston's community of enquirers into nature were physicians and ministers. Medical practitioners had the most education in the sciences, and ministers had the highest level of learning generally as well as being part of trans-Atlantic learned networks.

The Boston Puritan minister Increase Mather (1639–1723), an intellectual and political leader of the New England Congregational ministers, led in the formation of the first scientific society in America, the Boston Philosophical Society. (Mather was the author of a book on comets, *Kometographia* [1683], which showed familiarity with the current scientific literature.) The date of the Society's founding and its history and membership are largely unknown. Its end, according to the later account of a former member, Increase's son Cotton, was connected to the political crisis that enveloped New England beginning with the English government's suspension of the Massachusetts Charter in 1684. Pressure from the new rulers eventually drove Increase Mather into hiding. The Society was still in existence by late 1685 but ceased to function by 1687 at the latest.

Although none of its papers survive, the Society seems to have operated in a manner typical of the regional offshoots of the Royal Society such as the Dublin

Philosophical Society and the Oxford Philosophical Society, gathering and circulating accounts of natural events with a focus on unusual ones (the founding of the Society may have been connected with Increase Mather's scheme for gathering accounts of "illustrious providences" as demonstrations of God's power and care.) Like the Royal Society, it was primarily a voluntary body of men interested in natural science rather than of professional scientists or the entrepreneurs of Winthrop's group. The Boston group lacked the "star" scientists like Boyle and Hooke that the London group had, let alone a correspondence like Oldenburg's. Beyond the Mathers and the Reverend Samuel Willard (1640–1707), a future acting president of Harvard, the Society's membership is unknown. Interest in science continued after the collapse of the Society, driven by some of the same cultural factors driving the interest in science in England itself—the popularity of Newtonianism and the entertainment value of experimental philosophy.

Cotton Mather, who succeeded to his father's place of leadership, continued his interest in natural philosophy for the rest of his life, although there was no attempt to establish an institutional successor to the Boston Philosophical Society. Like his father, Mather viewed science in terms of "natural theology," the demonstration of the power and goodness of God through the study of nature, an approach that fit well with the new Newtonian science coming out of England. Unlike his father, Cotton Mather became a Fellow of the Royal Society and corresponded with *Philosophical Transactions*. Mather's *The Christian Philosopher* (1721) was one of many works in the Newtonian tradition using the properties of the created world to exalt the glory and providence of God, and was one of the first big works of natural philosophy coming out of New England. Along with his friend, the physician and future Fellow of the Royal Society Zabdiel Boylston (1679–1766), Mather also introduced smallpox inoculation to New England, an idea derived from Middle Eastern and African practices promoted in *Philosophical Transactions* and associated with the "new philosophy," which was distrusted by many religious conservatives.

The Scientific Revolution at Harvard University

There were few institutions of higher education in the English colonies. The oldest was Harvard, founded in 1636 in Massachusetts principally to train ministers for the New England colonies. It was joined by the College of William and Mary in Virginia in 1693 and Yale in Connecticut in 1701. Traditional natural philosophy played a role in the curriculum of these institutions, as it did in Europe. Harvard leaders, in the period when it was English America's only institution of higher education, attempted to keep up with changes in European science; Harvard president Leonard Hoar (1630–1675) communicated with Robert Boyle about establishing a chemical laboratory, although Hoar's forced resignation from the Harvard presidency shortly thereafter meant the project came to nothing.

In the early eighteenth century, Anglo-American colonial institutions, like other institutions in Britain itself, moved to Newtonian astronomy and natural philosophy. The most prominent institution was Harvard, whose leadership overlapped with the Boston ministerial community, many of whom were graduates. The leading mathematical scientist associated with late-seventeenth-century New England was Thomas Brattle (1658–1713), a Harvard graduate who became its treasurer. He was a correspondent of Flamsteed, and sent valuable astronomical observations to England. One of Brattle's cometary observations was even cited by Newton in *Mathematical Principles of Natural Philosophy*. Brattle had spent some time in London, where he had come to know Boyle and other members of the Royal Society.

The leading academic natural philosopher in the generation after Brattle was Thomas Robie (1689–1729). Robie was a mathematics tutor at Harvard and a correspondent of British natural philosophers. He came into conflict with the New England Puritan establishment over whether celestial phenomena should be primarily explained through natural causes or as omens. His *A Letter to a Certain Gentleman, desiring that a particular account be given of a wonderful Meteor* (1719) gave a natural explanation of a "meteor" (probably an aurora borealis) and deprecated reading religious meaning into it. This led to a controversy, in which the "moderate" position of Cotton Mather, asserting the compatibility of religious and natural explanations, seems to have been the one that prevailed. Robie's position, which paralleled that of Siguenza y Gongora in the earlier Mexican debate, led to some doubts as to his orthodoxy, which he remedied with the help of Harvard president John Leverett (1662–1724), who arranged for him to preach and publish a conspicuously orthodox sermon.

The most important move in establishing the new science at an institutional level was the establishment of the Hollis Chair in Mathematics and Experimental Philosophy at Harvard in 1728. Its first incumbent, Isaac Greenwood (1702–1745), was a friend and disciple of John Desaguliers. Greenwood was not a creative scientist, but in the tradition of Desaguliers he was a skilled and active popularizer of Newtonian physics. His lectures, both at Harvard and outside it, helped disseminate Newtonian ideas throughout New England, as did several textbooks and popularizations he published. His successor in the Hollis Chair, Winthrop's descendant John Winthrop IV (1714–1779), would be colonial America's leading astronomer.

British America Outside New England

New England, with its institutions of higher education and active intellectual culture of physicians and ministers, was the center of the Scientific Revolution in colonial British America. However, the revolution spread to other communities as well. Scientific activity in colonial Pennsylvania centered on the government official and bibliophile James Logan (1674–1751), the first recorded colonial American owner of Newton's *Mathematical Principles of Natural Philosophy*. Scientific leaders were more likely to be landowners than physicians or ministers in the South, where urban life was less developed and much of society and culture revolved around the great houses. As physicians were thin on the ground, land-owners were often responsible for the medical care of their families, servants, and slaves, leading in some cases to an interest in medical ideas. The Virginian William Byrd II of Westover (1674–1744), one of America's richest landowners, was admitted to the Royal Society at the age of 22 while in England. He contributed to *Philosophical Transactions* on a number of subjects, taking an empirical approach that emphasized natural history over the more theoretical subjects such as astronomy that dominated New England science. Like many students of colonial natural history, he remained focused on the potential for economic development and medical uses.

The dominant religious institution in the Southern colonies was the Church of England, and most Church of England ministers in the colonies came from England itself. Two Virginia ministers had the Royal Society or its leaders as patrons and contributed studies of the natural history of the South—John Clayton (1656 or 1657–1725) in Jamestown and John Banister (1649 or 1650–1692) in Bristol Parish.

SCIENCE IN THE FRENCH COLONIAL WORLD

French America had no institutions to rival the University of Mexico City or Harvard University. The centralization of French scientific life in Paris meant that scientists in the colonies were more likely to act as agents of Parisian institutions than to found their own scientific communities or carry out their own research agendas. The central institutions of French science—the Royal Academy of Sciences, the Paris Observatory, the Royal Botanical Garden—along with the French government sponsored many expeditions. Scientists were sent from Paris to Tycho Brahe's old observatory in Denmark, to Cayenne in Guiana, and to Goree, an island off the western coast of Africa, to conduct astronomical measurements and physics experiments. The physician Michael Sarrazin (1659–1734), who spent much of his career in the French colony at Quebec, sent many botanical specimens back to France, but his dream of establishing a botanical garden in Canada went unfulfilled for lack of support from Paris.

Among the most notable of the French colonial natural historians was the botanist Charles Plumier (1646–1704) of the Franciscan Minim order. Plumier's extensive research in the French Caribbean, however, was carried out at the behest of the French state, not his religious superiors. His publications, beginning with *Description of the Plants of America* (1703), were subsidized by the royal government. Plumier was a long-term associate of Joseph Pitton de Tournefort (1656–1708), the professor of botany at the Royal Botanical Garden, the center of the French botanical world, and a botanical explorer of the Levant. France was expanding in the Caribbean in the late seventeenth century, acquiring Saint-Domingue, the colony that would later become Haiti, from Spain in 1697, and the Royal Botanical Garden as a state institution was pressed into service to identify the potential resources of France's colonies.

THE VOC AND THE SCIENTIFIC COMMUNITY
IN THE INDIAN OCEAN AND EAST ASIA

One difference between the Dutch scientific community in the Indian Ocean region and the Spanish and Anglo-American communities in the Americas is that the clergy played only a marginal role in Dutch East Indian science. Medical practitioners were more common. The state also played a less central role. The Dutch Republic was organized on a federal basis, and the state was more limited in its sovereignty than the Spanish, French, or British states. The lead in colonization was taken by private companies, the Veneeringde Oostindische Compagnie, Dutch East India Company, or VOC, in the East and the West India Company in the West, although the VOC was far more successful. These companies were delegated powers ordinarily exerted by the state, such as the making of peace and war. The VOC became the largest private company in the world, employing nearly thirty thousand people and possessing a fleet of two hundred ships.

The VOC is the only rival of the Society of Jesus as the foremost institutional builder of global science in the early modern period. However, just as Jesuit science was shaped by its subordination to a religious mission, so VOC science was shaped by its subordination to a commercial mission. One difficulty faced by VOC scientists was the desire of the Company to control the flow of information, as well as commodities, from the territories it controlled to Europe. Communication with Europe, including European printers, was difficult anyway, and the Company could intervene to prevent the publication of research results if it thought they risked its economic position. Even possibly profitable industries could be blocked if the Company feared they would interfere with existing businesses. Lengthy delays also meant that VOC natural inquirers were largely isolated from the European scientific community.

The VOC did not have a scientific agenda like that of the Jesuit order, and the practice of natural science was largely at the discretion of individual employees. Natural history was the main science practiced by VOC employees. They were ideally positioned to gather information on plants and animals previously unknown to Europeans, and were connected to the flourishing Dutch markets for natural history specimens and exotica.

Institutionally, the VOC was a promoter and manager of botanical gardens both in its far-flung stations and in the Dutch Republic itself. VOC officials founded large botanical gardens in such centers as Batavia in what it now Indonesia and the African Cape. (The hard work of establishing and maintaining these gardens was done by indigenous workers and slaves.) The gardens were designed for the identification and acclimation of profitable plants. VOC plant handlers worked on projects to acclimate plants originating in one area to another, although the Company's commercial interests meant that certain plants were restricted to their area of origin to prevent price drops as more came on the market.

Three VOC Scientists—Drakenstein, Rumph, and Kaempfer

VOC employees could take numerous approaches to conducting and presenting science, depending on their interests, their position in the company, and the region or regions in which they operated. Three widely varying examples are Hendrik Adriaan van Rheede tot Drakenstein (1636–1691), Georg Rumph (1627–1702), and Engelbert Kaempfer (1651–1716).

Drakenstein was the creator of the twelve-volume *The Garden of Malabar in India* (1678–1693), one of the largest works of natural history produced in the seventeenth century (Fig. 8-1). Drakenstein was a colonial governor of the VOC fortress in Malabar from 1670 to 1677. Of noble background and, as a high VOC official, disposing of resources on an extensive scale, he could carry out a truly massive project, an example of "big science" in the seventeenth century. It involved the recruitment of European and Indian experts and technicians. The "brain trust" put together by Drakenstein included an Italian friar, Matthew of St. Joseph, two Dutch artists, a host of translators between Dutch, Latin, Portuguese, and Indian languages, and several indigenous physicians and botanical experts. Additionally, a host of manual workers gathered specimens, and the manuscript had to be shipped to the Dutch Republic to be printed. The first

Figure 8-1. *Hortus Malabaricus* **Coconut Palm.** A coconut palm from the *Hortus Malabaricus*.

volume appeared in 1678, and the last in 1703. The work included over seven hundred illustrations. As was often the case with VOC science, Drakenstein's project had commercial motivations, but it sheds light on internal VOC struggles as well. Embroiled in a conflict with the rival VOC governor of Ceylon, Drakenstein was interested in promoting the diverse range of useful and possibly profitable plants in Malabar. He also built a chemical lab in Malabar to extract possibly useful oils and essences from local plants.

Rumph, a German VOC scientist, wrote exhaustive works on the plants, animals, shellfish, and minerals of Indonesia. Amazingly, he accomplished much of this work while blind. After a career as a mercenary soldier and architect, he departed Europe in 1652, never to return. He spent most of his colonial career on the island of Ambon in the Banda Sea, a position ideally suited to his linguistic skills. He did not possess the power and wealth of Drakenstein, and much of the work he did himself or with indigenous people with whom he collaborated as an equal, not as a powerful patron like Drakenstein.

As a natural historian, Rumph was inspired not by Baconianism but by the ancients Aristotle and Pliny the Elder. He studied the flora, fauna, and minerals of Ambon, both observing them himself and consulting with the local inhabitants, for whose knowledge he had great respect. He lost his sight in 1670, and he and his manuscripts endured a number of disasters, including fire and earthquake, in addition to the problems posed by the difficulty of communication with Europe. He published little during his lifetime, mainly letters addressed to the German scientific society, the Academy of the Curious or Leopoldina, which admitted him in 1681 under the name "Plinius," which pleased Rumph. The Academy's correspondence-based practices were ideal for Rumph, who could never have been a full member of a scientific society that met regularly in a European capital. The *Ambonese Curiosity Cabinet*, on shellfish and minerals, was published shortly after his death in 1704. It contained thousands of items, many described for the first time to a European audience. Its extensively illustrated chapter on shells is presented in the form of a curiosity cabinet, reflecting Rumph's experience as a member of a network of collectors stretching back to Europe and enabling the printed work to serve as an advertisement for the shells themselves. His *Ambonese Herbal*, which dealt with potentially profitable plants, was suppressed for many years by the VOC and was only published in 1741. The fact that shells were viewed as artifacts that could be gathered at a particular place, while valuable plants could be cultivated in many different locations, may explain why the VOC prevented one work from being printed while allowing the other.

While Drakenstein and Rumph focused on a particular place, examining its natural history in depth, the work of the surgeon Kaempfer reflects his extensive travels, first in the service of a Swedish trade delegation to Persia and then as a VOC physician, which took him as far as the tiny Dutch base in the harbor of Nagasaki in Japan. Throughout his journeys he took copious notes of the societies through which he traveled. He was interested in checking the veracity of legends, and "debunked" the story of the "vegetable lamb" of Scythia, a medieval legend of a plant that had fruit in the form of a lamb. Examination of the plants of the region and conversations with its inhabitants revealed no such plant, which Kaempfer unhesitatingly described as a myth. His investigation of the electric "torpedo fish" of the Persian Gulf, on the other hand, found its powers to be all too real; he compared it to the accounts of the Mediterranean torpedo fish as described by classical authors including Pliny and Galen.

It was as a student of Japan, closed to all Westerners except for the small VOC delegation, that Kaempfer was best known in Europe. Like many medical practitioners, Kaempfer's principal interest in nature was in plants and their medical properties, an interest he shared with the Japanese physicians who were his principal botanical source. Kaempfer, like other VOC physicians through the history of the Deshima outpost, did not merely absorb Japanese knowledge from his Japanese medical associates, but disseminated Western knowledge. The Japanese were curious about Western medicine, and the Deshima surgeon was the one nontextual source for it.

Kaempfer's account of his travels, published in 1712, was by far the most important resource on Japanese plants available to Europeans until the late eighteenth century, when it was partially supplanted by the work of another VOC Deshima physician, Carl Thunberg (1743–1828). Kaempfer's fuller account of Japan was not published in his lifetime, but the manuscript was acquired by that omnivorous manuscript collector, Hans Sloane, who published an English translation in 1726.

NINE

THE SCIENTIFIC
REVOLUTION IN ASIA

The globalization of the Scientific Revolution was not restricted to those areas where European states exerted direct control, but extended to independent states as well. The time of the Scientific Revolution also saw increased European contact with the states and societies of Asia, from Europe's neighbors the Ottoman Empire and Russia to distant Japan. Although none of these societies was untouched by the Scientific Revolution, their reactions ranged from full acceptance to a brief flirtation followed by rejection. The role of government was central, but other sectors of society, including professional groups, religious minorities and curious individuals, participated as well. Astronomy, cartography, and medicine were among the leading sciences that attracted attention outside the West. Military modernization, a growing concern particularly for the western Asian states such as Russia and the Ottoman Empire that dealt with the Europeans on a regular basis, also motivated governments to launch projects for the acquisition of Western knowledge.

European dominance of long-distance shipping paradoxically worked against other countries' interest in European science. With the exception of Russia, the major Asian empires and states did not have ambitious shipping programs. Even the Ottomans were largely restricted to areas where traditional navigational methods continued to be effective, such as the Mediterranean. Japan and China were withdrawing from the sea, and many of the Indian Ocean powers were increasingly restricted by the power of first the Portuguese and then the Dutch, French, and British. Much of European science, such as the founding of the London and Paris Observatories, was driven by navigational needs. As fewer non-Western societies engaged in long-distance shipping (the most obvious exception was the Polynesians, but they had little contact with the rest of the world until the eighteenth century), they were uninterested in the navigational aspect of European science. However, the land equivalent of navigation, cartography, appealed to many states, Western and non-Western alike, that were in the process of acquiring new and poorly mapped lands, or wished for more accurate knowledge of the land they already had.

RUSSIA: ADOPTING THE REVOLUTION

Before the late seventeenth century, Russia had been largely culturally isolated from Europe. Its tradition of Christianity was Orthodox, looking toward Constantinople, rather than Catholic, looking toward Rome, and the struggles of the Reformation had little impact. The learned languages of Russia were Greek and Old Church Slavonic rather than Latin, and the literature of the Scientific Revolution was a closed book to most educated Russians, except for the few who had learned Latin. (Some Orthodox authorities even claimed Latin was literally the Devil's language!) What little printing went on was controlled by the Church and was devoted to theological texts. The Russian capital, Moscow, was geographically remote from the centers of European culture, and many Europeans thought of the Russians as incomprehensible barbarians, although they were willing to do business with them to acquire Russia's valuable resources of timber and furs.

Russia barely had a scientific culture at all. Interest in Greek texts focused on the Bible and the writings of the Church fathers, with little to no interest in natural philosophy. There were no universities on the Western model, and what education did take place was mostly in the monasteries, with a strong religious emphasis. Foreign technical experts—Italian architects and German artisans, among others—were invited into Russia but trained no Russian successors and had little impact on Russian scientific ignorance. The Patriarchate of Constantinople, the international leader of the Orthodox Church, was interested in reviving scientific studies in Russia, sponsoring the founding of a school where Aristotelian natural philosophy and Ptolemaic astronomy were taught in Greek and Latin, but it only had a few years of influence before everything changed.

Although Russian military and economic involvement with Central Europe and German immigration into Russia was gradually bringing Russian and Western culture closer together in the seventeenth century, the transformation that brought the Scientific Revolution to Russia took place in a relatively short span of years and was principally the work of one man, the Czar Peter I "the Great" (r. 1682–1735). Peter's concerns were primarily with national strengthening, military, naval, and economic. His interest in Western science was principally in its technical applications, particularly military and commercial. Navigation and maritime affairs were particularly important to the czar, both because he personally enjoyed sailing and because he wanted to build a powerful Russian navy in a country with little seafaring tradition. These issues were the focus of his famous visit to the West in 1697 and 1698—the first visit to Western countries made by a Russian czar, where he acquainted himself with many aspects of Western science and technology and may have met Isaac Newton. His return to Russia saw an acceleration of the westernization program in the sciences as in other fields.

Unlike countries further to the east, Russia was in direct contact with Europe and could adopt the latest European science with little relative time lag. Despite the differences between Russia's Orthodoxy and the varieties of Christianity practiced in the West, the common bond of Christianity also eased cultural transition. Peter was interested in the science practiced in the Protestant nations and France, which had accepted heliocentric astronomy, rather than the conservative, non-Copernican science of the Jesuits.

The creation of new institutions was central to Peter's reforms. The city of St. Petersburg itself was created and named after the czar to serve as a new capital for Russia, much closer to Europe than was the previous capital, Moscow. Naval and artillery schools brought the new mathematics and elements of physics to Russia. The Moscow School of Mathematics and Navigation was founded (with English instructors) in 1701, and was moved to St. Petersburg in 1715, where it became the Russian Naval Academy. The school introduced Arabic numerals to Russia and trained the cartographers who would map Russia's vast land empire as well as the navigators who would guide its ships. Another important institution was the artillery school founded in 1698. The artillery, along with the siege engineers, was always the most mathematically trained branch of an early modern military. Complementing the creation of new Russian institutions was a drive to get young upper-class men out of Russia to attend educational institutions in Europe so they could aid their country with new Western knowledge. This was a new phenomenon in Russian history, where previous intellectual connections had been primarily to the Orthodox world rather than to Germany or Western Europe; there was little tradition of a nonclerical intelligentsia.

The Petrine introduction of Western science revolutionized the Russian language by bringing in thousands of new words. Russian lack of interest in science and technology meant that the language in many cases literally lacked the words to discuss scientific topics. The new vocabulary introduced in Peter's reign stretched from navigation, shipbuilding, and military technology to medicine, mathematics, chemistry, and numerous other scientific and technical fields. New words added to Russian included such basic terms as *khimiia* for chemistry and *matematika* for mathematics. Innovations that the West had made even before the Scientific Revolution itself, such as the adoption of the Hindu/Arabic numerals, were also finally extended to Russia.

The principal institution standing in the way of Peter's changes, within and without the field of science, was the Russian Orthodox Church, which had almost completely dominated Russian intellectual and cultural life for centuries. The new changes were dangerous, particularly in that they were identified with the Western Christianity that good Orthodox Russians had always found schismatic and even heretical. For reasons similar to those of the Catholic Church, the Orthodox Church was also suspicious of scientific ideas such as heliocentrism. Church leaders allied themselves with conservative landowners against Peter's cultural revolution. Peter's program of adopting Western culture as well as science required a vigorous effort to forestall and suppress opposition among the

Church leadership. The Patriarchate of Moscow was abolished in 1700 and direction of the church was placed in the hands of a state-controlled Holy Synod, while recalcitrant monasteries were denied access to the printing press or even paper and ink. Russian seminaries remained conservative in their approach to science, but they had become marginal to Russian intellectual life.

The adoption of Western science in Russia culminated in the establishment of a scientific academy on the Western model, the Imperial Academy of Sciences of St. Petersburg, founded in 1724, the last year of Peter's reign. The gathering of scientists as members of the Academy, however, was only part of this vast effort to establish scientific and technological institutions in Russia: It also included a university, a library, a botanical garden, and an observatory. The Academy had a printing press and was meant to serve as a center for the translation of scientific and other Western works into Russian. Like the Berlin Academy and its later imitators, it was partly funded through a monopoly on the printing of almanacs. The personnel of the new Academy were almost entirely non-Russian, but more Russians would be added over time. Rulers after Peter were not as dedicated to the promotion of science as he was, but by the founding of the Imperial Academy Western learning had acquired a sufficient foothold to advance anyway. The Imperial Academy would attract such leading European savants of the eighteenth century as the Bernoulli brothers and Leonhart Euler. Russia had become a member, albeit a peripheral one, of the "Western" community of nations that exchanged scientific information and worked within the same intellectual framework.

CHINA: BORROWING EXPERTISE

China, more than any other country in Asia, was the subject of a determined attempt by Westerners to promote Western scientific ideas. These ideas were not those of the most advanced sectors of the Scientific Revolution such as Copernicanism or the mechanical philosophy, let alone Newtonianism. Instead, the Western ideas that were presented to the Chinese in the seventeenth century were those of the Jesuits, who accepted Ptolemaic and later Tychonic astronomy and physics based on Aristotle. Jesuit missionaries hoped that demonstrating the superiority of Western science, particularly astronomy and the mathematical sciences, would open the door for the Chinese to consider the Western religion of Christianity. The originator of this strategy was an Italian Jesuit, Matteo Ricci (1552–1610), who was not a trained astronomer, although he had studied with Clavius. Under Ricci's urging, the Jesuit headquarters in Rome began sending trained astronomers for the China mission. The earliest Chinese translators of Jesuit scientific materials—"heavenly learning"—were Chinese Christian converts. The Jesuits even presented a telescope to the Chinese emperor in 1634.

However, as in Russia, the real impact of Western science in China was shaped not by what Westerners wanted to offer, but what the Chinese were interested in taking. The initial appeal of Jesuit science was aimed at the Confucian intelligentsia, but the final decisions were taken by the Chinese state. Although the Jesuits translated Aristotelian natural philosophy into Chinese, with the exception of a few Christian converts the Chinese never displayed much interest in it. Although some Western physicians established practices in China, Western medicine also had little impact on Chinese medical thinking. What the Chinese were interested in were the mathematical disciplines—mathematics itself, astronomy, surveying, and cartography. The discipline that the state initially showed the most interest in was astronomy. Part of the legitimation of a Chinese emperor—his display of the "mandate of Heaven"—was an ability to construct an accurate calendar that would correctly predict astronomical events such as eclipses and conjunctions. By the late Ming, the calendar adopted at the beginning of the dynasty had developed serious problems, and many Chinese believed that a calendar reform was necessary. Using the learning of the Jesuits was not a break with Chinese practice: The Chinese had a long tradition of drawing on the astronomical expertise of the Indian and Islamic worlds to supplement their own astronomy. Using European experts was a continuation of that tradition, but the Europeans were interested in establishing a permanent institutional position for themselves from which they could promulgate their religion in a way previous foreign astronomers had not attempted.

Legitimation through astronomy was particularly important due to the change of China's ruling imperial dynasty from the Ming to the Qing in 1644. The Qing were the leaders of the Manchu people who invaded China during the collapse of the Ming government. Establishing the right of the new dynasty to the mandate was necessary, and the Jesuits were eager to ingratiate themselves with the new regime. Shortly after the accession of the Qing, they sponsored a contest between traditional Chinese astronomers, astronomers trained in the Islamic tradition, and Western Jesuits to correctly predict the onset, time, and duration of an eclipse. The contest resulted in a victory for the Westerners. With one interruption, Western Jesuits would head the Astronomical Bureau, part of the Board of Rites, until the suppression of the Jesuit order in the late eighteenth century. The first to occupy the position, Johann Adam Schall von Bell (1592–1666), wasted no time in firing the astronomers of the Islamic branch.

The acknowledged excellence of Western astronomical prediction, however, did not lead to increased interest in Western cosmology or theoretical astronomy. Chinese astronomers, like medieval Western astronomers, were principally interested in "saving the appearances," rather than speculation on the physical nature of the cosmos. When the head of the Astronomical Bureau, Schall von Bell's successor the Spanish Netherlands mathematician Ferdinand Verbiest (1623–1688), presented a treatise on Aristotelian natural philosophy in Chinese, *Studies to Exhaustively Master Principles*, to the emperor, it was rejected by both the emperor and the Confucian scholarly elite as the work of a technical expert with no real scholarly expertise or qualifications to deal with the theoretical issues in the text—a distinction reminiscent of the distinction between natural philosophers and mathematicians in medieval and Renaissance Europe. Unlike Western astronomy, Aristotelian natural philosophy offered no obvious advantages over Chinese thought. Even in applied science, Western ideas were not greeted with universal approbation or even interest. Song Yingxing (1587–1666) was one of the foremost Confucian literati scholars on scientific and technical subjects in the late Ming, but his encyclopedic *Exploitation of the Works of Nature* (1637) showed little interest in Western knowledge except to ridicule the idea of a spherical Earth and discuss Western gunmaking among other technological processes.

The type of Western astronomy practiced by the Jesuits was not a platform for the introduction of further advances such as Newtonian physics. Although Jesuits in China, like Jesuits elsewhere, had abandoned the Ptolemaic system in favor of Tychonianism by the mid-seventeenth century, they did not violate the Church's ban on Copernicanism until well into the eighteenth century. The Jesuits became isolated from the most intellectually active Copernican European astronomers in England, France and Central Europe.

The incorporation of the Jesuits into the Chinese bureaucracy also identified the Jesuits with the Chinese government rather than, as Ricci had hoped, with the Chinese intelligentsia. The interest of Confucian scholars in Jesuit science, along with other Jesuit teachings, diminished as the small Jesuit community in Beijing was increasingly composed of government officials rather than broadly educated intellectuals in the Ricci mold. However, the alliance with the Chinese government flourished in the late seventeenth and early eighteenth century.

Western Mathematical Science and Medicine in China During the Kangxi Reign

The fourth Qing Emperor, Kangxi (r. 1661–1722), had a strong personal interest in Western science, technology, and music. He took lessons in geometry and music from Jesuit instructors, establishing close relationships with some, including Verbiest. However, his interest went beyond viewing these activities as hobbies: Kangxi believed that these studies aided in the rule of the Empire. Shortly after taking power in 1667, Kangxi restored the Jesuits to control over the Astronomical Bureau but went far beyond that in attempting to incorporate the new Western knowledge in astronomy, harmonics, and mathematics into the Chinese canon. He was also interested in Western medicine, and was even treated with quinine, but this never extended to a program of reform of Chinese medicine. He did not share his contemporary Peter the Great's plan to entirely replace indigenous knowledge with the Western scientific tradition.

The introduction of this foreign knowledge posed problems for the Chinese intellectual class. One way of making the new Western astronomical and mathematical methods acceptable for Chinese scholars was to assert that they were ultimately Chinese in origin. The leader in this approach was the astronomer Mei Wending (1633–1721). Mei Wending was inspired by the challenge of Western mathematics to reexamine Chinese mathematical classics. This did not lead him to denigrate Western mathematics—both Chinese and Western mathematics were good. He developed a theory that ancient Chinese astronomy had been carried by Chinese to the West while it had been forgotten in China itself.

Therefore, this knowledge was being recovered by China rather than being introduced for the first time. Like his contemporary Rabbi Briel, Mei Wending saw the new knowledge as vindicating the wisdom of the ancient sages of his tradition rather than challenging it. Despite the partial success of this effort at "Sinifying" Western knowledge, the Jesuits' strange religion and their collaboration with the Manchus did lead to suspicion on the part of many Confucians, whatever the ultimate origins of their science.

A second phase in the promotion of Western science in Qing China was the dispatch of a group of Jesuits by the French king Louis XIV in 1685, a few years after the foundation of the Royal Academy of Sciences. These Jesuits, technical experts in mathematics, astronomy, and cartography, had the mission of not only spreading Christianity, but also of promoting French cultural and diplomatic power. Since the principal Catholic European power in Asia France was challenging was Portugal, the French Jesuits avoided the traditional route through Portuguese Goa and Macao in favor of one through the Protestant Dutch colonies of Capetown and Batavia. The scientific knowledge and skills they offered Kangxi were presented as a gift from his fellow monarch, Louis. The missionaries met with the Royal Academy of Sciences before their departure from Paris and were charged with corresponding with the Academy on Chinese scientific subjects, receiving scientific gifts such as astronomical tables and lenses from the Academicians. The French political goal was to undercut the Portuguese domination of Catholic European relations with China by establishing direct relations between the two monarchs. The prestige of the Chinese monarchy in Europe was great at the time, and an association with Kangxi might also benefit Louis at home. The Jesuits established themselves in the Chinese capital and made astronomical observations. Along with natural historical information, their observations were sent to France, where they were published under the sponsorship of the Royal Academy of Sciences.

Despite the initial success of Jesuit relations with Kangxi, their influence declined in the eighteenth century. The crisis for Kangxi's relationship with the West had initially nothing to with science. It was a religious issue, the Chinese rites controversy, in which the Jesuits supported a policy of adapting Christianity to Chinese culture by tolerating Christians performing Confucian rituals that the other missionary orders rejected. The issue was settled by Pope Clement XI in 1715. He came down against the Jesuit position. Although Kangxi was probably not interested in the theological issues at stake in the debate, the fact that it could be settled outside of China disturbed him, as it showed that some of his subjects put the authority of the pope above his own. The final victory of the anti-rites position made Christianity seem even more alien to China. The Jesuits were also drawn into the increasingly bitter factionalized court politics of the last few decades of Kangxi's reign, as his sons maneuvered to succeed him. The latter part of Kangxi's reign was marked by increased restrictions on the work of the missionaries, but they continued to serve the monarchy as an intellectual resource.

In 1713 Kangxi founded the Academy of Mathematics, dedicated to the publication of mathematical works drawing from both Western and Chinese traditions.

The Academy, staffed with Chinese and Manchu scholars, was a counterbalance to the Western and Chinese convert-led Bureau of Astronomy. Its sole mission was the creation of new, standardized mathematical works; it was not a scientific society or academy in the Western sense. The books it produced appeared under the emperor's authority and expressed his leading role in mathematics (a relationship similar to that of the Royal Academy of Sciences to Louis XIV in its early years). The Academy of Mathematics also gave the emperor's endorsement to Mei Wending's theory of the Chinese origins of Western mathematics and astronomy. The work of the Academy firmly integrated these branches of Western knowledge, in the form in which China had received them from the Jesuits, into the Chinese canon.

Despite the success of the Chinese and Manchu members of the Academy of Mathematics, the Western experts were still useful. In addition to astronomy, mathematics, and music, Kangxi was interested in drawing on Western expertise in cartography. The Qing were one of the great expansionist dynasties in Chinese history, and like Spain in Mexico and Peru and Russia in Siberia, they had acquired a large amount of poorly mapped territory. In the early eighteenth century, Kangxi launched a massive project for mapping all of China. Western Jesuits were involved as part of a Chinese-directed effort to produce a map of the empire up to the highest standards incorporating Western methods. The map produced, the *Kangxi Atlas*, was finished in 1717, before complete, accurate maps of France and Russia were available. (Kangxi sent a copy to Peter the Great as a gift in 1721, possibly as a way of asserting Chinese territorial claims in those areas where they might conflict with Russia's.)

The impact of Western science on China was limited. The indigenous tradition of natural investigation remained strong enough, and Western influence marginal enough, that Chinese natural investigators were not obligated to deal with Western ideas. Kangxi's reign marked the height of the early modern Chinese interest in "Western learning." His son and successor, the Yongzheng emperor (r. 1722–1735), lacked his father's interest in mathematics and the sciences, Chinese or Western. Although subsequent rulers continued to draw upon the technical expertise of the Jesuits, interest in the larger context of Jesuit astronomical and cartographic methods virtually disappeared. When Copernicanism was finally introduced to China in the mid-eighteenth century, it actually further damaged the intellectual prestige of Western astronomers: If the Westerners could not even make up their minds as to what occupied the center of the universe, why should they be trusted to establish correct theories?

IN THE SHADOW OF CHINA:
KOREA AND VIETNAM

Korea and to a lesser extent Vietnam looked to China for cultural leadership, including in astronomy. Both societies had a state astronomical bureau, although it was considerably more institutionalized in Korea, and regarded the prediction of the time and duration of eclipses and the maintenance of calendars as an important governmental function.

Korea was a far more closed society than China or Vietnam. Koreans had little direct contact with foreigners of any sort, including Westerners, and the influence of Western science was principally exercised indirectly through professional contacts between Korean astronomers and the Chinese Astronomical Bureau. Koreans were aware of European science through China as early as 1614, although the first Western astronomical manuals and instruments arrived in Korea only in 1631. Koreans adopted the new Sino-European calendrical system a few years after the Chinese did, with some difficulty as they were not able to directly employ Western or Chinese experts. Koreans adopted Western-influenced Chinese manuals of calendrical astronomy, and a regular system of Korean astronomical officials visiting Beijing and consulting with Western and Chinese astronomers led Korea to keep up with improvements in the system with only a few years' lag. However, the official-to-official restriction of Korean scientific interchanges meant that Korean intellectuals who were not officials, unlike their Chinese and Japanese counterparts, never had a chance to develop an interest in Western science.

Jesuit missionaries in Vietnam, following the example of the China mission, also sought to use astronomy to advance their cause. A Western Jesuit, Juan Antonio Arnedo, was appointed Court Astronomer and Editor of the Calendar in 1695 after the successful prediction of an eclipse. He was a man of some influence at the Vietnamese court, which he was able to use to protect missionaries. However, science was never as central to the Vietnam mission as it was in China itself.

JAPAN: A GRADUAL OPENING

Japan received Western science from two main sources. One was the Western Jesuits. Science played a relatively minor role in Jesuit missionary work in Japan itself compared to China, but Jesuit writings in classical Chinese, a language educated Japanese men knew, were exported to the island country. However, Japanese access to Western Jesuit writings was limited because the shogunate, the regime that governed the country, was suspicious of the connection of Western science with Western religion. Fearing that Japanese Christians would support an invasion of Japan by a Christian ruler such as the King of Spain, ruler of the nearby Philippines, the Japanese outlawed Christianity in their country in the early seventeenth century and tortured and executed many Christian missionaries as well as Japanese Christians. One Portuguese Jesuit missionary, Cristóvão Ferreira (c. 1580–1650), converted to Buddhism rather than become a martyr. He helped translate a book in Japanese ultimately adapted from Clavius's astronomical textbook, with some additional material on Western natural philosophy and meteorology. However, like the Aristotelian works written by Jesuits in China, his writings seem to have made little impression on Japanese thought.

The second way for Japanese to access Western learning was the tiny colony of Dutch traders in the harbor at Deshima. Fearing foreign invasion and social and political instability, the Japanese government had "closed the country" to foreign contact in the early seventeenth century. The only Western traders allowed in the country were the closely watched, tightly regulated Deshima community. The one way that a Western intellectual interested in Japan could win access to the country was by becoming physician to the Dutch colony, which recruited from all over Protestant Europe. Individual Japanese, mostly either translators who interpreted between Japanese authorities and the Dutch colony or physicians, became interested in "Dutch thought."

While in Russia and China, the key actor was the state, in Japan the state was one of a number of forces, including the actions of individuals and professional groups. Japan, which had adopted much of its high culture from China, had little difficulty with the fact that foreign knowledge was foreign. While Chinese intellectuals often hesitated to endorse "barbarian" knowledge, Japanese viewed foreign knowledge as legitimate. By the late eighteenth century, Japanese would even use Western knowledge to attack the supremacy of Chinese thought in Japanese culture. The superiority of Western learning in astronomy and medicine was evidence that Japanese needed to liberate themselves from the dominance of the Chinese tradition in other domains as well.

As in China, the Japanese state's interest in the new knowledge had primarily to do with astronomy and calendar-making. Since the legitimacy of the imperial dynasty was not connected to a "mandate of heaven" but to its supposed descent from the Japanese gods, the calendar was less of a priority, and by the seventeenth century it had not been updated for nearly eight hundred years and was severely out of harmony with the year. The state-sponsored reorganization of the calendar by mathematician Shibukawa Harumi (1639–1715) in 1684 remained based on traditional Chinese methods. Although Harumi was aware of Western mathematical astronomy and incorporated some Western data he obtained second-hand from a Chinese book, he rejected it as inferior theoretically to Chinese methods. Interestingly, the Japanese were sticking to traditional Chinese methods at a time when calendar-making under the Bureau of Astronomy in China itself was increasingly influenced by the West. The rise of a vigorous indigenous mathematical tradition, known as *wasan*, which arose without Western influence, had little impact on calendrical astronomy, as *wasan* masters scorned calendrical problems in favor of those of pure mathematics.

Harumi's reform did not permanently supply Japan with an accurate calendar, and in the early eighteenth century the shogunate became interested in the application of Western techniques to further refine the Japanese calendar. In 1720 the censorship regime was relaxed as the shogun of the time, Yoshimune (r. 1716–1745), believed that the application of Western techniques could result in an improved calendar. This relaxation was directed at shogunate officials who wanted to work with Western materials, rather than the educated public. The defeat of Japanese Christianity and the lessening of pressure from Western nations meant that the Christianity of Western science was less of a concern, although Western books, whether in their original language or in Chinese translation, were still carefully examined to see if they contained anything relevant to the proscribed religion. Although Western learning did not have a major influence on the next Japanese calendrical revision, in 1754, Japanese scholars continued to read Western works and were applying Western knowledge to calendar-making by the late eighteenth century, at a time when Japan was still closed off from direct contact with the West outside Deshima.

State control of astronomy meant that the principal way in which Japanese intellectuals outside the government became aware of Western science was through medicine. During the sixteenth century, some Japanese physicians had been interested in learning Western surgery, known as "red-hair" or "southern barbarian" surgery. Surgery was a subject in which the Chinese tradition that dominated Japanese medical learning had little interest, and unlike many other subjects, it survived the expulsion of the Catholic mission. In the seventeenth century, Western surgery was learned on the technical level, with little interest in Western anatomical theory. In 1740, Yoshimune commissioned two scholars to make a study of Dutch medical works, but it was not until the second half of the century that Japanese physicians began to seriously investigate Western theoretical medicine.

The transfer of medical knowledge between Europe and Japan and Asia generally was not a one-way process. One Deshima physician, Willem Ten Rhijne (1649–1700) published, in London, *The History of Arthritis*, a Latin book on East Asian medicine containing the first detailed description of acupuncture in a European language. It was widely reviewed in Europe, but it does not seem to have had an impact on European medical practice or theory.

SIAM: A BRIEF INTEREST

The Kingdom of Siam in the area of modern-day Thailand had extensive relations with Western powers in the seventeenth century. Siamese rulers received European traders and missionaries and even sent embassies to Europe. The two countries that they deal with the most were France and the Dutch Republic, two of the most scientifically advanced European countries. Despite these contacts, Siamese displayed little interest in Western science until the reign of King Narai (1656–1688). Narai had a keen interest in astronomy, which was one of the responsibilities of the Siamese government (Fig. 9-1). He collected clocks, star maps, astronomical tables, and other scientific instruments from the Europeans, and a Siamese embassy to France toured the Paris Observatory. Narai also received the French Jesuit mathematicians on their way to China in 1685, and expressed interest in establishing an observatory with Jesuit support. A Jesuit-staffed observatory with Western equipment, including a telescope, was begun at Lopburi. Narai himself observed an eclipse there on April 30, 1688. However, unlike the Chinese or Vietnamese rulers, Narai did not recruit Europeans into the astronomical

Figure 9-1. Narai Observatory. Telescopes in use at the court of Narai, the king of Siam. Shortly after this event, he was overthrown, and Western science in Siam suffered a massive setback.

bureaucracy, nor was his interest in Western scientific equipment widely shared among the Thai elite.

Shortly after the eclipse observation, Narai was overthrown and killed in an anti-French and anti-Catholic reaction that led to the departure of the French, including the Jesuits, and the partial closing of the country. Although sporadic contacts with the world of Western science would continue, mainly through the Dutch East India Company, the intense interest in Western ideas and techniques shown in the Narai era would not return until the nineteenth century.

THE OTTOMAN EMPIRE: MULTIPLE OPENINGS

No Asian state was closer to the heartlands of the Scientific Revolution and more closely involved with European political and economic life than the Ottoman Empire, an Islamic state that ruled southeastern Europe as far north as Hungary. (The Ottomans lost Hungary to the Austrian Habsburgs in 1687, the same year as the publication of Newton's *Mathematical Principles of Natural Philosophy*.) There were numerous ways in which the new science could make its way into the empire. The story of the Scientific Revolution in the Ottoman lands is really

Figure 9-2.   Istanbul Observatory. This illustration of the short-lived Ottoman observatory in 1577 shows Ottoman astronomers working with instruments similar to those of their Western contemporaries.

multiple stories, of which the two most prominent are the story of the Ottoman government and mainstream Muslim society, which only hesitantly engaged with the new science in a largely state-driven effort, and the story of the large Greek-speaking Christian population of the empire, which engaged with it much earlier, while not fully accepting it either.

The Ottomans were far more enmeshed in war with Europe than was any other non-Western society, fighting numerous wars with the Spanish and Austrian Habsburgs and the Republic of Venice, in addition to smaller European powers. Piracy, both Muslim and Christian, was endemic in the Mediterranean, with many Muslim vessels raiding Christian shipping from the Ottoman cities in North Africa and taking prisoners, who would be enslaved and sometimes convert to Islam, while Muslim captives and other travelers were enslaved or otherwise exposed to European culture and sometimes converted to Christianity, making a home in Christian societies. Muslim captives in Italy helped translate Arabic scientific and philosophical works. The Ottoman Empire was a frequent destination for traveling European savants and pilgrims, particularly from

France and Italy. The Ottomans had inherited the rich scientific tradition of medieval Islam, which drew from the same Greek and other ancient sources as did Western science. The fifteenth—and sixteenth-century sultans took a keen interest in education, founding numerous madrasas, particularly in the capital city Istanbul, including at least one medical madrasa. Christians and Jews who voluntarily converted to Islam also sometimes brought European science with them. The Hungarian Ottoman astronomer and convert Ibrahim al-Zigetvari translated a collection of astronomical tables by the French astronomer Noel Durret (d. 1650) into Arabic in 1660, the first Copernican work in an Islamic language.

Yet with all of these contacts with Europe, the Ottoman government and Muslim society took little interest in the Scientific Revolution. There were several missed opportunities to bring the new science to the Empire. The Italian engineer, anatomist, and painter Leonardo da Vinci (1452–1519) was invited to the service of the sultan but turned down the opportunity. Tycho Brahe at one time expressed interest in building an observatory in Ottoman Egypt, close to the site from which Ptolemy had made his observations, but the project, which would have been carried out principally through Venetian merchants resident in Egypt rather than Ottoman officials or scientists, came to nothing.

One reason for weak Ottoman interest in Western science was a diminishing interest in science generally. In the late fifteenth century, it had seemed for a moment like the Ottomans might be the heirs of the interest in science and particularly astronomy shown by the Central Asian Timurid dynasty, the sponsors of the last great classical Islamic observatory at Samarkand. One of the greatest of the Timurid astronomers, Ali Kuscu (1403–1474), relocated to Istanbul in 1472 and established a mathematical tradition in Ottoman education. But in the sixteenth century, and particularly in the reign of Suleiman the Magnificent (r. 1520–1566), the high culture of the Ottomans moved away from astronomy and mathematics in the direction of a strong emphasis on Islam and "religious sciences." The last attempt to establish a major state-sponsored observatory in the Islamic world, the Istanbul Observatory—contemporary with Tycho's observatory at Hven—had only a short life, from 1577 to 1580, killed by a failed astrological prediction and religious opposition (Fig. 9-2). The head of the Observatory, Taqi al-Din (1526–1585), had been a captive in Italy and incorporated some Western instruments into the Observatory, although it remained predominantly influenced by the Islamic tradition. Printing, a major mode of dissemination of scientific knowledge in the Latin Christian world, was also tightly restricted in the Ottoman Empire—Muslims did not print until the eighteenth century, as religious authorities feared the dissemination of thousands of copies of corrupted or erroneous versions of sacred texts. Printing was not outright banned, however, as Jews and Christians were allowed to maintain presses.

The Ottoman official attitude toward the new science was less hostile than indifferent. Ottoman Muslim religious authorities were more disinterested and suspicious of Western learning as a whole than specifically upset about particular aspects of the new science such as heliocentrism. Ottoman astronomers who were aware of Copernicanism generally treated heliocentrism as of minor importance, particularly since it did not raise the religious issues for Muslims that it did for Christians and Jews. Zigetvari's translation was of interest to Ottoman astronomers for its technical contributions to astronomical calculation, not its heliocentrism.

One area in which the Ottomans did take interest was the new geographic discoveries of the Europeans. One of the earliest maps showing the Atlantic coastline of South America is the "Piri Reis" world map (see Figure 3-1), named after its creator, the Ottoman admiral Piri Reis (d. 1553). He seems to have derived this information from captured Western mariners, and Piri Reis claimed that sources for his map included a map made by Columbus himself and information derived from a sailor with Columbus who had subsequently been captured by the Ottomans. The map was presented to the Ottoman sultan Selim I in 1517. Ottoman interest in Western geographic knowledge continued, with the creation of some major works in the sixteenth century and the translation of the multivolume study of world geography by the Dutch VOC mapmaker Willem Janszoon Blaeu (1571–1638), *Atlas Major* (1662–1672), made by Abu Bakr ibn Behram el-Dimaski (d. 1691) in the seventeenth. El-Dimaski's introduction discussed the main European cosmographical systems, those of Ptolemy, Tycho, and Copernicus, and defended the Islamic world against European assertions that it had stagnated in astronomical knowledge. The Ottoman encyclopedist Haji Khalifa (1609–1657) also drew on Western knowledge in his geographic writings. Despite their interest in geography, the Ottomans, unlike the Russians and Chinese, were not interested in the application of European cartographic techniques to their own far-flung empire—possibly because they feared knowledge of the empire falling into the hands of Christian European experts.

By the early eighteenth century, Ottoman interest in Western observational astronomy and cosmology was increasing. The opening of the first printing house for books in Turkish, the Muteferrika Press, in 1727, was part of this movement, known in Ottoman historiography as the "Tulip period." The Press published several Western-influenced works on astronomy and geography. The founder of the press, a Hungarian convert to Islam from Christianity named Ibrahim Muteferrika, published a lengthy astronomical supplement to Khalifa's geographic work *Cihannuma* (1632). Muteferrika gave the most detailed description of the Ptolemaic, Copernican, and Tychonic systems yet available in Turkish before coming down on the side of Ptolemy. (The first Ottoman Muslim savant to come down forthrightly on the side of heliocentrism was Osman ibn Abdulmennan in his translation of Bernhard Varenius's *General Geography* [1650], published in 1751. Abdulmennan pointed out that it is more sensible to roast meat by rotating it on skewers than to rotate the fire around the meat!) Ottoman envoy Yirmisekiz Mehmed Celebi (d. 1732) visited the Paris Observatory twice in 1721. Celebi had some knowledge of astronomy, and conversed with the director, Jean Domenico Cassini (the son of the Gian Domenico Cassini who had founded it). Celebi observed the instruments and submitted a report to Constantinople for the benefit of Ottoman astronomers. Despite this interest and the religious acceptability of heliocentric astronomy, however, the empire continued to use the tables of the late Timurid astronomer Ulugh Beg (1394–1449) as its official calendrical resource until the end of the eighteenth century.

In addition to astronomy, there is some evidence that Ottoman physicians were aware of new developments in Western medicine. In keeping with the Ottoman bias toward practical applications, Ottoman medical specialists were interested in new therapies, including "chemical medicines" ultimately derived from Paracelsianism, rather than changes in anatomical or physiological knowledge or medical theory.

The Ottomans and Western Military Technology

When the Turkish government began to take an interest in Western science, its motives were pragmatic, based on an interest in Western technology. As competitors with the Western powers, the Ottomans had always been interested in new developments in Western military technology. By the middle of the eighteenth century, Ottoman leaders had become aware of the need for military modernization: Ottoman armies were no longer competitive with the best European armies and were being forced to give up territory to advancing Austrian and modernized Russian forces. European artillerists were hired to improve the accuracy of Ottoman cannon, which required the introduction of some new mathematics. The first in a series of institutions designed to introduce Western technological knowledge to the Ottoman army was the Corps of Bombardiers, founded in 1735. It was headed by a Westerner, the French count Claude Alexander de Bonneval (1675–1747), who had defected to the Ottomans and converted to Islam, taking the name Humbaraci Ahmet Pasha and helping to reorganize the Ottoman artillery. The Corps included an educational division with a strong mathematical component, including geometry and altitude measurement, taught via a combination of Ottoman and Western textbooks. However, unlike Peter the Great's military modernization, which had also begun with an artillery unit, the Praeobrazhensky Guards, the Ottoman program did not lead to interest in the more theoretical branches of knowledge or the full adoption of Western science, let alone the founding of a scientific academy like that of St. Petersburg. The Corps was disbanded shortly after Ahmet Pasha's death. The full impact of the Scientific Revolution would only be felt by Ottoman Muslims beginning in the late eighteenth century, but military institutions would continue to lead the way.

Greek Christians and Jews in the Ottoman Empire and the Scientific Revolution

Despite official Ottoman disinterest, the science of the Scientific Revolution did make its way into the empire. The people most actively interested in the new science were not Muslims but members of religious minorities, particularly Greek

Christians and to a lesser extent Jews who had the opportunity to study science in a Western context. The University of Padua in the Venetian territories benefited from Venice's long-term involvement with the Greek East and admitted both Jews and Greek Christians from the Ottoman lands. Other Italian universities also admitted Ottoman Greek students.

The opening of the Ottoman Empire's Greek population to the new science took place in two phases. The first, in the early seventeenth century, was a revival of interest in the Greek scientific classics. This was sponsored by the Orthodox Church, which had a great deal of self-government and dominated Greek cultural and intellectual life in the empire. Orthodox leaders believed that at a time when Greeks had no independent polity, identification with classical Hellenic culture would help ward off pressure to convert to either Islam or Roman Catholicism. This phase did not draw on post-Copernican Western science or even alternative classical natural philosophies such as Epicureanism but was basically Aristotelian and Ptolemaic, like the science of prerevolutionary Latin Europe.

The second phase acquainted Ottoman Greeks with current developments in Western science. Two of the leading writers who brought Western scientific knowledge to the Greek population of the Ottoman Empire were the Padua-educated Alexander Mavrocordatos (1636–1709) and Crysanthos Notaras (1663–1731). Mavrocordatos taught an advanced form of Aristotelianism associated with Padua and introduced the circulation of the blood, the discovery of another Padua Aristotelian, William Harvey, to Ottoman Greek speakers. He made his career in the Ottoman administration. Notaras was a churchman. He spent time in Paris, where he visited the Paris Observatory and received instructions on how to construct an astrolabe from the head of the Observatory, Jean Domenico Cassini. On his return to the empire, Notaras became Patriarch of Jerusalem and wrote the first book in Greek to give a full presentation of Copernican astronomy, *Introduction to Geography and the Sphere*. Although Notaras did not fully endorse the Copernican system, he presented it as an accurate description of the universe and even included a diagram combining Copernican astronomy with vortex-based Cartesian physics. He also attempted to spread Western scientific instruments and scientific education through the Orthodox world.

Like the Catholic Church, Orthodox religious authorities in the Ottoman Empire resisted some aspects of the new science, such as heliocentrism, more effectively than their fellow Orthodox clergy in Russia. The Galileo of the Greek Orthodox world was Methodios Anthrakites (1660–1736), probably also educated at the University of Padua. After returning to the empire, he established himself as a teacher and wrote a three-volume textbook, *The Way of Mathematics*. The book presented, without endorsing, Copernicanism and incorporated some Cartesian elements as well. Anthrakites was summoned to Constantinople by the Holy Synod, the governing body of the Greek Orthodox Church. Unlike the powerful Notaras, Anthrakites was excommunicated and banned from teaching, but only temporarily, as he (like Galileo) publicly repented and even burned some of his own books. The Synod reaffirmed that only Aristotelian science was permissible, but ongoing contacts between Greek Orthodox scholars and the West meant that the prohibition was ultimately unenforceable. *The Way of Mathematics* itself was published in Greek in Venice in 1749. Language barriers and the dominance of the Greek and Turkish intellectual establishments by their respective religious authorities, however, meant that these Greek writings had little influence on the Turks and other Muslim peoples in the empire.

Another route by which the new science entered the Ottoman Empire was through the Jewish community, which had connections throughout the Christian and Islamic worlds. For Jewish physicians and scientists, as for other Jews, the Ottoman realms and other Muslim-ruled territories offered a relatively tolerant refuge from growing persecution and hostility in the Christian world. Western-trained Jewish physicians practiced in the Ottoman world. There is some evidence that a Western-educated Jew, David ben-Shushan, transmitted Western astronomical knowledge to Taqi al-Din. However, Jewish physicians in the Ottoman lands often continued to address Western audiences, Jewish and non-Jewish, rather than Ottoman ones, partly because of the more developed printing and bookselling industry of the West. Tobias Cohn (1652–1729), a German-born, Padua-trained physician, became physician to the sultan and composed his medical and scientific encyclopedia, *Ma'aseh Tuviyyah* (1707), in Turkey, but it was published in Venice and was principally aimed at a Western Jewish audience.

INDIA: A LATE OPENING

Although Western missionaries, physicians, and traders were an increasingly common presence in seventeenth-century India, European science had little impact. Most of India in the late sixteenth and seventeenth centuries was ruled by the Moguls, a Muslim dynasty of Central Asian origin that ruled from the northern Indian capital of Delhi. Jesuit missionaries were active at the courts of the Mogul rulers Akbar (r. 1556–1605) and Jahangir (r. 1605–1627), but unlike the Chinese rulers the Mogul court was more interested in European art and humanist and religious learning than in science. Many Indian experts were involved in the creation of the natural histories of India by Europeans such d'Orta and Drakenstein, but these efforts seem to have had little influence on Indian intellectual life. The English East India Company, which was supplanting its Dutch rivals in India by the late seventeenth century (and attracting investment money from the Royal Society), did not produce figures like Drakenstein and d'Orta with an interest in Indian science or the spreading of Western knowledge until later in the eighteenth century. Bernier—an individual adventurer, not a representative of an institution like the Jesuits or the East India Company— translated works of Gassendi and Descartes into Persian, the language of much of the northern Indian Muslim elite, for the use of his patron Danishmand Khan Shafi'a Yazdi (1578–1657), an official at the Mogul court, but the availability of these works did not result in an Indian interest in mechanical philosophy. India also lacked the state astronomical bureaus of East Asia with their interest in new

and more accurate methods, nor did it, as yet, face the Western military challenge that forced the Ottomans to keep up with Western technology. It was a
politically, religiously, and socially pluralist society where interest in Western
science was taken up by a few members of the elite without having a great impact
on the rest of the population.

The greatest evidence of interest in Western science in early modern India
was the observatory of the Hindu prince Jai Singh II (1688–1743), ruler of Jaipur.
Jai Singh's observatories, originally built for astrological purposes, brought
together indigenous Indian, Islamic, and Western astronomical traditions as well
as Hindu, Muslim, and Western astronomers. Indian astronomy in the period
was undergoing a minor scientific revolution of its own, as the Hindu and Islamic
astronomical traditions were brought together more closely than ever before,
and Jai Singh's interest in European astronomy was an extension of this multicultural approach. Although the basic layout of his observatories was Indian and his
instruments were originally constructed on Indian models, Jai Singh was interested in European instruments and even the telescope. He bought one for his
collection and observed, among other things, the four Galilean satellites of
Jupiter. Jai Singh made only moderate use of the telescope, however, possibly due
to the poor quality of the telescopes available in India, and did not use telescopic
sights for his astronomical instruments. He was interested enough in European
astronomy that he employed European assistants, mainly trained in Jesuit methods and cosmology rather than the post-Keplerian astronomy practiced in the
most advanced centers in Europe itself. Jai Singh sent a delegation to Portugal to
acquire instruments and compare Indian astronomical tables to European ones.
The delegation, led by the Jesuit missionary priest Father Emanuel de Figuerado,
arrived in Lisbon in January 1729 but did not make it to the leading observatories
in Greenwich and Paris, returning to India the next year. The tables eventually
issued by Jai Singh's observatory and completed between 1727 and 1735 were
closely modeled on the 1702 tables of the French astronomer and mathematician
Philippe de La Hire (1640–1718), a member of the Royal Academy of Sciences,
rather than the more accurate tables created by Flamsteed. The tables, known as
the *Zij-I Muhammad Shahi* after the reigning Mogul emperor, remained in use in
parts of India into the late nineteenth century. The observatory itself seems to
have been abandoned shortly after Jai Singh's death in 1743.

Despite the European influence on Jai Singh, his astronomy remained in the
Indian and Islamic tradition, making only limited use of new instruments and ad-
hering to a basically Ptolemaic cosmology. Like the Chinese Bureau of Astronomy,
Jai Singh was also isolated from the most modern astronomy by the fact that
the European astronomers he worked with were Catholic Jesuits educated in
the anti-Copernican tradition. Nonetheless, the expedition to Portugal and the
subsequent adoption of La Hire's tables are evidence of the growing reach of
European astronomy.

CONCLUSION

THE SCIENTIFIC REVOLUTION IN WORLD HISTORY

The Scientific Revolution, as the foundation for the science practiced everywhere on the globe today, is a central event in world history. It impact has not been limited to Europe and its colonies but has affected societies around the world. All of us continue to live in the world it shaped.

THE SCIENTIFIC REVOLUTION AND THE HISTORY OF SCIENCE

The Scientific Revolution is the great dividing line in the history of science, separating the rapidly developing science of the modern era from the far more slowly and hesitantly developing natural philosophy of the premodern era. Although we no longer believe the solar system is at the center of the universe, the model of the solar system we employ is still basically that of Copernicus, Kepler, and Newton, with its heliocentrism, elliptical orbits, and gravitational interactions. Geocentric astronomy survives only as a curiosity upheld by fringe conservative religious groups. The "Newtonian" model of a science as a search for a set of mathematically expressible laws originating in the seventeenth century has dominated the history of physics and had effects on other sciences as well.

The Scientific Revolution also established institutions and practices that have shaped subsequent science. This was not a linear progression. Universities, dominant in the Middle Ages but somewhat marginal for much of the scientific development of the sixteenth and seventeenth centuries outside medicine, made a remarkable comeback, establishing themselves as central institutions of scientific research in the nineteenth and twentieth centuries. Scientific societies, by contrast, have become more honorary distinctions for their members than active players in scientific development. Becoming a Fellow of the Royal Society now is less entrance into a dynamic scientific community than it is a mark of honor for a distinguished scientific career. *Philosophical Transactions* continues to be published but is a journal of at best minor importance. The scientific journal as a whole, however, has flourished in the centuries since the Scientific Revolution, although it now faces the challenge of adapting to the online world.

On a more fundamental level, the Scientific Revolution also established a culture of scientific development. The prestige and fame won by scientists like Newton and Galileo encouraged emulation, contributing to the development of science as not just an interesting avocation but a life's work. Although the profession of science in the eighteenth-century West was nothing like the modern scientific profession in size and wealth, it was the largest in world history to that date. The idea, established in the seventeenth century, that scientific development is the key to economic growth and social stability has also persisted, to the point where its participation in the international world of science is considered a key marker of a society's level of development.

THE REVOLUTION IN GLOBAL SCIENCE

Before the Scientific Revolution, thought about the natural world was a matter of loosely connected traditions that dominated particular cultural areas and civilizations. Each had its areas of strength; each served the function that its society assigned to it. However, beginning in the seventeenth century, the "Western" scientific tradition founded in Europe began to establish a narrow edge over others, beginning in astronomy and the related disciplines of cartography and navigation. The installation of a Westerner over the Chinese Astronomical Bureau, one of the world's major scientific institutions, in the mid-seventeenth century was an early sign that this change had come to be recognized cross-culturally, and helped prompt more gradual shifts in Korea, Vietnam, and Japan. Most important was the wholesale adoption of Western science by Russia in the era of Peter the Great.

The three centuries following the Scientific Revolution would see the further development of Western science with a rapidity unparalleled in history. In every area, Western science would see breakthrough after breakthrough until the narrow edge it had during the Scientific Revolution would expand to cast all other scientific traditions in the shade. This could be ascribed to the political dominance of the West in the nineteenth century, which saw the suppression of many non-Western traditions and cultures, just as the scientific traditions of Native America had been crushed by Western force in the sixteenth century. However, the Western religion of Christianity did not defeat rival universal religions, Islam or Buddhism, or even many local, nontextual religions in the way that Western science defeated rival scientific traditions. Western science triumphed not simply because of Western power but also because it simply worked better and engaged nature at a deeper level than its erstwhile rivals.

THE SCIENTIFIC REVOLUTION
AND THE SCIENCE OF THE WORLD

Europeans established direct, ongoing connections between Afro-Eurasia and the Americas for the first time and pioneered the sea connection of the western, southern, and eastern Afro-Eurasian coasts from Scandinavia to Japan. This enabled European science to be the first to extend its data-gathering across all inhabited continents except Australia. This affected a wide variety of sciences. The most obvious case was geography, where for the first time the world could be mapped as a whole (although the far south and the interior of Africa remained for the eighteenth and nineteenth centuries). In natural history, a whole new hemisphere of plant and animal life was open for examination as well as the flora and fauna of far-distant regions of Africa and Asia. European botanists could compile the first collections of information about plants, whether physical in the form of a botanical garden or herbarium or textual in the form of a book, that could claim worldwide scope. Zoologists became aware for the first time of the massive diversity of the world's fauna. Creatures as exotic as the rattlesnake, the opossum, and the chimpanzee could be studied and dissected. Building on the achievement of botanists and zoologists during the Scientific Revolution, natural historians in the eighteenth century would establish universal systems of classification still in use today. But the impact of globalization was felt in other sciences as well. In astronomy, the southern sky was revealed, and astronomical observations could be taken from a far wider range of positions on the Earth's surface, enabling far more precise and useful observations. European sailors with compasses could examine the variations in the Earth's magnetic field across many seas. While the Scientific Revolution influenced other civilizations, it also occurred at a time when European global reach was expanding in an unprecedented way. The eighteenth century would continue in the path set by the Scientific Revolution, with massive coordinated programs to observe the rare transits of Venus across the face of the sun and obtain for the first time an accurate idea of the distance of the Earth and the sun, a project first conceived of by Edmond Halley.

THE SCIENTIFIC REVOLUTION
AND EUROPEAN DOMINANCE

By the late seventeenth century, thanks to the Scientific Revolution, European science in a few areas, notably astronomy, navigation, and cartography, had acquired a slight but unmistakable edge over science elsewhere, an edge that would continue to spread to more fields and continue to grow through the following centuries. In the nineteenth century, Europeans established domination over India, much of China and the Islamic World, Africa, Southeast Asia, and several other areas of Afro-Eurasia, an even more sweeping assault on the rest of the world than that characteristic of the age of Columbus and da Gama. The connection of these two facts is unclear. Economic and technological factors were far more central to the development of European empire than was science *per se* however.

Some historians and cultural critics have argued that the Scientific Revolution led to a more exploitative attitude to nature that was related to more exploitative attitudes toward subject populations, including the European poor, women, and non-European peoples. The idea promoted by the mechanical philosophy of the material world as essentially "dead" made it easier to exploit than it had been when it was viewed as in some sense living, as it had been by some alchemical philosophers or Aristotelians. However, brutal exploitation existed long before the Scientific Revolution, and a deeper understanding of the matter theory of the period, including the continuing influence of alchemical theory, renders the identification of the Scientific Revolution as a whole with strict mechanical philosophy untenable. Certainly the Scientific Revolution coincided with such radical steps in European exploitation of the rest of the world as the conquest of much of the Americas and the establishment of the Atlantic slave trade, so at the very least the new scientific attitude does not seem to have made Europeans less exploitative.

THE SCIENTIFIC REVOLUTION AND "EUROCENTRISM"

Whatever its relation to the brutal reality of European domination, science played an important role in the establishment of an ideology of European superiority, sometimes referred to as "Eurocentrism." The superiority of European science, which first began to manifest itself with the Scientific Revolution, was used as evidence of the superiority of Western civilization both over the other civilizations of Afro-Eurasia and over the rest of humanity generally.

The creation of a "European" history of science can be traced to the humanists, with the neglect or denigration of the Arab contribution to science in favor of a narrative that traces its development from the Greeks to the early modern period. This narrative never completely relegated to obscurity the Arab contribution to science, but it did put the Arabs into the position of conservers of the Greek tradition for those who were really able to make use of it, medieval and early modern Christian Westerners. Champions of this view included Francis Bacon, who thought that neither the medieval scholastics nor the Arabs had made any contributions to science worth mentioning.

The idea, still present in popular culture if no longer in the work of serious historians, of the Scientific Revolution as the work of a stream of "scientific geniuses" stretching from Copernicus to Newton (or from Archimedes to Newton) also reinforced the idea of European superiority, as these geniuses were European (and male) geniuses. (The heroic narrative of "genius" also obscured the key role of institutions and cultures, as well as the contributions, individual and collective, of the many figures who were not part of the canon of "geniuses," such as De Acosta, Halley, and Flamsteed.)

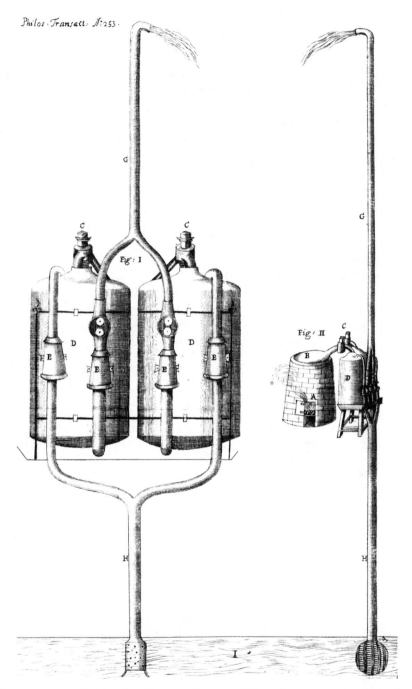

Steam-engine Design by Thomas Savery. This early steam-engine design by Thomas Savery appeared in the pages of *Philosophical Transactions,* linking the late Scientific Revolution with the early Industrial Revolution.

By establishing the dominance of European science, the Scientific Revolution also created the narrative of the history of science as a fundamentally European one. Since early modern scientists found their inspiration in Aristotle or Archimedes rather than the fifth-century BCE Chinese natural philosopher Mozi, Aristotle and Archimedes are part of the "mainstream" history of science in a way Mozi is not. Philosophers such as Mozi and the numerous scientific practices characteristic of non-Western civilizations tend to be ghettoized in the area of "non-Western science," which has both set up barriers between non-Western and Western sciences and obscured the enormous differences between non-Western traditions.

THE SCIENTIFIC REVOLUTION
IN THE MODERN WORLD

All of us, Western or not, are heirs of the Scientific Revolution. The modern world is impossible to imagine without it. The dream of Francis Bacon, of human life endowed with new discoveries and powers, has been fulfilled beyond Bacon's wildest dreams. No longer does any state possess Peter the Great's or Kangxi's power of choice, to accept or reject the new science. No one can imagine going back to the old regime in science—the truest mark of the success of a revolution.

CHRONOLOGY

1406	Western rediscovery of Ptolemy's *Geography* with a Latin translation by Jacobus Angelus of Scarparia.
1417	Humanist and papal secretary Poggio Bracciolini discovers a complete manuscript of Lucretius's Epicurean Latin epic *On the Nature of Things*, making it known for the first time since the fall of Rome.
1450?	Approximate date of Johann Gutenberg's introduction of printing with movable type.
1453	Constantinople, capital of the Byzantine Empire, falls to the Ottoman Turks.
1471	Marsilio Ficino publishes a Latin translation of portions of the Hermetic corpus.
1484	Ficino publishes a complete translation of Plato's works into Latin.
1492	Christopher Columbus's first voyage to America.
1498	Vasco da Gama's circumnavigation of Africa opens the sea route between Europe and the Indian Ocean and East Asia.
1503	Spanish King Ferdinand of Aragon founds the Casa de Contratación, repository of navigational and cartographic knowledge.
1507	First European map referring to the newly discovered continents as "America" after Florentine explorer Amerigo Vespucci issued from the town of St. Die in the Duchy of Lorraine.
1515	The arrival of the first rhinoceros in Europe since the fall of the Roman Empire, a diplomatic gift to Portugal from the Sultan of Gujarat.
1517	The 'Piri Reis' map, one of the earliest surviving maps incorporating the eastern coastline of South America, presented to Ottoman Sultan Selim I; Protestant Reformation begins.
1523	Establishment of the post of senior cosmographer at the Casa de Contratación.
1525	Publication of a massive complete edition of the ancient physician Galen's writings using techniques of humanist scholarship.

1526   Publication of Gonzalo Fernández de Oviedo's *Natural History of the Indies*, the first work devoted to American natural history published in Europe.

1530   Publication of Otto Brunfels' innovative herbal, *Living Images of Herbs*. Publication of Girolamo Fracastoro's *Syphilis, or the French Disease*, which gives the disease its name.

1531   Publication of Latin translation of Galen's *On Anatomical Procedures* sparks interest in anatomy.

1537   Papal bull *Sublimis Deus* declares that the Natives of the Americas are human beings with souls. Founding of a chair of navigational mathematics at the Portuguese University of Coimbra, of which the first incumbent is Pedro Nunes.

1539   Georg Rheticus visits Copernicus, urging the publication of his manuscript, which Copernicus entrusts to him.

1540   Founding of the Society of Jesus, known as the Jesuits.

1542   Establishment of the Roman Inquisition. Possible date of the founding of the Neapolitan Secret Academy, the earliest known scientific society.

1543   Publication of Copernicus, *De Revolutionibus*. Publication of Andreas Vesalius, *De Humanis Corporis Fabrica*.

1544   First publication of Pier Andrea Mattioli's commentary on the ancient botanist Dioscorides, the most popular and frequently reprinted herbal of the sixteenth century.

1545   First university botanical garden founded at the University of Pisa.

1546   Foundation of the botanical garden at the University of Padua.

1548   Following a political crisis at Naples, the Secret Academy is shut down.

1550   Dispute between Bartolomé de las Casas and Juan Ginés de Sepúlveda at Valladolid on the question of whether the inhabitants of the New World are natural slaves.

1551   Collegio Romano founded in Rome by Ignatius Loyola. Erasmus Reinhold issues the *Prutenic Tables*, a set of astronomical tables based on Copernican assumptions.

1553   Establishment of a chair of navigation and cosmography at the Casa de la Contratación.

1554   Mercury amalgamation process for refining silver developed by Bartolome de Medina in Peru.

1559   Establishment of the Catholic Church's Index of Forbidden Books. Royal decree forbids Spanish students from studying at foreign universities.

1562   Publication of the works of the ancient skeptical philosopher Sextus Empiricus in Latin translation contributes to the spread of skeptical ideas.

1563   Garcia d'Orta's *Dialogues on the Simples, Drugs, and Medical Matters of India* is the first scientific book published in India.

1567   Philip II of Spain offers a monetary prize for the solution of the longitude problem.

1568   Foundation of the botanical garden of Bologna.

1569   Publication of Gerhardus Mercator's world map, the first to use the "Mercator projection."

1570	Publication of Abraham Ortelius's cartographic collection *Theater of the World*, the first global atlas. First edition of Christoph Clavius's *Commentary on the Sphere of Sacrobosco*, the influential Jesuit astronomy textbook.
1571–1577	Francisco Hernández's scientific exploration of Mexico.
1572	New star inspires astronomical and astrological debate.
1572–1575	Establishment of the Roman commission that will create the Gregorian calendar.
1575	University of Leiden founded.
1576	King Frederick II of Denmark grants Tycho Brahe the island of Hven to found his observatory, Uraniborg.
1577	The appearance of a comet, whose parallax will be used by Tycho and others to show that it is above the moon, and that contrary to Aristotle the heavens are subject to change. Founding of the Leiden Botanical Garden. Publication of John Dee, *General and Rare Memorials Pertayning to the Perfect Arte of Navigation*.
1582	Announcement of the Gregorian Reform of the calendar by Pope Gregory XIII in the bull *Inter Gravissimas*. The new calendar is adopted by Catholic countries.
1585	Simon Stevin publishes *The Tenth*, setting forth system of decimal fractions. Thomas Harriot leaves England for Sir Walter Raleigh's colony in Virginia.
1588	Tycho's *Of More Recent Phenomena of the Ethereal World* sets forth the Tychonic system of the motions of the sun and planets. Publication of Thomas Harriot's *A Briefe and True Report of the New Found Land of Virginia*.
1589	Galileo Galilei wins mathematics chair at University of Pisa.
1589–1591	Appearance of the standard ten-volume edition of the works of Paracelsus edited by the physician Johannes Huser.
1592	Galileo Galilei becomes professor of mathematics at the University of Padua.
1594	First permanent university anatomy theater founded at the University of Padua.
1595	First allusion to Copernicus in a Jewish work, Rabbi Judah Loew's *The Paths of the World*.
1596	Founding of Gresham College in London.
1597	After a falling out with the king, Tycho Brahe abandons Uraniborg and leaves Denmark for the court of the Holy Roman Emperor.
1598	Philip III of Spain increases the value of the longitude prize.
1599	*Certaine Errors of Navigation* by the English mathematician Edward Wright explains the mathematical basis of the Mercator projection for the first time.
1600	Giordano Bruno burned at the stake in Rome. Publication of William Gilbert's *On the Magnet*.
1601	Death of Tycho Brahe in Vienna. Johannes Kepler inherits his astronomical data and succeeds him as Imperial Astronomer.

1602	Founding of the VOC, the Dutch East India Company. Jesuit missionary Matteo Ricci makes a map for the emperor of China incorporating Western knowledge.
1603	Prince Federico Cesi founds the Accademia dei Lincei.
1604	New star inspires Kepler to write *Of the New Star*, setting forth what becomes the widely accepted theory that new stars are caused by burning of celestial waste.
1608	Hans Lipperhey applies for a patent on the telescope in the Netherlands.
1609	Founding of the first university chair in anatomy separate from surgery at Padua. Foundation of a chair of chemical medicine at the University of Marburg, the first chair requiring laboratory work.
1610	Publication of Galileo's *The Starry Messenger*, announcing his telescopic discoveries.
1611	Galileo joins the Accademia dei Lincei. Solemn convocation at the Jesuit Collegio Romano honors Galileo's telescopic discoveries. Jesuit General Claudio Acquaviva requires Jesuits to defend the authority of Aristotle in philosophy. Kepler publishes *Dioptrics*, the first examination of the optics of telescopes.
1613	Publication of Galileo's *Letters on Sunspots* leads to a feud with the Jesuit astronomer Christoph Scheiner, eventually poisoning Galileo's heretofore good relations with the order.
1614	Isaac Casaubon demonstrates that the Hermetic writings originated in early Christian era. Publication of John Napier's *Description of the Marvelous Canon of Logarithms*, setting forth his invention of logarithms.
1616	Copernicus's *On the Revolutions* put on the Index of Forbidden Books; Galileo admonished not to teach or publicly hold Copernican doctrine.
1618	The first comets to be observed through the telescope. Beginning of the Thirty Years' War. The comets will frequently be seen as a sign of the forthcoming disasters of the war.
1619	Foundation of Savilian Professorships of Geometry and Astronomy at Oxford. Publication of Kepler's *Harmonies of the World*, setting forth his Third Law. René Descartes inspired to found a new philosophy.
1621	Founding of the botanical garden at the University of Oxford.
1625	Publication of the first work of microscopic science, a broadsheet on the bee by Francesco Stelluti. Spanish Inquisition denounces Johannes Baptista Van Helmont, partly for his role in the weapon-salve controversy. He will spend most of the next two decades under house arrest.
1626	Founding of the French Royal Botanical Garden, although the garden was not in operation until 1640.
1627	Publication of Kepler's *Rudolphine Tables*, astronomical tables based on his theories and the most accurate to date.
1628	Publication of William Harvey, *On the Motion of the Heart*, setting forth the theory of the circulation of blood.
1629	Publication in Amsterdam of the first Copernican work by a Jew, Joseph Delmedigo's *Sefer Elim*.

1631	Pierre Gassendi observes the transit of Mercury across the face of the sun. First arrival (via China) of Western astronomical tools and manuals in Korea.
1632	Publication of Galileo's *Dialogue on the Two Great Systems of the World*, espousing Copernicanism. First published description of the slide rule.
1633	Trial and conviction of Galileo. Jesuit scientist Athanasius Kircher arrives in Rome. Founding of the first university observatory at Leiden.
1634	Jesuit missionaries present a telescope to the Chinese emperor.
1635	Nicolas-Claude Fabri de Peiresc coordinates widely scattered observations of a solar eclipse through French diplomats.
1636	The Dutch Republic offers a prize for the solution to the longitude problem.
1638	Publication of Galileo's *Discourse on Two New Sciences* in Leiden. Descartes publishes *Discourse on Method* and associated scientific works. Establishment of the first observatory in the Southern Hemisphere at Recife.
1642	Beginning of the English Civil War.
1645	Western Jesuit Schall von Bell appointed head of Chinese Imperial Astronomical Bureau.
1647	Blaise Pascal's *New Experiments on the Void* demonstrates the existence of vacuum.
1648	Thirty Years' War ends with Treaty of Westphalia.
1649	John Wilkins arrives at Oxford University as Master of Wadham College, founding an active scientific circle there. Queen Christina of Sweden lures Descartes to Stockholm, where he dies the next year.
1651	Foundation in the German city of Schweinfurt of the Academy of the Curious into Nature.
1654	First public demonstration of an air pump, by Otto von Guericke. Walter Charleton's *Physiologia Epicuro-Gassendo-Charletoniana* introduces Gassendist atomism to England.
1655	Publication of Isaac La Peyrère's *Prae-Adamitae*, the foundation for the "polygenist" view of humanity.
1657	Founding of the Florentine Accademia del Cimento. Guericke demonstrates the vacuum by evacuating the space between two brass hemispheres and then showing that teams of horses cannot pull the hemispheres apart. Alchemist John Winthrop Jr. first becomes governor of Connecticut, a position he will hold with one brief interruption until his death in 1676.
1658	Publication of the complete works of Pierre Gassendi. Christiaan Huygens' paper setting forth his discovery of Saturn's rings read at a meeting of the Montmor Academy.
1660	Founding of what would become the Royal Society in London. First translation of a Copernican work (a set of astronomical tables) into Arabic by Ibrahim al-Zigetvari.
1661	Marcello Malpighi's *On the Lungs* describes the circulation of blood through the capillaries.

1662	The Royal Society receives a charter from King Charles II.
1663	Works of Descartes placed on the Catholic Church's Index of Forbidden Books.
1665–1666	Plague of London kills the American alchemist George Starkey and drives Newton to the country. Newton's *annus mirabilis*.
1665	Appearance of the first issues of *Journal des Scavans* and *Philosophical Transactions*, edited by Henry Oldenburg. Publication of Robert Hooke's *Micrographia* with the results of his microscopic observations.
1666	Founding of the Royal Academy of Sciences in Paris. Fire of London drives the Royal Society from Gresham House and destroys many of William Harvey's manuscripts at the London College of Physicians.
1667	End of the Accademia del Cimento. Margaret Cavendish becomes only woman to attend a Royal Society meeting until the twentieth century. Foundation of the Paris Observatory. Body of René Descartes returned to France and given a public burial. Emperor Kangxi restores Jesuit control of the Astronomical Bureau.
1668	Newton devises the reflecting telescope. Louis XIV invites Gian Domenico Cassini to come to Paris and run the Observatory.
1669	Cassini arrives in Paris; he never returns to Italy. Newton appointed to the Lucasian Chair of Mathematics at Cambridge.
1670	First appearance of *Miscellanea Curiousa*, a periodical sponsored by the College of the Curiosities of Nature. It concentrates on medical issues.
1673	First letter of Antoni van Leeuwenhoek published in *Philosophical Transactions*. Publication of François Poulain de la Barre's tract *The Equality of the Two Sexes,* arguing for the equality of the sexes on Cartesian grounds.
1675	Founding of Greenwich Observatory. Thomas Shadwell's play *The Virtuoso* ridicules the Royal Society, and particularly Robert Hooke. Christiaan Huygens and Hooke both design and supervise the creation of spring watches, provoking s bitter priority dispute.
1677	Publication of Leeuwenhoek's description of the male sperm. Death of Henry Oldenburg leads to the collapse of most of the Royal Society's foreign correspondence and eventually the suspension of *Philosophical Transactions*.
1679	Edmond Halley visits Johannes Hevelius's observatory in Danzig to evaluate the quality of Hevelius's observations made with instruments not fitted with telescopic sights. Shortly after Halley's departure, Hevelius's observatory burns down.
1680	Gottfried Kirch becomes the first astronomer to discover a comet through the telescope. Leeuwenhoek unanimously elected to the Royal Society. Debate in Mexico between Carlos de Siguenza y Gongora and Eusebio Kino over whether comets were divine signs.
1681	Increasingly harsh anti-Protestant policies of Louis XIV cause Huygens to leave Paris and return to the Netherlands.
1682	Appearance of the comet that later becomes known as Halley's Comet. The Royal Society purchases two hundred shares of the Royal African Company, England's slave trade monopoly company.

1683	Founding of the Boston Philosophical Society. Publication of Dutch physician Willem ten Rhijne's *History of Arthritis*, a discussion of East Asian medicine, including the first detailed description of acupuncture in a European language.
1684	Edmond Halley's visit to Isaac Newton leads Newton to formulate theory of universal gravitation. *New Division of the World among the Different Species or Races of Men that Inhabit it* by French Gassendist physician and traveler François Bernier expounds early scientific racism. Shibukawa Harumi employs Chinese-language Jesuit works among other Chinese and Japanese works in creating Japan's first native calendar.
1685	Goverd Bidloo publishes *Anatomy of the Human Body*, the first atlas of the human body to incorporate microscopic data. French Jesuit scientific mission leaves for China.
1686	Elias Ashmole founds the Ashmolean Museum in Oxford, England's first public museum, to house the Tradescant collection.
1687	Publication of Newton's *Mathematical Principles of Natural Philosophy*. Holy Roman Emperor Leopold I recognizes the Academy of the Curious into Nature as the "Leopoldina."
1688	French Jesuit mission led by mathematical experts arrives in the Chinese capital.
1690	Posthumous publication of William Petty's *Political Arithmetick*, which gives the discipline its name.
1691	Death of Robert Boyle, whose will establishes the Boyle Lectures. Foundation of John Dunton's periodical the *Athenian Mercury*, which includes scientific popularization and runs until 1697.
1692	First Boyle Lectures delivered by Richard Bentley, with help from Newton.
1695	Hans Sloane takes over and revitalizes *Philosophical Transactions*. Western Jesuit Juan Antonio Arnedo appointed court astrologer in Vietnam.
1697	Fontenelle becomes secretary to the Royal Academy of Sciences, a position he will hold until 1740.
1698–1701	Edmond Halley's Atlantic voyages as captain of the *Paramore* in search of astronomical and geomagnetic information.
1699	Reorganization of the Royal Academy of Sciences, with the admission of Cartesians including the Oratorian Nicolas Malebranche. Thomas Savery's steam engine demonstrated at a meeting of the Royal Society. The Royal Society sells its shares in the Royal African Company, ending its direct financial participation in the slave trade.
1699–1701	Maria Sibilla Merian and her daughter Dorothea gather natural historical knowledge and specimens in the Dutch colony of Surinam.
1700	Founding of the Berlin Academy of Sciences, with Leibniz as its first president. Denmark, Prussia, and the other Protestant states of the Holy Roman Empire adopt the Gregorian calendar.
1701	Founding of the Moscow School of Mathematics and Navigation. Founding of the first Spanish scientific society, the Royal Society of Medicine and other Sciences of Seville.
1702	Royal Academy of Sciences begins to publish annual reports.

1703	Newton becomes president of the Royal Society.
1704	Publication of Newton's *Opticks*. First appearance of *The Ladies' Diary*, an English periodical with the purpose of introducing educated women to mathematics and science.
1705	Halley's *Synopsis of the Astronomy of Comets* predicts the return of the comet of 1682 in 1758.
1707	Publication of Tobias Cohn's Hebrew textbook of medicine and natural philosophy spreads knowledge of modern science among the Jewish community. Publication of Hans Sloane's natural history of Jamaica.
1709	Newton causes the expulsion of Flamsteed from the Royal Society for nonpayment of dues.
1710	Maria Winkelmann petitions the Berlin Academy for an appointment as astronomer following the death of her husband, Gottfried Kirch, but is denied on account of her gender. William Whiston is expelled from Cambridge and forfeits his chair for heresy. The Royal Society obtains a loose authority over the Greenwich Observatory.
1712	Edmond Halley publishes abbreviated version of John Flamsteed's astronomical data, igniting feud between Flamsteed on one side and Halley and Newton on the other that will continue until Flamsteed's death in 1719. Publication of a report of the Committee of the Royal Society chosen by Newton, backing Newton against Leibniz in the controversy over the origin of the calculus.
1713	Kangxi founds the Imperial Academy of Mathematics.
1714	Halley takes over editorship of *Philosophical Transactions* from Sloane, reorienting it from natural history to mathematics, astronomy, and physics. British Parliament founds the Board of Longitude with the establishment of a monetary prize for the discovery of a successful method for finding the longitude at sea.
1715	Moscow School of Mathematics and Navigation moves to St. Petersburg and becomes the Russian Naval Academy.
1715–1716	Controversy between Gottfried Wilhelm Leibniz and the English Newtonian Samuel Clarke over the religious implications of Newtonian natural philosophy.
1717	Completion of the Kangxi map of China.
1719	Death of Flamsteed, Halley succeeds him the next year as Royal Astronomer; Thomas Robie's *A Letter to a Certain Gentleman, desiring that a particular account be given of a wonderful Meteor* sets off a controversy in New England about whether meteors should be read as divine signs.
1720	Japanese Shogun Yoshimune liberalizes the law banning foreign books, increasing the exposure of Japanese intellectuals to Western science.
1721	Publication of Cotton Mather's Newtonian *The Christian Philosopher: A Collection of the Best Discoveries in Nature, with Religious Improvements*. Ottoman envoy Yirmisekiz Mehmed Celebi makes two visits to the Paris Observatory and writes a report to Istanbul on Western astronomical techniques.
1723	Last appearance of Leeuwenhoek in *Philosophical Transactions*, the year of his death. Methodios Anthrakites summoned before the Holy Synod

of the Orthodox Church and excommunicated for publishing a book with Copernican and Cartesian content.

1724   Foundation of the St. Petersburg Academy of Sciences.

1725   Posthumous publication of Flamsteed's star catalogue in a version authorized by him.

1727   Death of Isaac Newton. He receives burial in Westminster Abbey and an elaborate state funeral attended by thousands. Newton is succeeded as president of the Royal Society by Sir Hans Sloane. London merchant Thomas Hollis endows the Hollis Chair in Mathematics and Natural Philosophy at Harvard University. Its first holder, Isaac Greenwood, will give public lectures and otherwise promote natural philosophy in New England.

1727–1730   Jai Singh's astronomical delegation to Portugal.

1728   Founding of the Muteferrika Press in Istanbul, the first press in the Ottoman Empire for Muslim readers, which will publish several books introducing Western geography and astronomy to the Ottoman Muslim public.

1752   Britain and its colonies adopt the Gregorian calendar.

1753   Sweden adopts the Gregorian calendar.

BIBLIOGRAPHY

Ames-Lewis, *Francis*, ed. *Sir Thomas Gresham and Gresham College*. Aldershot: Ashgate, 1999.

Azzolini, Monica. *The Duke and the Stars: Astrology and Politics in Renaissance Milan*. Cambridge, MA: Harvard University Press, 2013.

Barrera-Osorio, Antonio. *Experiencing Nature: The Spanish-American Empire and the Early Scientific Revolution*. Austin: University of Texas Press, 2006.

Ben-Zaken, Avner. *Cross-Cultural Scientific Exchanges in the Eastern Mediterranean*. Baltimore, MD: Johns Hopkins, 2010.

Beuchot, Mauricio. *The History of Philosophy in Colonial Mexico*. Translated by Elizabeth Millán. Washington, DC: Catholic University of America Press, 1998.

Biagioli, Mario. *Galileo, Courtier: The Practice of Science in the Age of Absolutism*. Chicago, IL: University of Chicago Press, 1993.

Boss, Valentin. *Newton and Russia: The Early Influence, 1698–1796*. Cambridge, MA: Harvard University Press, 1972.

Bottela-Ordinas, Eva. "Debating Empires, Inventing Empires: British Territorial Claims Against the Spaniards in America, 1670–1714." *The Journal for Early Modern Cultural Studies* 10 (2010): 142–168.

Brentjes, Sonja. *Travellers from Europe in the Ottoman and Safavid Empires, 16th–17th Centuries: Seeking, Transforming, Discarding Knowledge*. Farnham, Surrey: Ashgate, 2010.

Brown, Jeremy. *New Heavens and a New Earth: The Jewish Reception of Copernican Thought*. New York: Oxford University Press, 2013.

Burns, William E. *An Age of Wonders: Prodigies, Politics and Providence in England 1657–1727*. Manchester and New York: Manchester University Press, 2002.

Butterfield, Herbert. *The Origins of Modern Science*. Revised edition. New York: Free Press, 1965.

Campbell, Mary Baine. *Wonder and Science: Imagining Worlds in Early Modern Europe*. Ithaca, NY: Cornell University Press, 1999.

Canizares-Esguerra, Jorge. *Nature, Empire and Nation: Explorations in the History of Science in the Iberian World*. Stanford, CA: Stanford University Press, 2006.

Carrubba, Robert W. "Engelbert Kaempfer and the Myth of the Scythian Lamb." *The Classical World* 87 (1993): 41–47.

Carrubba, Robert W., and John Z. Bowers. "Engelbert Kaempfer's First Report of the Torpedo Fish of the Persian Gulf in the late Seventeenth Century." *Journal of the History of Biology* 15 (1982): 263–274.

Chakrabarti, Pratik. *Medicine and Empire, 1600–1960.* New York: Palgrave Macmillan, 2014.

Chaplin, Joyce. *Subject Matter: Technology, Matter and Science on the Anglo-American Frontier.* Cambridge, MA, and London: Harvard University Press, 2001.

Cieslik, Hubert. "The Case of Christovao Ferreira." Available online at http://pweb .cc.sophia.ac.jp/britto/xavier/cieslik/cie_ferreira.pdf. Accessed December 11, 2013.

Cohen, H. Flores. *The Scientific Revolution: A Historiographical Inquiry.* Chicago, IL, and London: University of Chicago Press, 1994.

Cook, Alan. *Edmond Halley: Charting the Heavens and the Seas.* Oxford: Clarendon Press, 1998.

Cook, Harold J. *Matters of Exchange: Commerce, Medicine and Science in the Dutch Golden Age.* New Haven, CT: Yale University Press, 2007.

Cracraft, James. *The Revolution of Peter the Great.* Cambridge, MA, and London: Harvard University Press, 2003.

Crane, Nicholas. *Mercator: The Man Who Mapped the Planet.* London: Phoenix, 2003.

Crosby, Alfred W. *The Measure of Reality: Quantification and Western Society, 1250–1600.* Cambridge: Cambridge University Press, 1997.

Davis, Natalie Zemon. *Trickster Travels: A Sixteenth-Century Muslim between Worlds.* New York: Hill and Wang, 2006.

Davis, Natalie Zemon. *Women on the Margins: Three Seventeenth-Century Lives.* Cambridge, MA: Harvard University Press, 1995.

Delbourgo, James. "Slavery in the Cabinet of Curiousities: Hans Sloane's Atlantic World." British Museum. Available online at http://www.britishmuseum.org/pdf/ delbourgo%20essay.pdf Accessed December 31, 2013.

Dew, Nicholas. "Scientific Travel in the Atlantic World: The French Expedition to Goree and the Antilles, 1681–1683." *British Journal of the History of Science* 43 (2010): 1–17.

Eamon, William, and Francoise Paheu. "The Accademia Segreta of Girolamo Ruscelli: A Sixteenth-Century Italian Scientific Society." *Isis* 75 (1984): 327–342.

Fernandez-Armesto, Felipe. *Amerigo: The Man Who Gave His Name to America.* New York: Random House, 2008.

Findlen, Paula. *Possessing Nature: Museums, Collections and Scientific Culture in Early Modern Italy.* Berkeley and Los Angeles: University of California Press, 1994.

Findlen, Paula, ed. *Athanasius Kircher: The Last Man Who Knew Everything.* New York and London: Routledge, 2004.

Fontenelle, Bernard le Bovier de. *Conversations on the Plurality of Worlds.* Translated by H. A. Hargreaves. Berkeley: University of California Press, 1990.

Force, James. *William Whiston: Honest Newtonian.* Cambridge: Cambridge University Press, 1985.

French, Peter. *John Dee: The World of an Elizabethan Magus.* New York: Dorset Press, 1989.

Goodman, Grant Kohn. *The Dutch Impact on Japan.* Leiden: E. J. Brill, 1967.

Govier, Mark. "The Royal Society, Slavery, and the Island of Jamaica: 1660–1700." *Notes and Records of the Royal Society* 53 (1999): 203–217.

Grafton, Anthony, with April Shelford and Nancy Siraisi. *New Worlds, Ancient Texts: The Power of Tradition and the Shock of Discovery.* Cambridge, MA: Harvard University Press, 1992.

Gratton-Guiness, Ivor. *The Norton History of Mathematical Sciences: The Rainbow of Mathematics.* New York: W. W. Norton, 1998.

Greenblatt, Stephen. *The Swerve: How the World Became Modern.* New York: Norton, 2011.

Harkness, Deborah. *The Jewel House: Elizabethan London and the Scientific Revolution.* New Haven, CT, and London: Yale University Press, 2007.

Hellyer, Marcus. *Catholic Physics: Jesuit Natural Philosophy in Early Modern Germany.* Notre Dame, IN: University of Notre Dame Press, 2005.

Hill, Ruth. *Sceptres and Sciences in the Spains: Four Humanists and the New Philosophy (ca. 1680–1740).* Liverpool: Liverpool University Press, 2000.

Hodges, Ian. "Western Science in Siam: A Tale of Two Kings." *Osiris* Second Series, vol. 13 (1998): 80–95.

Hostetler, Laura. *Qing Colonial Enterprise: Ethnography and Cartography in Early Modern China.* Chicago, IL, and London: University of Chicago Press, 2001.

Ihsanoglu, Ekmeleddin. *Science, Technology and Learning in the Ottoman Empire: Western Influence, Local Institutions, and the Transfer of Knowledge.* Aldershot: Ashgate, 2004.

Irving, Sarah. *Natural Science and the Origins of the British Empire.* London: Pickering and Chatto, 2008.

Jacob, James. "The Political Economy of Science in Seventeenth-Century England." In Margaret C. Jacob, ed. *The Politics of Western Science, 1640–1990.* Atlantic Highland, NJ: Humanities Press, 1990: 19–46.

Jacob, Margaret C. *Scientific Culture and the Making of the Industrial West.* New York: Oxford University Press, 1997.

Jami, Catherine. *The Emperor's New Mathematics: Western Learning and Imperial Authority during the Kangxi Reign (1662–1722).* Oxford: Oxford University Press, 2012.

Jardine, Lisa. *The Curious Life of Robert Hooke: The Man Who Measured London.* New York: HarperCollins, 2004.

Keevak, Michael. *The Pretended Asian: George Psalmanazar's Eighteenth-Century Formosan Hoax.* Detroit, MI: Wayne State University Press, 2004.

Kennedy, Rick. "Thomas Brattle and the Scientific Provincialism of New England, 1680–1713." *The New England Quarterly* 63 (1990): 684–600.

Kennedy, Rick. "Thomas Brattle, Mathematician-Architect in the Transition of the New England Mind." *Winterthur Portfolio* 24 (1989): 231–245.

Landes, David. *Revolution in Time: Clocks and the Making of the Modern World.* Cambridge, MA: Harvard University Press, 1983.

Laqueur, Thomas. *Making Sex: Body and Gender from the Greeks to Freud.* Cambridge, MA: Harvard University Press, 1990.

Laqueur, Thomas. "Sex in the Flesh." *Isis* 94 (2003): 300–306.

Lattis, James M. *Between Copernicus and Galileo: Christoph Clavius and the Collapse of Ptolemaic Cosmology.* Chicago, IL, and London: University of Chicago Press, 1994.

Lewis, Rhodri. "William Petty's Anthropology: Religion, Colonialism and the Problem of Human Diversity." *Huntington Library Quarterly* 74 (2011): 261–288.

Lindberg, David C., and Robert S. Westman, eds. *Reappraisals of the Scientific Revolution.* Cambridge: Cambridge University Press, 1990.

Lynch, William T. *Solomon's Child: Method in the Early Royal Society of London.* Stanford, CA: Stanford University Press, 2001.

Malcolmson, Cristina. *Studies of Skin Color in the Early Royal Society: Boyle, Cavendish, Swift.* Farnham, Surrey: Ashgate, 2013.

Merchant, Carolyn. *The Death of Nature: Women, Ecology and the Scientific Revolution.* San Francisco, CA: Harper and Row, 1980.

Merwick, Donna. *Possessing Albany, 1630–1710: The Dutch and English Experiences.* Cambridge: Cambridge University Press, 1990.

Morrison, Robert. "A Scholarly Intermediary between the Ottoman Empire and Renaissance Europe." *Isis* 105 (2014): 32–57.

Neal, Katherine. "Mathematics and Empire, Navigation and Exploration: Henry Briggs and the Northwest Passage Voyages of 1631." *Isis* 93 (2002): 435–453.

Newman, William R. *Gehennical Fire: The Lives of George Starkey, an American Alchemist in the Scientific Revolution.* Cambridge, MA: Harvard University Press, 1994.

Newton, Isaac. *The* Principia: *Mathematical Principles of Natural Philosophy.* Translated by I. Bernard Cohen and Anne Whitman. Berkeley: University of California Press, 1999.

Nicolaidis, Efthymios. *Science and Eastern Orthodoxy: From the Greek Fathers to the Age of Globalization.* Translated by Susan Emanuel. Baltimore, MD: Johns Hopkins, 2013.

Norton, Marcy. *Sacred Gifts, Profane Pleasures: A History of Tobacco and Chocolate in the Atlantic World.* Ithaca, NY: Cornell University Press, 2008.

O'Brien, Patrick. "Historical Foundations for a Global Perspective on the Emergence of a Western European Regime for the Discovery, Development and Diffusion of Useful and Reliable Knowledge." *Journal of Global History* 8 (2013): 1–24.

Osler, Margaret J., ed. *Rethinking the Scientific Revolution.* Cambridge: Cambridge University Press, 2000.

Otremba, Eric. "Inventing Ingenios: Experimental Philosophy and the Secret Sugar-Makers of the Seventeenth-Century Atlantic." *History and Technology: An International Journal* 28 (2012): 119–147.

Pagden, Anthony. *The Fall of Natural Man: The American Indian and the Origins of Comparative Ethnology.* Cambridge: Cambridge University Press, 1982.

Park, Katherine. "The Rediscovery of the Clitoris." In David Hillman and Carla Mazzio, eds. *The Body in Parts: Fantasies of Corporeality in Early Modern Europe.* New York and London: Routledge, 1997: 170–193.

Patai, Rafael. *The Jewish Alchemists: A History and Source Book.* Princeton, NJ: Princeton University Press, 1994.

Pedersen, Olaf. *The Two Books: Historical Notes on Some Interactions Between Natural Science and Theology.* Edited by George V. Coyne S. J. and Tadeusz Sierotowicz. Vatican City: Vatican Observatory Foundation, 2007.

Petersson, R. T. *Sir Kenelm Digby: The Ornament of England, 1603–1665.* London: Jonathan Cape, 1956.

Porter, Roy, ed. *The Cambridge History of Science, Volume Four: Eighteenth-Century Science.* Cambridge and New York: Cambridge University Press, 2003.

Portuondo, Maria M. *Secret Science: Spanish Cosmography and the New World.* Chicago: University of Chicago Press, 2009.

Qaisar, Ahsan Jan. *The Indian Response to European Culture and Technology, A.D. 1498–1707.* Delhi: Oxford University Press, 1982.

Rabinovich, Oded. "Chameleons Between Science and Literature: Observation, Writing, and the Early Parisian Academy of Sciences in the Literary Field." *History of Science* 51 (2013): 33–62.

Ruderman, David B. *Jewish Thought and Scientific Discovery in Early Modern Europe.* Detroit, MI: Wayne State University Press, 1995.

Russell, G. A., ed. *The 'Arabick' Interest of the Natural Philosophers in Seventeenth-Century England*. Leiden: E. J. Brill, 1994.

Saravia, Luis, ed. *History of Mathematical Sciences: Portugal and East Asia II*. Hackensack, NJ: World Scientific, 2004.

Saravia, Luis, and Catherine Jami, eds. *The Jesuits, the Padroado and East Asian Science (1552–1773)*. Hackensack, NJ: World Scientific, 2008.

Schafer, Dagmar. *The Crafting of the 10,000 Things: Knowledge and Technology in Seventeenth-Century China*. Chicago, IL: University of Chicago Press, 2011.

Schaffer, Simon. "The Information Order of Isaac Newton's Principia Mathematica: The Hans Rausing Lecture 2008." Uppsala: Uppsala University, 2008.

Schiebinger, Londa. *The Mind Has No Sex? Women in the Origins of Modern Science*. Cambridge, MA: Harvard University Press, 1989.

Schiebinger, Londa. "Skelettestreit." *Isis* 94 (2003): 307–313.

Schiebinger, Londa, and Claudia Swan, eds. *Colonial Botany: Science, Commerce and Politics in the Early Modern World*. Philadelphia: University of Pennsylvania Press, 2005.

Schleiner, Winfried. "Early Modern Controversies about the One-Sex Model." *Renaissance Quarterly* 53 (2000): 180–191.

Shirley, John W. *Thomas Harriot: A Biography*. Oxford: Clarendon Press, 1983.

Siraisi, Nancy G. *Avicenna in Renaissance Italy: The Canon and Medical Teaching in Italian Universities after 1500*. Princeton, NJ: Princeton University Press, 1987.

Smith, Pamela H., and Paula Findlen, eds. *Merchants and Marvels: Commerce, Science and Art in Early Modern Europe*. New York: Routledge, 2002.

Stearn, William T. "Engelbert Kaempfer (1651–1716)—Pioneer Investigator of Japanese Plants." *Curtis's Botanical Magazine* 16 (1999): 103–115.

Stearns, Justin. "Writing the History of the Natural Sciences in the Pre-modern Muslim World: Historiography, Religion, and the Importance of the Early Modern Period." *History Compass* 9 (2011): 923–951.

Stearns, Raymond Phineas. *Science in the British Colonies of America*. Urbana: University of Illinois Press, 1970.

Stolberg, Michael. "A Woman Down to Her Bones: The Anatomy of Sexual Difference in the Sixteenth and Early Seventeenth Centuries." *Isis* 94 (2003): 274–299.

Stone, Richard. *Some British Empiricists in the Social Sciences, 1650–1900*. Cambridge: Cambridge University Press, 1997.

Stuurman, Seip. "Francois Bernier and the Invention of Racial Classification." *History Workshop Journal* 50 (2000): 1–21.

Sugimoto, Masayoshi, and David L. Swain. *Science and Culture in Traditional Japan, A.D. 600–1854*. Cambridge, MA: MIT Press, 1978.

Thrower, Norman J. W. *The Three Voyages of Edmond Halley in the Paramore 1698–1701*. London: Hakluyt Society, 1981.

Varey, Simon, ed. *The Mexican Treasury: The Writings of Dr. Francisco Hernández*. Stanford, CA: Stanford University Press, 2000.

Vucinich, Alexander. *Science in Russian Culture*. Stanford, CA: Stanford University Press, 1963.

Westman, Robert S. "The Melanchthon Circle, Rheticus, and the Wittenberg Interpretation of the Copernican Theory" *Isis* 66 (1975): 164–193.

Williams, Gerhild Scholz, and Charles D. Gunnoe, Jr., eds. *Paracelsian Moments: Science, Medicine and Astrology in Early Modern Europe*. Kirksville, MO: Truman State University Press, 2002.

Woodward, Walter W. *Prospero's America: John Winthrop Jr., Alchemy, and the Creation of New England Culture, 1606–1676.* Chapel Hill: Published by the University of North Carolina Press for the Omohundro Institute of Early American History and Culture, 2010.

Yates, Frances. *The Occult Philosophy in the Elizabethan Age.* London and New York: Routledge, 2001.

FURTHER READING

Applebaum, Wilbur. *The Scientific Revolution and the Foundations of Modern Science.* Westport, CT: Greenwood, 2005.

Ball, Phillip. *Curiosity: How Science Became Interested in Everything.* Chicago, IL, and London: University of Chicago Press, 2012.

Burns, William E. *Knowledge and Power: Science in World History.* Boston, MA: Pearson, 2011.

Burns, William E. *Science and Technology in Colonial America.* Westport, CT, and London: Greenwood Press, 2005.

Christianson, John Robert. *On Tycho's Island: Tycho Brahe, Science and Culture in the Sixteenth Century.* Cambridge: Cambridge University Press, 2003.

Coudert, Allison P. *Religion, Magic and Science in Early Modern Europe and America.* Santa Barbara, CA: Praeger, 2011.

Danielson, Dennis. *The First Copernican: George Joachim Rheticus and the Rise of the Copernican Revolution.* New York: Walker, 2006.

Dear, Peter. *Revolutionizing the Sciences: European Knowledge and its Ambitions, 1500–1700.* Second edition. Princeton, NJ, and Oxford: Princeton University Press, 2009.

Debus, Allen G. *Man and Nature in the Renaissance.* Cambridge: Cambridge University Press, 1978.

Dobbs, B. J. T., and Margaret Jacob. *Newton and the Culture of Newtonianism.* Atlantic Highlands, NJ: Humanities Press, 1994.

Drake, Stillman. *Galileo: A Very Short Introduction.* Oxford and New York: Oxford University Press, 2001.

Freely, John. *Aladdin's Lamp: How Greek Science Came to Europe Through the Islamic World.* New York: Vintage Books, 2009.

Gingerich, Owen. *The Book Nobody Read: Chasing the Revolutions of Nicholas Copernicus.* New York: Walker, 2004.

Hall, A. Rupert. *The Revolution in Science 1500–1750.* London and New York: Longman, 1983.

Hall, Marie Boas. *The Scientific Renaissance 1450–1630.* New York: Dover, 1994.

Henry, John. *The Scientific Revolution and the Origins of Modern Science.* Second edition. New York: Palgrave, 2002.

Jacob, James. *The Scientific Revolution: Aspirations and Achievements.* Amherst, NY: Humanity Books, 1999.

Jacob, Margaret C. *The Scientific Revolution: A Brief History with Documents.* Boston, MA, and New York: Bedford St. Martin's, 2009.

Jardine, Lisa. *Ingenious Pursuits: Building the Scientific Revolution.* New York: Doubleday, 1999.

Kearney, Hugh. *Science and Change: 1500–1700.* New York: McGraw-Hill, 1971.

Langford, Jerome J. *Galileo, Science and the Church.* Third edition. Ann Arbor: University of Michigan Press, 1992.

Levenson, Thomas. *Newton and the Counterfeiter: The Unknown Detective Career of the World's Greatest Scientist.* Boston: Houghton Mifflin Harcourt, 2009.

Moran, Bruce T. *Distilling Knowledge: Alchemy, Chemistry and the Scientific Revolution.* Cambridge, MA, and London: Harvard University Press, 2005.

Rossi, Paolo. *The Birth of Modern Science.* Translated by Cynthia De Nardi Ipsen. Oxford: Blackwell, 2001.

Shapin, Steven. *The Scientific Revolution.* Chicago, IL, and London: University of Chicago Press, 1996.

Shea, William R., and Mariano Artigas. *Galileo in Rome: The Rise and Fall of a Troublesome Genius.* New York: Oxford University Press, 2003.

Vollman, William T. *Uncentering the Earth: Copernicus and The Revolutions of the Heavenly Spheres.* New York and London: W. W. Norton, 2006.

Westfall, Richard S. *The Construction of Modern Science: Mechanisms and Mechanics.* Cambridge: Cambridge University Press, 1977.

Westfall, Richard S. *The Life of Isaac Newton.* Cambridge: Cambridge University Press, 1993.

CREDITS

INDEX